Unforgettable

THE BOLD FLAVORS OF
PAULA WOLFERT'S
RENEGADE LIFE

◦ ❖ ◦

Emily Kaiser Thelin

Foreword by Alice Waters

Photography by Eric Wolfinger ◦ Design by Toni Tajima
Editing by Andrea Nguyen ◦ Recipes by Paula Wolfert

GRAND CENTRAL
Life & Style
NEW YORK · BOSTON

Grand Central Life & Style
Hachette Book Group
1290 Avenue of the Americas, New York, NY 10104
grandcentrallifeandstyle.com
twitter.com/grandcentralpub

Originally published in 2017 in hardcover by Mortar & Pestle, Berkeley, California
First Grand Central hardcover edition: October 2017

Grand Central Life & Style is an imprint of Grand Central Publishing.
The Grand Central Life & Style name and logo are trademarks of Hachette Book Group, Inc.

The publisher is not responsible for websites (or their content) that are not owned by the publisher.

The Hachette Speakers Bureau provides a wide range of authors for speaking events. To find out more, go to www.hachettespeakersbureau.com or call (866) 376-6591.

Print book interior design by Toni Tajima

Recipes reprinted by permission of Houghton Mifflin Harcourt from *The Slow Mediterranean Kitchen* (2003), *The Cooking of Southwest France* (2005), and *Mediterranean Clay Pot Cooking* (2009); and by permission of HarperCollins from *Mediterranean Cooking* (1994), *The Cooking of the Eastern Mediterranean* (1994), *Mediterranean Grains and Greens* (1998), and *The Food of Morocco* (2011)

Library of Congress Control Number: 2017948583

ISBNs: 978-1-5387-2988-5 (hardcover); 978-1-5387-2987-8 (ebook)

Printed in the United States of America

WOR

10 9 8 7 6 5 4 3 2 1

"Good food is memory."
—Paula Wolfert

To the 1,112 people who
supported our crowdfunding campaign
to make this book possible,
your generosity and faith are
truly unforgettable.

Contents

Foreword
by Alice Waters

FROM THE TIME I DEVOURED Paula Wolfert's extraordinary first book, *Couscous and Other Good Food from Morocco,* and then started cooking from it, I have been convinced that she is simply one of those rare people who know the exact way food should be. This book beautifully demonstrates her irresistible food, set out on the table the way I like to see it, the way I like to eat it, the way it *should* be eaten.

Always with Paula, every element was thoroughly researched and thought out, tested over and over, clearly and logically recorded, and beautifully executed.

Throughout her career, over and over, Paula has given us hope by serving us recipes that partake of this kind of simplicity—even those recipes of hers that are the most exacting and time-consuming—surprising us again and again with the generosity and breadth of her curiosity and the precision and focus of her perfectionism; surprising us, while skillfully steering us past the shallows of food fashion into the deep harbors of ancient food traditions that depend on such timeless values as patience, frugality, loyalty, and community, values that are inimical to the fast-food values that pervade the modern world.

Emily Kaiser Thelin and her extraordinary collaborators, Eric Wolfinger, Andrea Nguyen, and Toni Tajima, have gifted us with an inspiring and beautiful book: a critical survey of a very public career, an anthology of wonderful recipes, and an intimate biography of a brave and complicated person who is now facing the challenges of Alzheimer's disease with the same shrewd appetite for understanding that she brought to all her researches into food and cooking. By her pioneering example she continues to be a worthy mentor to us all.

Introduction

IN AN IMPOSSIBLY NARROW LANE in the crowded ancient medina of Marrakech, a motor scooter zipped past, a horned ram bleating between the driver's legs, bound for sacrifice for the Muslim holiday of Eid al-Adha. I jumped to get out of the way and promptly collided with a family headed home for the holiday, a small lamb chewing on weeds while straddling the shoulders of the man. I cinched my coat tighter against the wet, cold December day and pushed on against the crowds.

It was December 2008. I had come to Morocco on an assignment for *Food & Wine* to profile legendary cookbook author Paula Wolfert, a longtime contributor to the magazine whom I had edited as a staffer there since 2006. This was the culinary equivalent of a journey through the Arabian dunes with T. E. Lawrence or a trip to Kitty Hawk with the Wright Brothers—the chance to tour the place where a titan of my field first made her name. She and I had met in person only twice before, once at a food conference and then for lunch at her house in Sonoma. She had returned to Morocco because her publisher, HarperCollins, had suggested she update her first book, the 1973 landmark *Couscous and Other Good Food from Morocco*.

In *Couscous*, Paula writes how Eid al-Adha, the Festival of the Sacrifice, "occurs on the tenth day of the twelfth month of the Muslim calendar year and commemorates the sacrifice of Abraham. Every Moroccan tries to get hold of a sheep . . . a kid or, if he is very poor, a fowl. The point is to make a sacrifice and then enjoy it." As a resident of Morocco in the late 1960s, she purchased and fattened her own live lamb for the holiday and, working from a cookbook published by *House & Garden* magazine—decades before DIY butchery—taught herself to cut up the carcass. Any odd bits that she'd butchered badly, she chopped to make *kefte*, delicious Moroccan meatballs.

I had been looking forward to this trip for months, but when I arrived, Paula e-mailed profuse apologies that she had been delayed and wouldn't be able to join me until the next day. I wandered the medina alone—for as long as I could stand it. I loved it but felt I might drown in the riptide of rams, goats, carpet sellers, spice merchants, and charcoal smoke. I retreated to the rooftop café of my hotel to sip hot mint tea.

When we met the next morning, the holiday was over. The rams and goats were gone, but the crowds were denser than ever. Paula tucked her bobbed chestnut hair behind her ears, linked her arm in mine, and together we traversed the Djemaa el-Fna, Marrakech's vast central square. Although the square teemed with people, the tension I had felt the day before melted away. She led me first to the best stall for *merguez* sausages, where men stood working the open-air grills, the sweet scents of paprika, cumin, and grilled lamb infusing the smoke.

"You can tell this stall is good because so many Moroccans have lined up for it," she observed. To anyone who tried to sell us something we didn't want, she smiled and sang out, "La, barak Allahu fik!" Even to my untrained ear, Paula's Arabic sounded surprisingly poor, her consonants blunted by her Brooklyn edge, her vowels as broad as a Texas cowboy's. But she put feeling into it. Hearing her, sellers burst out laughing and gave us a wide swath. What had she said to them? I wondered, because the day before, nothing I did or said in any language could buy me a minute's peace.

"It means 'God will grant you every wish if you leave me alone.' It's only used in Morocco," she revealed with her characteristic mirth. "They can't believe a Westerner knows it."

We headed to another stall for *mechoui*, Marrakech-style roast lamb. She sailed up to the wizened old operator, laid a hand on his arm, and proceeded to pepper him with questions in English, French, and Arabic about how he prepared it. I feared he might be insulted by the examination, but as her questions grew ever more detailed, down to the kind of cumin he used, he burst into a delighted grin.

"You know our food!" he exclaimed, and hugged her.

❖

Paula Wolfert may be the most influential cookbook author you've never heard of. It's a food biography cliché to claim that the subject changed the way we eat—except Paula really did, in ways that have gone overlooked by many people until now. She never had a restaurant. She never had a television show. But over nearly four decades, from 1973 to 2011, she published eight seminal cookbooks,

Paula in her home kitchen in the 1970s.

three reissues, and countless articles on the traditional foods of the Mediterranean. Her work had a quiet but incalculable influence on our grocery shelves and on our approach to cooking. She helped popularize foods we now take for granted: the couscous, preserved lemons, and tagines of Morocco; the duck confit and cassoulet of France; and the *muhammara* (Syrian red pepper–nut spread), sumac, pomegranate molasses, and mild red pepper flakes—Aleppo, Marash, and Urfa—of the Middle East. But more, she legitimized a basic approach to cooking that all good chefs now embrace: a respect and reverence for foods of tradition and place.

When Paula started in the 1970s, she was one of a generation of cookbook authors who worked in the wake of Julia Child's 1963 *Mastering the Art of French Cooking* to introduce Americans to yet more authentic international cuisines. She joined women like Marcella Hazan, Madhur Jaffrey, and Diana Kennedy, who championed genuine Italian, Indian, and Mexican cooking, respectively.

But three qualities put Paula in a class by herself: her curiosity, her rigor, and her vision.

After publishing *Couscous* in 1973, Paula did not stay long in Morocco—or in any country. Her inquisitiveness kept her moving: to Southwest France, to Spanish Catalonia, to Sicily, to the Middle East. She ultimately circled the Mediterranean many times, helping introduce the very concept of Mediterranean cuisine to the American culinary mainstream. A marketing consultant might have warned her that she was watering down her brand by refusing to stay in one place. But her favorite settings were places of discovery—uncharted territory, overlooked ingredients, whatever everyone else couldn't see. As she liked to put it, "All my life I've been drawn to The Other."

In her explorations, she showed an unusual ability to bond quickly with women home cooks (and chefs of both genders) all over the Mediterranean, coaxing from them their most cherished recipes and cooking secrets. She included her favorite finds in her books. Though she often finessed them to polish their flavors, she never dumbed them down.

By refusing to apologize for obscure ingredients or complex techniques, she challenged Americans to become better cooks. Her rigor ensured her obscurity; for years, mainstream cooks found her books too challenging. (Some of her most iconic recipes are indeed complicated. Her instructions for cassoulet, first published in *Food & Wine* magazine in 1978, go on for pages and call for six kinds of pork.)

But her exactitude made her a hero to our most forward-thinking chefs. Julia Child called her "one of the few food writers whose recipes I trust." Thomas Keller told me that Paula's "fortitude," her refusal to dilute a recipe or its history, makes her work "relevant for generations of professional chefs and home cooks." Alice Waters says Paula's books altered the menus at Chez Panisse many times, and helped her articulate the idea of treating vegetables as a main dish. Jerusalem-born, London-based chef Yotam Ottolenghi describes Paula as having "paved the way to Morocco for so many of us." Pioneering Italian chef Mario Batali credits her with introducing the very idea of authenticity to an America that had little interest in epicurean traditions. "She's a lot of fun to have a drink with, too," he added. Few cookbook authors enjoy the devotion of such vaunted chefs.

She was a visionary who saw where American food trends were going often decades before they occurred. She has a reputation as a free spirit who wrote books according to her whims. But she cannily positioned each one to offer something new. Her scouting put her further and further ahead. Only now have some of her best finds caught on, like foraged greens and Aleppo peppers. In no small part thanks to her, duck confit is currently available at Costco. To paraphrase historian Ron Chernow on Founding Father Alexander Hamilton, she was a messenger from a future we now inhabit.

And yet Paula is little known outside an elite circle. As a line cook in the late 1990s, I had never heard of her when a chef who was teaching me how to make a Moroccan carrot salad said she had adapted it from *Couscous*. When I asked who Paula Wolfert was, she pulled me off of the line and into her office, pushed the book into my hands, and insisted that I read it that night. At home, I stared at the photo of Paula on the back and wondered at her fortitude. Who was this woman who'd had the bravery to master three hundred years of one country's cooking, to become the first to codify that cuisine in English?

❖

In 2010, I left *Food & Wine* to move to California with my fiancé, now husband. By then, Paula lived in Sonoma, and as we became closer, I began to interview her for a potential biography. But something strange was going on with her mind.

She was known for her keen memory: At the peak of her career, she could re-create whole recipes from two scribbled lines. She could take one bite of a flatbread in Tunisia and compare the leavening to equivalents in Egypt, Turkey, Israel, or Algeria. In conversation, she could recall names of hundreds of friends she had made in her travels. She had also studied close to a dozen languages in order to converse with cooks she met throughout the Mediterranean. But now, at age seventy-two, she struggled to remember the basics of any of them. When she tried to read in English, she said, words floated on the page. Like everyone else who loved her, I dismissed it as a side effect of aging. Even her doctors told her nothing was wrong. Finally, in 2013, she received a diagnosis of dementia, probably Alzheimer's.

When she told me, I felt as bleak as I had that first day in Marrakech without her. But characteristically, she bucked me up. "I refuse to feel sorry for myself," she said. "This illness takes forever, and I'm determined to make it take as long as I can." She then quoted her beloved grandmother, "You can't win a war if you're not willing to fight."

As her editor at the magazine, I'd learned to parse out our phone calls like Halloween candy. They provided such pleasure, but I knew they could suck up a good part of the day. Before her diagnosis, she all but lived to talk about food but also about love, politics, reality television, life. Now in our calls she filled me in on her strategies for her illness.

In a strange way, dementia is today where food was when Paula began her culinary career: we don't know what we don't know, and we might pay dearly for our ignorance. Research into its prevention, treatment, and cure is woefully underfunded when compared with what goes toward conquering other major diseases, such as cancer and AIDS. Yet more and more Americans are succumbing to dementia as the population lives longer.

"More of us will have to 'come out' to fight for a cure," she said. "But too many are afraid."

Paula's illness inspired me to act. I sent out a proposal to write her biography to nearly a dozen publishers. A consensus emerged among them: her story was interesting but her time had passed.

So I took a page from Paula's renegade example and banded together with three gifted food professionals: photographer Eric Wolfinger, book designer Toni Tajima, and author Andrea Nguyen, who served as editor. We have assembled this culinary biography to honor Paula's incredible life and to highlight her contributions to American epicurean history. Thanks to our Kickstarter campaign, more than eleven hundred of her fans and colleagues funded our endeavor. Paula donated her recipes and opened her personal archive, which included articles both by her and about her, plus many letters, faxes, and e-mails.

When we started in 2011, Paula was already having memory trouble. But she had many prompts in her cookbooks and archives to help us. We took enormous pleasure in preparing dishes for her, which provoked more surprising recollections. Those kitchen forays also reminded us of what an unforgettable adventure cooking Paula's recipes can be.

OPPOSITE:
Paula and the
author, May 2016

Choosing which recipes to include proved much harder. Paula had published upward of a thousand, which had been curated from more than ten thousand dishes she had tasted on the road. How I yearned to include, for example, her romantic *éclade de moules* from *The Cooking of Southwest France*, which involves igniting fistfuls of fresh pine shoots in a wide forest clearing, or her fanciful egg omelet with hop shoots from *Mediterranean Grains and Greens*, though I've never seen a hop shoot in my life.

Ultimately, I followed Paula's criteria, which she expressed eloquently and practically in her fourth book, *Paula Wolfert's World of Food*: "When I develop recipes, I always look for ways to create what I call the Big Taste . . . food that is deeply satisfying, and that appeals to all the senses. I like dishes that leave their flavor with me, whose tastes and aromas I will never forget."

This cookbook is not a Greatest Hits of Paula Wolfert's cookery, as there are far too many of them. These are the recipes that celebrate Paula's life and the ideas and foods she cherishes. The book is organized chronologically, and many of the chapters include recipes to help illustrate her discoveries. Many of the recipes are in line with her new diet—a regimen nourishing for anyone, not just dementia sufferers. But they were primarily selected because they tell her story. Menus are suggested to help explain the choices, but they are optional, as each recipe is equally delicious on its own. Ultimately, I chose stories and recipes that I hope you will always remember.

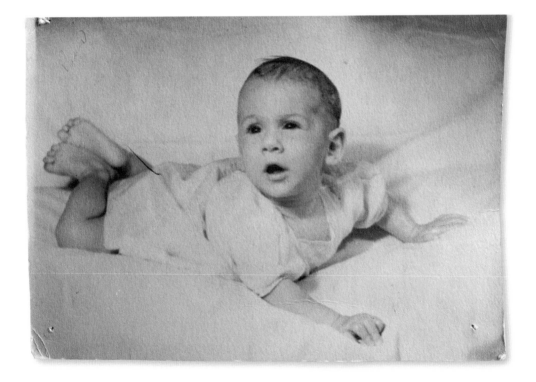

The Hell
Out of Flatbush

NEW YORK ❧ 1938 to 1955

"I live in a dark, fearful world. I have a photo of myself
from when I was only five days old that I've studied carefully, and that look is already there in my eyes—that
look of apprehension. Sure, I venture into the wilds of
Dagestan, and cross deserts, and risk the backroads of
Syria as a Jew, but no matter where I go or what I do,
I'm frightened—of exactly what, I never know."

—Paula Wolfert, quoted in James Villas's
Between Bites: Memoirs of a Hungry Hedonist

I SAW PAULA WOLFERT for the first time in 2005. Circled by a cluster
of admirers, she was standing near the back of an auditorium at a
conference at the Napa campus of the Culinary Institute of America.
I immediately recognized her from her books. A young freelance
writer, I nervously approached, then was startled to realize she
looked more nervous than I. She clearly didn't know anyone to whom
she was speaking, and her brown eyes revealed a vulnerability and a
tentativeness that belied her decades of experience. I had an impulse
to reach out with a calming hand. But when I introduced myself,
she smiled warmly and touched my arm with her soft palm, instead
reassuring me.

Paula's profound contrasts—her fear and boldness, her affection
and rigor—were seeded in her childhood, but not for reasons you
might expect. Born Paula Miriam Harris on April 7, 1938, she was the
eldest daughter of Sam and Frieda Harris, a comfortably middle-class

OPPOSITE:
Paula as an
infant, 1938

Jewish couple who lived in the comfortably middle-class Jewish section of the Brooklyn neighborhood of Flatbush.

Mel Blanc, the original voice of Bugs Bunny, said he modeled the character's voice on a Flatbush accent. Set in the heart of the borough, the neighborhood was home to an eclectic mix of strictly segregated groups: Jews, Italians, Irish Catholics, and Dutch Protestants. (Flatbush, from the Dutch for "flat woodland," was settled by the Dutch in the seventeenth century.) In her first years, Paula knew only the Jewish part of town, its high-rises and its many other middle-class Jewish families. Paula had a younger sister and brother, but until she was

With her parents, Sam and Frieda Harris, on a summer road trip, c. 1941

five, she was an only child. Her father managed several Harlem hotels and was said to be able to get along with anybody. He may also have given Paula some of his entrepreneurial spirit. Her mother, Frieda, was a housewife who valued good looks over adventure; from Paula's earliest years she and her mother did not get along.

For much of her childhood, Paula struggled to fit in. She was born walleyed, her right eye turned outward from her left. Her parents took her to a preeminent ophthalmologist, who said he could correct the problem cosmetically with surgery, though she had to wait until she turned sixteen. Today her eyes appear normal, but she has never had stereoscopic vision, so she lacks depth perception. Her left eye is farsighted, her right eye nearsighted. When she is particularly nervous or excited, she cannot fully control which eye her brain uses to see.

Her personality, even now, mirrors this unusual split. Especially when she is keyed up, she flips back and forth from near to far and back again: from infectious warmth to bristling impatience, vulnerability to boldness, anger to joy, boredom to intense engagement. To a certain extent, she knows her own extremes. For example, she chose "soumak" (a Slavic spelling of sumac) for her e-mail and Twitter handle because the Mediterranean spice can be either "very sweet, or poisonous," she said with a delighted cackle. That range is part of what makes her so magnetic—and may have made her a handful growing up.

In the years before the surgery to align her eyes, she came up with strategies to compensate for her strange appearance. To win over wary strangers, she developed a disarming warmth and a vocal range that could swing from booming life of the party to intimate whisper, the better to draw people in. As an adult, she created workarounds for her visual impairments. Incredibly for someone so accomplished in the kitchen, all her life she avoided chef's knives. Even as an adult, she avoided any kitchen tasks that required depth perception, from chopping herbs with a chef's knife to flipping an omelet in a pan, knowing she could hurt herself. "I was very scared of big knives, of my fingers getting in the way," she admits.

But as a child, the kitchen didn't interest her much. She didn't eat well growing up. In keeping with the dominant food culture of postwar America, her childhood home was not big on traditional flavors. Everything was "boiled or broiled," Paula has joked—if it was cooked at all. Her mother preferred to diet. "I grew up on melon, iceberg lettuce, and cottage cheese," Paula has often said. Perhaps because the pickings were so slim, she had little appetite as a kid and was regarded as skinny. To fatten her up, Frieda strangely gave her orange juice.

With her mother
c. 1941

❖

In 1943, when she was five, Paula experienced good food for the first time. In a setting that may have inspired her entire career, she learned to equate good food with love. Her mother sent her to stay with her paternal grandparents, Bertha and Max Harris, who then lived in rural New Jersey. Paula does not know why she was sent away, and no one else who might remember is alive, but that year Frieda was pregnant with Paula's little sister, and she may have lacked the stamina to keep up with her enthusiastic firstborn.

Paula's grandparents had emigrated from the Balkans in the early 1900s and had never much assimilated (beyond their last name, which was Americanized at Ellis Island from Himowitz). They came from the Romanian and Serbian sides of the Danube River and still spoke to each other in Romanian. They understood English well enough to listen to radio shows, however, and tuned in almost every day, as they lay on their bed with Paula between them. She loved to feel the warmth and shaking of their bellies as they laughed at the best jokes. They doted on her, getting her a pet goat when they discovered she was afraid of dogs. In their Victory Garden, they gave Paula her first Technicolor tastes of freshly harvested vegetables like eggplants

With her grandmother, Bertha Harris, in her Victory Garden in New Jersey, c. 1943

and red peppers, many of them seldom seen in 1940s grocery stores. In the kitchen, Bertha introduced her to the earthiness and gentle spice of Balkan dishes like *ajvar* (recipe, page 20), an eggplant relish, and *ćevapčići* (recipe, page 24), small sausages. Paula's earliest culinary memory is of her grandmother slowly cooking eggplants on the stove. Balkan cooking blends many elements from the Mediterranean: North African, southern European, and Turkish, among other cuisines. These memories were seared into Paula's brain, fueling her entire career, though she wasn't yet aware of their impact.

Before this book project, Paula often boasted to me that she had published more eggplant recipes than any other cookbook author she knew. I asked for the one that had started her love of nightshade vegetables, but she couldn't recall her grandmother's recipe, until September 2015. We were in the midst of this book project when one of Paula's longtime friends, cookbook author Diana Kennedy, sent her a manuscript for her memoir that, by chance, included a recipe for *ajvar*, the Serbian eggplant and bell pepper spread. Paula made the dish, only to realize it tasted eerily close to the relish her grandmother had made.

"This is really crazy!!!" Paula e-mailed me. "I knew my grandmother's dish, but never its proper name."

What was even crazier, as a picture in her e-mail showed, Paula had published her own recipe for *ajvar* forty years earlier, in her second book, *Mediterranean Cooking*, but never made the connection to her grandmother. She had learned it in the 1960s from a woman in Yugoslavia who used green bell peppers, not red ones like Bertha did. Paula's palate is so precise that such a seemingly minor difference might well have prevented her from recognizing the link. *Ajvar* is also a Serbian term; her grandmother spoke Romanian. It's possible that Bertha called the spread *zacuscă*, a term Paula only recently found online.

As a five-year-old, Paula adored her grandmother's relish as an unusually delicious treat. She speculates that she might have liked it because the dish tasted so much more complex than its few humble ingredients—a tenet of all Paula's recipes. "I think I loved it because two plus two equaled so much more than four," she said.

Landing on Kennedy's *ajvar* recipe gave her new energy. For several weeks after her initial discovery, Paula tinkered with Kennedy's version to see if she could bring it even closer to her memories of Bertha's. As she worked, her family remarked they had not seen her so happy in the kitchen in years.

I was happy, too. Just as she had done when I was her editor, she crowded my inbox with revision after revision, each one looking more delicious. Finally, at our next photo shoot, she showed me how she made the spread. She grilled the eggplants and peppers over low coals until they collapsed, peeled them, then worked them to a pulp with her bare hands (see photo on page 23). "Can you see why this would have gotten a little girl excited?" she asked. Then she seasoned the pulp with a heady mix of crushed garlic, cider vinegar, paprika, salt, and pepper. It tasted wonderful. Moreover, I had rarely seen Paula so at ease while cooking anything.

❖

Despite her forty years as a food authority, Paula has never relaxed in the kitchen. She's too much of a perfectionist. The only time I'd seen her that comfortable was in Morocco, when she found a good cook to teach her a dish she had read about, *chaariya meftoun*, short noodles steamed like couscous, often served with a stew. She had written a brief description of it in her first book but wanted to see it made after watching a YouTube video of Moroccan cooking star Choumicha preparing it, a viewing that convinced Paula it was going to be the next hot dish. Before we left the States, we contacted a dozen people in the hope of finding someone to help us, to no avail.

But Paula has magical good luck. After landing in Marrakech, she left her ATM card in the airport bank machine. The next person in line recognized her name; the woman's American parents had raised her in Morocco and had cooked from *Couscous*. "Let me know if I can help with anything during your stay," she insisted. A few days later, striking out in our hunt for *chaariya*, Paula e-mailed her. "Yes," the woman wrote back, "my Berber housekeeper makes an excellent version. Come for lunch."

When we pulled up to the woman's suburban development, I was skeptical. But then the housekeeper, Malika, greeted us at the door dressed in a bright blue silk Berber tunic. "I think this is going to be good," Paula said. "You can tell she cares."

What followed was a master class in how Paula gets her recipes. In the kitchen, which was scented with Malika's freshly ground spices, Paula pulled out her notebook but didn't write much down; instead, she peppered Malika with questions: Where was her saffron from, her cumin, her almonds? And where was she from, and how had she learned so much about cooking? Malika opened up about her almonds but also her recent struggles to support her family, how before she'd found this job she'd worked as a janitor at a school, her young son strapped to her back. Malika and Paula joked, they hugged. Paula gave her a tomato peeler as a thank-you gift. By the time the noodles steamed, they seemed like grandmother and granddaughter. Moreover, a kind of otherworldly, almost holy glow pulsed in the room. Paula started to cry. We all started to cry.

"That's how I wrote all of my books!" Paula said. "Hugging, kissing, and measuring spoons."

I suspect that Paula's cookbooks are so exceptional because she bonds with good food the way she bonds with her favorite people, like her grandmother. The best dishes are synonymous with love itself.

"To me, good food is memory," Paula once told food writer Peggy Knickerbocker. "One time or another, I've had a fling with each of the recipes in my books."

❖

Paula could only stay with her grandparents that one year. In 1944, when she was six and back in Flatbush, she resumed a diet of orange juice, cottage cheese, iceberg lettuce, and broiled meat—with occasional forays for Chinese food, or for oysters, surf and turf, and cheesecake (recipe, page 27) at Lundy's in Sheepshead Bay. Paula also met her new sister, Ruby, born in Paula's absence, whom their mother seemed to like better. That year, Paula tried to get rid of Ruby by pushing her down the stairs. It's possible her jealousy of Ruby inspired her lifelong fear of being replaced. When sororicide didn't work, she launched a campaign to escape her family.

At age seven, after her grandparents moved to Manhattan, she ran away to their midtown apartment by riding the subway. Her grandmother lovingly played along, "hiding" her in the basement and telling her she'd feed her onion sandwiches. ("They'll smell me out!" the young Paula protested.) But that night Bertha took her back to Brooklyn. Concerned about her reckless behavior, her mother sent her to a preeminent psychiatrist, a relative, who told her parents, "She's a renegade. Do not worry about her."

❖

At age eleven, Paula fled the Jewish section of Flatbush to explore her first foreign country: the Irish Catholic neighborhood around the corner. She swiftly befriended several girls, joining their tours of the neighborhood Irish bars to bring their fathers home for supper.

Compared to her block of cookie-cutter brick high-rises, she loved the exotic landscape of low-slung bungalows, laundry hanging on the line, and chickens in a few of the backyards. The ornate baroque Catholic church, with its incense-laden Latin Mass, proved a particular draw. "It was so gaudy compared to the boring synagogue," she said. "I loved it! And I wanted to learn everything about it!"

Within six months, with guidance from her friends and the church priest, Paula had taken enough catechism classes to convert to Catholicism. She completed three of the rituals leading up to conversion that Easter, when she was baptized, confirmed, and took her first communion (and ate the communion wafer, her initial culinary adventure in the church).

"It didn't taste like the body of Christ, I'll tell you that," she said. "They warn you it might stick to the inside of your mouth because you can't chew. It certainly wasn't salty. But it was all *very* exciting."

But before she could complete the final steps to convert, her mother found out and brought a halt to Paula's plan. It is likely Paula's primary goal was to stick it in the eye of her secular Jewish parents, particularly her mother. Frieda sent her to another preeminent psychologist, her cousin's cousin. Paula didn't care for him but found that as long as she went twice a week, her mother left her alone. Preteen Paula was quickly proving herself to be highly unconventional and doggedly curious.

Paula wasn't just a sensualist yearning for transcendence, however. She also had incredible drive. Research soothed her anxieties. Unable to escape physically, she dove into books. It helped that her father recognized his daughter's keen mind: In 1945, when President Franklin Roosevelt died, Sam encouraged his eight-year-old daughter to write down her thoughts. When she was a preteen, he encouraged her cultural curiosities by buying her anthropology books, such as *Patterns of Culture* by Ruth Benedict. Paula devoured Benedict's pioneering work alongside her Nancy Drew books.

When the Korean War broke out in 1950, Paula left her school grounds and raced to the nearby public library to learn everything she could about the land, feeling keenly betrayed by her teachers who had never taught her about the place. She hated to be kept from the truth. Her grandmother's one flaw, Paula discovered, was that Bertha sometimes told tall tales, like the one about how bears were

With her father
c. 1947

brought into her village from the countryside and the local men would lie down on the animals to absorb their strength. Was this true? Paula yearned to visit the Balkans to find out. While researching the region in her beloved public library, Paula discovered stories of Balkan bards called *gusle* players. In the Homeric tradition, the blind singers recited tales of heroism, the telling lasting for hours, even days. If they sensed the audience growing bored, they tweaked their tales to reengage them. (These bards influenced Paula's imagination so much that she became something of a food lover's *gusle* player: she can talk about food for hours, and on the rare occasions when she senses she's losing an audience, she's willing to embroider her epic tales.) She taught herself rudimentary Serbian and pledged to see the *gusle* players of Montenegro and Macedonia on their home ground.

In her early teens, Paula met a veritable partner in crime while exploring another nearby congregation, the Dutch Reformed church across from her school. One Halloween, while playing in the church graveyard, she encountered Loretta Foye, a Dutch Irish girl from the remote Brooklyn waterfront neighborhood of Red Hook who swiftly became her best friend and math tutor. "Red Hook was *really* exotic," Paula recalls. "I would have never graduated from high school if Loretta hadn't gotten me through algebra and trigonometry." Loretta was also two years older and was enrolled at Columbia University when Paula was still a sophomore at Erasmus Hall, Flatbush's acclaimed public high school. But they stayed in touch, and Paula started to dream of following her friend to Manhattan.

Then Paula's parents gave her the worst possible news: at the end of her junior year, the family would be moving to the suburbs of Westchester, north of Manhattan. If she moved with them, she would have to spend her senior year in an even duller and more homogeneous place than Flatbush. "I wanted so much to be in New York City," she said. "The suburbs just weren't part of my scenario." When she was fifteen, she even found a German boyfriend who lived in Manhattan, in Yorkville. She came up with a cunning solution to the Westchester move: after both her sophomore and junior years, she enrolled in summer school classes and was able to graduate a year and a semester early.

After she turned sixteen in April 1954, she underwent the long-awaited surgery to align her eyes cosmetically. In January of the following year, she graduated from high school. Since Barnard College wouldn't take students at midyear, she enrolled at Columbia University's School of General Studies and chose English as her major. She took a room at a women's boardinghouse in Greenwich Village. In Manhattan, she finally discovered like-minded souls: the Beats.

Paula's family at the dinner table in 1952, celebrating her brother's first birthday. LEFT TO RIGHT: Frieda, Paula, Ruby, Howard (in high chair), grandparents Bertha and Max, and father Sam.

Paula's Childhood Favorites

❖ ❋ ❖

Paula's earliest years were not crammed with delicious foods. On the contrary, she grew up on a regimen dominated by 1950s diet foods and orange juice—except the year she turned five, when she lived with her grandparents. Her grandmother, Bertha Harris, had a limited but loving repertoire of Balkan dishes, with their layered, lingering flavors deeply rooted in tradition, made a lifelong impression on her granddaughter. The first two dishes here reflect that influence. The cheesecake reminds her of one she enjoyed at Lundy's, a restaurant in Sheepshead Bay, Brooklyn, where her parents took her and her siblings on special occasions.

FIRST COURSE OR SIDE
Ajvar

MAIN COURSE
Ćevapčići

DESSERT
Ricotta Cheesecake

Ajvar

Proust had madeleines; Paula Wolfert has eggplants. Her love of nightshades was seeded in her childhood, and this is her best guess at her grandmother's recipe for a Balkan eggplant spread she often made when Paula was growing up. Tangy and only faintly garlicky, it's an ideal accompaniment to just about anything: grilled skewered meats (like the sausages that follow), grilled fish or vegetables, or spread on bread in a turkey or tofu sandwich.

---

3 or 4 red sweet peppers, such as bell or Corno di Toro (about 4 ounces | 115 g each)

1 green bell or poblano pepper (about 4 ounces | 115 g)

2 eggplants (about 12 ounces | 350 g each; see notes)

2 garlic cloves, peeled

½ teaspoon flaky sea salt

¼ cup (60 ml) extra-virgin olive oil, plus more for topping

1 tablespoon unfiltered cider vinegar

Heaping ¼ teaspoon freshly ground black pepper

Pinch of mild red pepper flakes, preferably Aleppo or Marash (optional)

Pinch of cayenne pepper (optional)

Makes about 2 to 2½ cups (about 550 g)

⏱ The spread can be refrigerated for up to 1 week (its flavor improves daily).

Light a medium-low fire in a charcoal or gas grill. Set the red and green peppers and the eggplant on the grill and cook slowly, turning occasionally, until they are nicely charred on all sides and soft to the point of collapsing, about 30 minutes. As they finish cooking, transfer the vegetables to a large bowl, cover with a plate or plastic wrap, and let steam and cool.

Using your fingers or a paring knife, peel the eggplant and the peppers. Remove any large seed pockets in the eggplant, and then stem and seed the peppers. Transfer the vegetables to a large bowl. Using your hands, pull the peppers and eggplant apart into chunks, then crush and massage them between your fingers to form a coarse paste. Set aside.

Using a mortar and pestle, the back of a heavy knife and a cutting board, or a mini food processor, crush together the garlic and salt, forming a paste. Add the garlic paste, olive oil, vinegar, black pepper, and the red pepper flakes and cayenne, if using, to the eggplant mixture and mix well. Taste and adjust the seasoning with more vinegar, salt, and black, red, and cayenne pepper if needed.

Transfer to a jar and top with a ¼-inch (6-mm) layer of olive oil. Cover tightly and refrigerate at least overnight before serving. Season lightly once more before serving.

recipe continues →

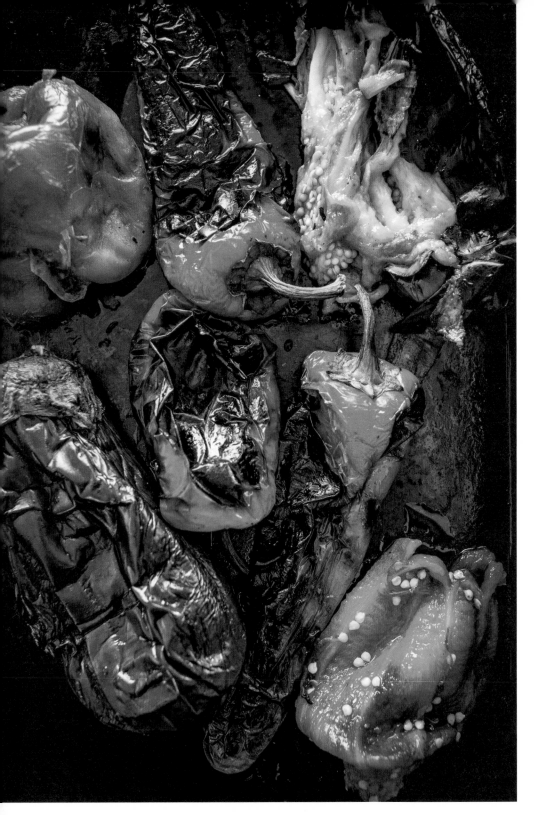

NOTES The fresh red and green peppers can be charred on the stove top by setting them directly on a gas burner with the flame turned to medium-high and rotating them as they blacken. If the skin is fully charred but the flesh is not yet tender, transfer the peppers to a foil-lined sheet pan and bake in a 400°F (200°C) oven until soft to the point of collapsing, 10 to 25 minutes longer, depending on the thickness of the peppers.

The eggplants can be cooked in a 400°F (200°C) oven; pierce them a few times with a sharp knife, set them on a foil-lined sheet pan, and bake until soft to the point of collapsing, 30 to 40 minutes.

From her many years of cooking with eggplants, Paula has found the best-tasting ones, especially for grilling or roasting whole, each weigh about 12 ounces (350 g) and feel firm to the touch.

Ćevapčići

Although she didn't know it when her grandmother made these sausages for her, Paula was tasting her future: *Ćevapčići* (pronounced Che-VAHP-chi-cee) is a diminutive of the word *ćevap*, or sausage; common to many Slavic languages, it comes from the Persian word *kabāb*. Paula published dozens of kebab, *köfte*, and kibbe recipes from around the Mediterranean—plus an Indonesian version of meat on skewers, beef *satay* (recipe, page 72).

These small sausages are gently spiced with paprika, red pepper flakes, and garlic, threaded on skewers, and quickly grilled. Club soda makes them light and silky. When Paula was a child, her grandmother would offer these sausages with *ajvar* (recipe, page 20) as well as sour cream for drizzling on top, chopped onions for sprinkling, and puffy flatbreads called *lebenje*.

---

1 or 2 garlic cloves, peeled

¾ teaspoon flaky sea salt

1½ pounds (675 g) ground beef, preferably 80 percent lean

1 teaspoon hot smoked paprika (pimentón de la Vera picante)

½ teaspoon freshly ground black pepper

¼ teaspoon mild red pepper flakes, preferably Aleppo or Marash

3 tablespoons (45 ml) club soda

OPTIONAL FOR SERVING

Soft, fluffy pitas (such as pide), Ajvar (page 20), Turkish Yogurt Sauce (page 315), thinly sliced red onion half-moons

Makes 20 sausages, enough to serve 4 to 6

Using a mortar and pestle, the back of a heavy knife and a cutting board, or a mini food processor, crush together the garlic and salt, forming a paste. Transfer the garlic to a large bowl and add the beef, paprika, black pepper, and red pepper flakes. Using your fingertips, gently rub the seasonings into the meat, distributing them evenly. Using a rubber spatula, gradually fold in the club soda until a smooth consistency is achieved.

Dampen your hands with water and form the meat into 20 sausages, each about 1 inch (2.5 cm) in diameter and 3 inches (7.5 cm) long. They should look like short, chubby hot dogs.

You may pack each sausage around a skewer (if using bamboo skewers and a charcoal or gas grill, be sure to soak the skewers in water for 30 minutes before using). But it is also fine to grill them without skewers.

recipe continues →

Light a medium-high fire in a charcoal or gas grill, preheat a stove-top grill pan over medium-high heat, or preheat the broiler. Grill or broil the sausages, turning them a few times, until just cooked through, about 5 minutes total. Serve the sausages hot or warm with the bread, Ajvar, yogurt sauce, and onion, if desired.

NOTE To vary the flavor, use a mixture of two parts ground beef to one part pork (or lamb) instead of all beef and cook for 6 to 8 minutes.

Ricotta Cheesecake

Paula has never had much of a sweet tooth and always struggled to find enough favorite desserts for the sweets chapters in her cookbooks. But she fondly remembers the cheesecake at Lundy's restaurant in Sheepshead Bay, one of her family's favorite spots when she was growing up. She never learned the restaurant's recipe, but she says this crustless ricotta cheesecake recipe (from her book *Mediterranean Clay Pot Cooking*) reminds her of it. She learned this recipe many years later, at a restaurant called La Villa on the island of Corsica.

You can make this in a glass pie plate instead of clay, but the earthenware both insulates the cheesecake and absorbs excess moisture, which prevents cracking. Baked in glassware, the cheesecake may form a crack or two on its surface, but it will taste equally delicious. Dot a few fresh berries over any cracks, and no one will ever know.

---

1 tablespoon unsalted butter

4 large eggs

½ cup (100 g) sugar

1 pound (450 g) whole-milk ricotta, preferably sheep's milk

2 teaspoons grated lemon zest

½ teaspoon pure vanilla extract

Pinch of flaky sea salt

2 tablespoons poire Williams, eau-de-vie de Mirabelle, or dark rum

Preheat the oven to 450°F (230°C). Grease a 9- or 10-inch (22.5- to 25-cm) cazuela, tagine base, or glass pie plate with the butter.

Serves 6 to 8

In a food processor, combine the eggs and sugar and process until light and creamy, about 20 seconds. Add the ricotta, lemon zest, vanilla, and salt and process until smooth and thick. Scrape the filling into the prepared cooking vessel.

Bake until puffed but still a bit wiggly in the center, about 20 minutes. Turn off the oven and, without opening the oven door, let the cake finish baking in the receding heat for 20 minutes. It will lose its puffiness and its surface will turn a lush golden brown. Remove the cake from the oven, sprinkle the top with the poire Williams, and let cool for about 30 minutes. Cut into wedges and serve warm.

Life as
a Beatnik

NEW YORK ❖ 1955 to 1959

PAULA IS A DILIGENT RESEARCHER AND COLLECTOR. For this book project, she handed me boxes filled with clippings, notebooks, ephemera, and other clues on the cultural and culinary trends that mattered to her. While perusing these archives to find out about her beatnik years, I found an article she had printed out about Jack Kerouac's *On the Road*. Paula had underlined the following passage, which doubles as a motto for this period—and for the rest of her life:

> Hitchhiking is spontaneous prose. It's a form of winging it and just knowing that you're going to meet the person or you're going to find the junction up ahead where it all makes sense. And it doesn't make sense right now, but that's all right, just keep on moving.

❖

In January 1955, sixteen-year-old Paula arrived at Columbia University, primed for adventure. Allen Ginsberg wouldn't publish *Howl* until 1956, and Jack Kerouac wouldn't release *On the Road* until the fall of 1957. Their works were in progress that January (and Kerouac was out of town) when she met Ginsberg, Peter Orlovsky, and other players in the renegade, avant-garde beatnik scene. She found the Beats to be kindred spirits in their quest for authentic sensory experiences.

Paula didn't just share their disenchantment with postwar consumerist American culture. She also liked writers. She wanted to

OPPOSITE:
Paula in 1955

express herself on the page, but her vision problems and natural impatience made it hard for her to organize her thoughts. Through the Beats, she would eventually find an even more renegade career path for a woman in the 1950s: restaurant chef.

At Columbia, she barely went to class. At night, she and her Brooklyn friend Loretta donned black leotards, tights, and flats—accessories for the right Beat look. If their local West End Bar was too full of Sarah Lawrence girls, they'd hitch a ride on a motorcycle or in a taxi to the White Horse Tavern in the Village. She recalled, "We were like pilot fish, looking around for larger things to happen to us." Long into the night they smoked and talked literature and philosophy, and flirted. Paula was fascinated; she had never heard such intellectual conversations before. Although it would later annoy her that the men talked over the women, at first she didn't notice.

To fund their nights out, Paula helped Loretta run a weekly poker game out of Loretta's apartment, the two of them sharing a cut from each of the betting pots. Loretta put Paula in charge of snacks. Paula knew so little about cooking that, on Loretta's advice, she acted boldly. "I threw a pot roast into a hot oven for a half hour and called it roast beef," she recounted.

But even among the Beats, Paula had conflicting desires. She loved the rebel life, but she also wanted to marry a smart, good-looking guy with an Ivy League degree and earning potential. "I went to college to earn my MRS," she often joked. One day she clarified, "You have to understand, this was the 1950s, the last time that men were the breadwinners, women were the housewives. I didn't know what I wanted, but I wanted to get married because that was how I thought I'd get on with my life." She wanted to do what was expected of her in order to explore options for the unexpected.

In June 1957, a friend of a friend, a dashing aspiring writer named Michael Wolfert, walked into the West End and slid into her booth. Shy and sensitive, he whispered when he spoke, drawing his listeners in close. He had just graduated with honors from Harvard, with a double major in literature and government. Back when Harvard was still rumored to impose strict quotas on Jews, he was a major catch. Paula loved writers: Michael not only had his own novel in the works and a job on the copy desk at the *New York Post* but also a literary pedigree, with a Pulitzer Prize–winning father and a poet mother.

Michael shared Paula's conflicting desires. He was a Communist sympathizer with the capitalist ambition to write the Great American Novel, earn a good living, *and* remain a member of the proletariat. He lived in the shadow of his charismatic father, Ira, a leftist war correspondent and novelist who hobnobbed with Hemingway in Spain.

Michael wanted to live abroad and write novels as Ira had, and he was drawn to Paula's fearlessness. "I was freer, and he was looking to be free," she said.

Their courtship was swift. He read James Joyce's *Ulysses* to her in bed; she told him about her beloved *gusle* players. He shared a new book about them by some Harvard professors and pledged to help her see them one day.

Six months later, in December 1957, they wed. She was nineteen and he was twenty-one. If that sounds young today, it was normal for the times. Paula chose to wear pink instead of white because, as she explained, "I didn't think I was pure and I didn't want anybody to think I was." Her mother's cousin, a Brooklyn rabbi, refused to perform the ceremony "because everyone knew I was this wildcat," she said. A substitute was found.

Michael Wolfert

Although they received several thousand dollars cash in wedding presents, they skipped a honeymoon to save the money for travel. "We wanted to see the world," Paula said. They formed a loose plan to move to another capital of Beat life, Tangier, where the rent would be lower and Michael could finish his novel in the shadow of the great Beat writers there like Paul Bowles. To save more, Michael got a higher-paying job at a marketing firm and found them a rent-controlled apartment on the Upper East Side.

❖

Paula finally had the freedom she had long craved. Yet she didn't know what to do with it. She wanted to do *something*—she felt a bit jaded with life as a spectator to her husband's Beat friends. If anything, their disregard for the women among them appears to have driven Paula to find a way to stand out. On her mother's advice, she took a career aptitude test, which suggested she would be good with her hands. She bought some clay and some sculpting supplies and attempted a self-portrait. Embarrassed by the attempt, she threw out the clay and the supplies.

Then on New Year's Day 1958, the new bride prepared her first meal. She turned to *The Glamour Magazine After Five Cookbook* (most likely a wedding gift from her mother). Typical of American postwar food, the recipes showed little regard for tradition, even flavor. With

a newlywed's naïveté, Paula turned to the menu for January 1: egg drop consommé, pork chops with bananas, and sugared pineapple. Per the pork recipe, she browned the chops and braised them in a mix of sour cream, sherry, and bananas. Disgusted with the results, she threw out the dish and the book and reported the fiasco to her mother. "If you're going to keep that Harvard man, you have to learn to cook," Paula remembered Frieda saying. Paula can't recall exactly how she ended up there, but whether through an ad in the yellow pages or the advice of a friend, she found herself signing up for six classes at Dione Lucas's cooking school.

Few know the name Dione Lucas today, but in the late 1950s, Paula could have hardly found a better teacher. Lucas was a kind of precursor to Julia Child, attempting to bring classic French cooking to the American masses via books and television. A *New York Times* story on her at the time said, "while more American cooks jump on the bandwagon for Redi-Mix cakes, Instant Meatballs and Heat 'n' Gulp TV dinners, Dione Lucas, a small, indomitable figure, marches steadily in the opposite direction." Lucas was the first woman to appear on an American cooking show and the first woman to be awarded a Grande Diplôme from Le Cordon Bleu. Her technique was said to be unparalleled. She was justly famous for her omelets and at one time owned a popular Upper East Side restaurant called the Egg Basket.

Lucas held her classes at her elegant apartment in The Dakota, the iconic New York apartment building. Before each class commenced, she had her students change into house slippers, perhaps to protect the floors. With a schoolmarmish bun and manner, Lucas cut an intimidating figure. But she was generous with her charges. In those days, cooking classes were typically demonstrations, and the rarer participation classes called for a few students to work together on just part of a dish. Lucas gave each of her pupils the opportunity to cook an entire dish from start to finish alone, with her supervision.

Paula's life changed during the class on sole Dugléré (recipe, page 42), an obscure but delicious nineteenth-century seafood dish invented by Parisian chef Adolphe Dugléré, who, according to *Larousse Gastronomique*, had studied under Carême, cooked for the Rothschilds, and invented *pommes Anna*. On completing the dish, Paula took one bite and realized what she needed to do: drop out of college and become a chef. "I loved its silky sauce," she said. "The tomato flavor was so surprising to me. I had never had fish prepared like that before. It was so rustic and yet so elegant."

When Paula and I cooked the dish together in 2015, it was clear that Lucas's version of sole Dugléré was a kind of ur–Paula Wolfert preparation: layered with rich, often surprising flavors, its components each relied on techniques that seemed unorthodox, even somewhat questionable. I was convinced it would not work until everything finally came together. The pivotal dish also evoked her grandmother's *ajvar* in its use of tomato and hot red pepper, ingredients that remained key throughout her career. As we worked in her home kitchen fifty-seven years later, Paula remembered both Lucas's impeccable technique and her coldness. "That's good," she said approvingly. "But she was not a nice woman."

Paula volunteered to become Lucas's unpaid full-time assistant, then threw herself into her new métier. On Lucas's recommendations, and with Michael's encouragement, she spent hundreds of dollars of her and Michael's wedding money on a *batterie* of pans and other equipment, including her first clay pot, a *triperie* for making tripe (photo, page 262). She started a small cookbook library, as Lucas advised, tracking down hard-to-find volumes by Elizabeth David and Henri-Paul Pellaprat (founder of Le Cordon Bleu and mentor to Lucas). In the evenings, she taught herself more recipes. Whether homemade sausage or fish set in its own aspic, none proved too daunting. The only challenge was using chef's knives; her cosmetic eye surgery had not blessed her with depth perception, so she often cut herself (a *New York Times* story on Lucas's classes mentions a Mrs. Wolfert being "rushed to the bathroom for first aid" after cutting herself while chopping a lobster). But she purchased two carbon-steel Sabatier chef's knives and a cleaver she still owns (photo, page 38).

Finding ingredients proved to be another obstacle: in 1950s New York, only a few odd health food stores and European butchers sold the rarer cuts and fresh vegetables. Paula visited them all. If any technique questions came up, she brought them to Lucas the next day.

Lucas was full of knowledge, but she was not kind. Her unbending nature, however, fueled Paula's perfectionism. Lucas once told *Time* magazine, "It's best to cook a strudel when you feel mean. The beast stands or falls on how hard you beat it. If you beat the dough 99 times, you will have a fair strudel. If you beat it 100 times, you will have a good strudel. But if you beat it 101 times, you will have a superb strudel."

"I used to quote her, 'A cook follows a recipe. A chef improves it.' That line really stuck with me," Paula said.

By late 1958, Paula was told she needed gall bladder surgery—probably from eating all the butter and eggs. When she returned to The Dakota after her recovery, Lucas announced perfunctorily that she had hired a replacement and her services were no longer required. Paula was devastated.

❖

Within a few months, however, Paula resourcefully turned to Lucas's chief rival, James Beard, the second major food authority then working in America. Michael's father, Ira Wolfert, published with Alfred A. Knopf, and his editor, Angus Cameron, was also Beard's. In many ways Lucas's foil, Beard was a natural writer and performer. Through books and television shows, he promoted the notion, still new in the United States, that cooking should be a pleasure—one that men could enjoy as much as women. Privately, he supported a tiny circle of Manhattan food writers and chefs by getting them work through his consulting and catering jobs. In the spring of 1958, Beard invited Paula to audition for him by cooking a three-course lunch at his Greenwich Village townhouse for himself and his friend, one of Paula's newest cooking heroes, the food writer Paula Peck.

"So I knock on the door," she said. "He knows I'm coming. But I did *not* know that he was gay." Paula had plenty of gay friends among the Beats, but none in that crowd could prepare her for the food titan.

Even in ordinary attire, Beard stood out: he was well over six feet tall and weighed over 250 pounds. At home he often wore flamboyant attire such as kimonos—or nothing at all. That day he had on an open-collared shirt with long, frilled cuffs and a number of gold chains draped over his chest. Paula held in her surprise as she quietly followed him into the living room, where they reviewed the menu. But Beard proved to be fun-loving and welcoming in every way Lucas was not, and Paula soon felt at ease.

The menu Beard planned for Paula's audition revealed her mastery of 1950s cooking, though she was just one year into her new calling. Around this time, Beard's doctors had discovered an irregular heartbeat and warned him to eat a healthier diet. But he evidently wasn't interested in heeding their advice. He chose a first course of lobster bisque ("with two cups of cream," Paula said), chicken Raphael for the main course ("three cups of cream and six egg yolks"), and a strawberry tart with *crème pâtissière* (even "more cream and eggs"). By then, she'd made the bisque and tart countless times for Lucas. Paula was unfamiliar with the 1910s American chicken dish but felt confident enough to figure it out.

Beard was so impressed with the meal that within weeks he dispatched Paula to her first catering gigs. At the Connecticut home of a Broadway director, she was to cater a lunch for 150. Paula had never cooked for so many, but Beard shared fail-safe recipes, including his Cognac-spiked walnut roll (recipe, page 45). When Paula arrived, however, the hostess, Mrs. Joshua Logan, was so shocked at her youthful appearance that she called out, "Oh my god, they've sent me a child!" and took to her bed, convinced that her luncheon was ruined. ("I looked about twelve at the time," Paula admitted.) But Paula would not be daunted: she cleverly sent up a slice of the walnut roll and persuaded her otherwise.

In addition to Beard's referrals, Paula also took on catering gigs of her own. Through Beat contacts she catered a Manhattan cocktail party where Jack Kerouac showed up. She served a Spanish tapas menu that included sizzling, garlicky shrimp (recipe, page 40). Kerouac came into the kitchen, glanced in her direction, and said, "Great legs."

"I could hardly believe it," Paula said, grinning at the memory. "Of course, I was serving whole shrimp [with the legs intact], so I didn't know if he meant mine or theirs!"

When summer rolled around, Paula's dream of becoming a professional restaurant chef came true. Beard got her a job as sous chef at Chillingsworth restaurant on Cape Cod. Paula moved to Massachusetts for the summer, and Michael came to visit her on weekends. Her chef was John Clancy, another of Beard's protégés, an ex-marine admired for his strong French technique. His menu was straightforward, only a dozen dishes, most of them French classics like duck à l'orange and lobster *à l'américaine*. Clancy manned the hot line. Paula worked *garde manger* (the pantry station), where she oversaw salads, starters, and desserts. Since salad spinners hadn't yet been invented, she spun the lettuce dry in a French wire basket in the gardens—and nearly threw out her shoulder. She also ladled out the soups, which included French onion and gazpacho garnished with a generous dollop of mayonnaise (a Beard recipe).

In August, the restaurant received a glowing review from the new restaurant critic at the *New York Times*, Craig Claiborne, who was friendly with Clancy. "To the residents of Cape Cod in search of imaginative food and relief from fish-net décor," he wrote, "the East Brewster restaurant called Chillingsworth is heartily recommended." He praised the canapés and gazpacho and found fault only with the "overly pungent" strips of orange rind in the duck sauce.

Then one day Clancy asked Paula to run the lunch line by herself. She should have aced it: lunch was all omelets, Dione Lucas's specialty. But the rush hit and she panicked.

"Now, I prided myself on my omelets," she said. "But then, twelve or twenty orders came in at once. I didn't even know how to use the stoves to get twelve omelets going. I started to cry."

Her eyes were part of the problem: She could never fully control which eye to use, especially in stressful situations. Clancy told her she wasn't ready to be a chef. Although she finished the summer, she felt so worn down by August that she swore she'd never cook professionally again.

Paula neglected to mention any of this to her mentor. Back in New York, Beard was consulting for The Four Seasons, a new restaurant that would change American fine dining. Beard helped pick the debut chef, Albert Stöckli from Switzerland, and suggested Paula as *garde manger* cook. Stöckli agreed, but she turned down the position.

It is incredible to imagine that Paula got so close to becoming a line cook at The Four Seasons. I have mentioned this to many chefs, most of whom pointed out that had she had taken that job, she probably would have burned out on food altogether, and might never have written a single book.

As she remembered it, Beard was furious. She knew she was burning a bridge, but she was ready to explore new worlds. In the fall of 1959, ready to fulfill the plan to move to Tangier that they had formed at the start of their marriage, she and Michael boarded a Yugoslav freighter bound for Morocco. She felt sure they would never live in New York again.

In 1959, eager to
leave New York
for Tangier

Retro Dinner Party

❖ ❀ ❖

As a young bride in the late 1950s, Paula got her start in food as a professional caterer and restaurant chef working under two of the greatest culinary minds of the era, Dione Lucas and James Beard. These three classics are a small sample of the many dishes she mastered.

FIRST COURSE

Sizzling Shrimp with Garlic and Pimentón

MAIN COURSE

Sole Dugléré

DESSERT

Walnut Roll

Sizzling Shrimp with Garlic and Pimentón

As noted earlier, when Paula served these shrimp to Jack Kerouac at a 1959 Manhattan cocktail party, his response was, "great legs." Though she likes to feign uncertainty about whether he meant the shrimp's legs or hers, the compliment remained fresh in her memory nearly sixty years later.

In her book *Mediterranean Clay Pot Cooking*, she updated the recipe with guidance from Spanish food expert Janet Mendel. It's one of Paula's simplest: shell-on shrimp sautéed in nothing more than olive oil, garlic, red pepper flakes, and *pimentón de la Vera* (Spanish smoked paprika), served with the heady oil in which they're cooked. The shrimp don't sizzle as much as, say, fajitas, but they release similarly enticing scents as they cook. Shell-on shrimp provide such a nice brininess, the dish hardly needs added salt, but peeled shrimp also work. Any size shrimp will do.

---

1 cup (240 ml) extra-virgin olive oil, preferably Spanish

1 tablespoon finely chopped garlic (from 3 cloves)

1 teaspoon mild red pepper flakes, preferably Aleppo or Marash

1 pound (450 g) shrimp, preferably shell on (see note)

2 tablespoons hot water

½ teaspoon flaky sea salt

¼ teaspoon sweet smoked paprika (pimentón de la Vera dulce)

Crusty bread, for serving

Serves 4 to 6

In a 12-inch (30-cm) cazuela or heavy frying pan, combine the oil, garlic, and pepper flakes. Set over medium-low heat to warm slowly (on a diffuser if using a cazuela), gradually raising the heat to medium-high until the oil is hot and the garlic starts to sizzle and just turns golden, about 3 minutes.

Add the shrimp and cook, turning once, until firm and white throughout, 2 to 5 minutes; the timing depends on their size. Remove the pan from the heat. Sprinkle the shrimp with the hot water, salt, and paprika. Serve at once, directly from the cazuela or on plates. Accompany with the bread for mopping up the cooking juices.

NOTE Set the shrimp out at room temperature for 10 to 15 minutes before cooking so they are not ice-cold when they hit the pan.

Sole Dugléré

After tasting this elegant dinner party dish in a 1958 class taught by famed New York cooking instructor Dione Lucas, Paula decided to drop out of college and become a restaurant chef. She had not made the dish again for decades when we cooked it together in 2015. She swore she had no memory of it, yet when we assembled the fillets, her hands knew what to do. The recipe is unusual, as the fish fillets are first poached in white wine in the oven and then draped in a thick, creamy sauce and broiled. As I prepared the sauce with her, I feared it would taste heavy, even gluey. But she reassured me. Presto! It emerged from the broiler tasting surprisingly silky and redolently spiced. You'll want to serve this dish with crusty bread to savor each bit of the sauce.

6 tablespoons plus
2 teaspoons unsalted butter
(90 g total), plus more
for greasing

3 Roma tomatoes (about
9 ounces | 255 g total), halved
lengthwise and seeded

6 (4-ounce | 115-g) skinless
sole (Dover, petrale, or grey)
or flounder fillets

Flaky sea salt

Cayenne pepper

6 black peppercorns

3 bay leaves, halved

1 thin yellow onion slice,
separated into 6 strands

¼ cup (60 ml) dry white wine

3 tablespoons (25 g)
all-purpose flour

1 cup (240 ml) fish stock

¼ cup (60 ml) heavy cream

1 tablespoon finely chopped
fresh flat-leaf parsley

Freshly ground black pepper

2 tablespoons freshly grated
Parmigiano-Reggiano cheese

Serves 4 to 6

Preheat the oven to 350°F (180°C). Butter a shallow broiler-safe baking dish 10 to 12 inches (25 to 30 cm) in diameter. Line the bottom with parchment paper and lightly butter the parchment.

Using the large holes of a box grater, and with the cut side against the grater, grate the tomato halves and discard the skins. Set aside.

Arrange the sole fillets on a work surface and pat dry. Sprinkle each fillet with a pinch or two of salt and cayenne pepper, then top each fillet with 1½ teaspoons of the butter, 1 peppercorn, and 1 bay leaf half. Starting from a narrow end, roll up each fillet into a snug cylinder and place, seam side down, in the prepared baking dish. Top each fillet with 1 onion strand. Pour the white wine into the dish.

Poach the fish in the oven for 15 minutes. Remove from the oven and spoon out all but about 1 tablespoon of the wine from the dish.

recipe continues →

Set the fish aside in the dish and keep warm. Position an oven rack 7 inches (17.5 cm) from the heating element and preheat the broiler.

In a small saucepan, melt 3 tablespoons (45 g) of the butter over medium-high heat. Add the flour and whisk for 30 seconds to blend thoroughly without coloring. Add the stock, cream, and grated tomato and bring to a boil, whisking constantly. Turn down the heat to medium and cook, whisking constantly, until thickened, about 5 minutes. Add the parsley, then whisk in the remaining 2 teaspoons butter, ½ teaspoon at a time, whisking after each addition until melted. Season with salt and black pepper and remove from the heat.

Spoon the sauce over the fish fillets and sprinkle evenly with the cheese. Broil until the sauce begins to brown, about 4 minutes. Serve immediately directly from the baking dish or transfer the fillets to individual plates with a generous serving of sauce.

Walnut Roll

Lightly sweet and spiked with Cognac, this crowd-pleasing, fail-safe dessert works for any occasion from a potluck to a holiday feast (it would make an ideal gluten-free *bûche de noël*, the French yule log cake). Its user friendliness is why Paula's early mentor, food titan James Beard, recommended she make ten of the rolls for a dinner party for 150 that she catered as a nineteen-year-old in 1958 (she had never cooked for that many people before).

Today Paula avoids sugar because of her dementia. To adjust for a low-sugar diet, here is a deliciously indulgent but lighter version: Whip 1½ cups (360 ml) heavy cream with 2 tablespoons Cognac, 1 teaspoon grated orange zest, and a pinch of salt until stiff peaks form, then fold in ½ cup (60 g) chopped walnuts. Use this mixture in place of the filling, then omit all but the final dusting of confectioners' sugar.

CAKE

Unsalted butter, for greasing

5 large eggs, separated, at room temperature

½ cup (100 g) granulated sugar

Pinch of salt

1¼ cups (150 g) finely chopped walnuts

½ teaspoon baking powder

FILLING

½ cup (120 ml) whole milk

1½ cups (180 g) chopped walnuts

1 cup (240 ml) heavy cream

½ cup (115 g) unsalted butter, at room temperature

⅔ cup (130 g) granulated sugar

2 tablespoons Cognac, Armagnac, or Grand Marnier

....

Confectioners' sugar, for dusting (optional)

Preheat the oven to 375°F (190°C). Butter an 11-by-17-inch (28-by-43-cm) jelly roll or rimmed cookie pan. Line the pan with parchment paper, allowing about 2 inches (5 cm) to overhang each end; butter the paper.

To make the cake, using a stand mixer fitted with the whisk attachment (or a handheld mixer and a large bowl), beat together the egg yolks, granulated sugar, and salt on medium-high speed until pale yellow, about 3 minutes. Using a rubber spatula, fold in the walnuts and baking powder until well mixed.

Wash and dry the whisk attachment and reattach it to the mixer. In a clean bowl, beat the egg whites on medium-high speed until

Makes one 11-inch (28-cm) roll; serves 8 to 15

The cake can be frozen for up to 2 weeks. Thaw at room temperature before serving.

recipe continues →

stiff peaks form. Using the spatula, fold the whites into the yolk mixture just until no white streaks are visible. Transfer the batter to the prepared pan, spreading it in an even layer.

Bake until a toothpick or cake tester inserted into the center comes out clean, about 15 minutes; expect the cake to be thin. Remove the cake from the oven, cover it immediately with a lightly dampened kitchen towel, and refrigerate for 30 minutes.

Meanwhile, prepare the filling: In a small saucepan, heat the milk over medium heat until steaming hot. Remove from the heat. Put the walnuts in a small heatproof bowl, pour the hot milk over them, and let cool to room temperature, about 15 minutes.

Using the stand mixer fitted with the whisk attachment (or a handheld mixer and a medium bowl), beat the cream on medium-high speed until stiff peaks form. Transfer the cream to another bowl. Fit the mixer with the paddle attachment and beat the butter on high speed until light and fluffy. (Or use the handheld mixer and a large bowl.) Add the granulated sugar in two or three batches, beating after each addition until light and fluffy. Add the milk and walnut mixture and Cognac and beat just until incorporated. Using the rubber spatula, fold in the whipped cream just until combined.

Remove the cake from the refrigerator and lift off the towel. Dust the top of the cake with confectioners' sugar, if using. Lay a sheet of parchment 20 inches (50 cm) long on the cake. Firmly grip the ends of the pan, including the overhanging paper, and quickly invert the pan onto a work surface. Lift off the pan and then slowly peel off and discard the parchment from the bottom of the cake. Scoop the filling onto the cake and, using an offset spatula, spread the filling in an even layer. Starting from a narrow end, and using the second sheet of parchment on the work surface as an aid, roll the cake up like a jelly roll.

Wrap the rolled-up cake in aluminum foil and refrigerate until firm, at least 15 minutes or up to 12 hours. Before presenting to guests, transfer the roll to a platter and dust the top with more confectioners' sugar, if using. Cut crosswise into slices to serve.

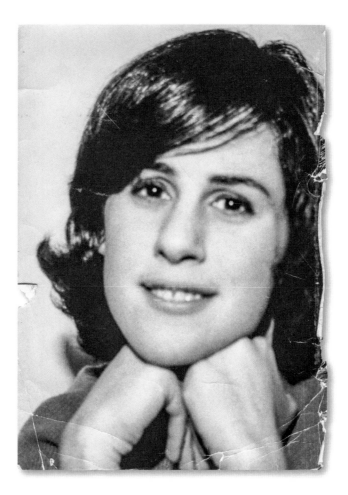

Escape to Tangier

TANGIER AND PARIS
❖ 1959 to 1969

"A French writer once said that 'a recipe has a hidden side, like the moon.' In every recipe there's a little something that makes it special, and, hopefully, better."

—Paula Wolfert, in *Mediterranean Grains and Greens*

ON MY SECOND DAY WITH PAULA in Marrakech in 2008, we received a late-afternoon cooking lesson at a hotel with one of its chefs. Although we were promised an expert in modern Moroccan fusion cooking, we met a woman who was in over her head: she served us a first course of barely cooked carrots under a mound of confectioners' sugar, garnished with rose petals. Paula feigned enthusiasm for as long as she could, but before the chef could start a second course, Paula pled fatigue. We left hungry and discouraged. "No one likes the old ways anymore," she lamented. We returned to the Djemaa el-Fna, the medina's central square, for something to eat. The sun had set, the sky had turned a topaz blue, and the square, lit with charming strings of lights, was more packed than ever. Again Paula sang out "La, barak Allahu fik," and the crowds melted away.

As we moved towards the food stalls, she raised her head like an eagle, scanned for the biggest lines, grabbed my hand, and swooped us in. Flying from one stall to the next, within thirty minutes, we'd filled up on snail soup, roast lamb with cumin, and, for me, a small piece of *sellou*, a gingery cake. "I hate that dessert," she said, waving off a taste. "It's much too sweet."

OPPOSITE:
At the Beat Hotel
in Paris, 1961

49

Each snack evoked fresh memories of her Moroccan adventures. As she recounted them, I noticed the flavors in the foods all the more, her tales enriching them like a spice. While I lingered over my ginger tea, she admired the charming light strings over the stalls. "They didn't have these when I first came here in 1959," she said. "They didn't have electricity in the medina." Then she asked if she had gotten me some snail soup.

"See," she said, "I remember everything from fifty years ago. I just can't remember anything from five minutes ago."

❖

Paula hadn't been diagnosed with dementia that December 2008 when we were in Marrakech together. But she remembered the past much better than the present, which is a symptom of the condition. She told me how, on a bright fall day in 1959, the freighter that she and Michael boarded in New York docked in Casablanca for a night before sailing on to Tangier. The couple took a bus to Marrakech to spend the night there. On the drive in, Paula marveled at women washing clothes in a river by the road and at a man in a *djellaba*, the traditional long, hooded robe worn by men and women, walking alongside his donkey. In 1959, Morocco was still a feudal country: Paula was told the country had only freed its slaves with independence from France and Spain just two years earlier. To her, Marrakech felt like an unwelcome trip back in time. The entire Marrakech medina lacked plumbing or electricity, including the main square. In the blistering midday heat, Paula and Michael took in the swarm of snake charmers, henna artists, and food hawkers.

"I wasn't very fond of Marrakech at that time," she told me. "Marrakech was the fourteenth century. It was fascinating, but it wasn't a place I wanted to live. Tangier was the future."

Because Tangier had only just come under Moroccan rule, among the only signs of Moroccan life were the daily calls to prayer and the annual celebration of Ramadan.

Had Paula wanted to explore the foods of the Mediterranean, she couldn't have picked a better perch. Tangier stands sentry to the Mediterranean Sea. Its white cliffside homes look over the cerulean Straits of Gibraltar, the only passage into the Mediterranean from the Atlantic. On clear days you can see Spain. Because of its strategic importance, multiple Mediterranean countries have ruled it. From 1923 to 1956, while France and Spain ruled separate partitions of Morocco, nine countries ruled Tangier simultaneously. This international protectorate, or interzone, issued some capricious edicts. ("One year," Paula told me, "Belgium decided that carrying live chickens home upside down was cruel, so they insisted residents carry the chickens head up.") It also provided a haven to nonconformists—smugglers, political refugees, homosexuals, beatniks—of nearly every stripe.

Tangier stoked Paula's lifelong love of learning new languages. She could explore four countries in a single conversation: Tanjaoui, the local dialect, blended Moroccan Arabic, or Darija, with French, Spanish, and English. "You could start a sentence in one language and end in another and everybody understood you," she said. She had taught herself Serbian, studied Spanish in school, and picked up some French with Dione Lucas. Now she began classes in French and Arabic.

"Tangier in the 1960s was more than a city: It was a state of mind," Paula wrote in a 1995 story for *Saveur*, "a place people came to reinvent themselves and to live out their most eccentric fantasies. The phone book listed several 'countesses' and 'barons' who were actually courtesans and butcher boys. The phone company didn't care. The phones didn't work anyway."

With a letter of introduction from a poet friend of Michael's parents, Paula and Michael came under the wing of Paul Bowles. The American writer and composer had settled in the city in the late 1940s with his wife, Jane, and stood as the center of Beat life there. He found the Wolferts a nearby apartment and jobs at the American School of Tangier, Michael as an English teacher and Paula as a library assistant. At night, they joined the city's lively dinner parties, hosted dinners of their own, and danced to Elvis Presley records.

Paula dined out the rest of her life on her time in Tangier—on her days of rubbing shoulders with Bowles, Tennessee Williams, and other artists. But even by age twenty-one, she appears to have grown a little exasperated with them. In her reminiscences, they often come off as a boys' club of hedonistic, overgrown teenagers.

The city had a seamy underside—pedophilia, drug abuse, orgies conducted at scenic beaches and at cocktail parties. Whatever made Paula uncomfortable, she turned her blind eye to and moved on. At three o'clock every afternoon when the kef (a more potent form of marijuana) was chopped fresh, rolled, and passed at Paul Bowles's house, she would leave. "From my point of view, those weren't good stories. They were just things that were happening," she said.

Michael explored Tangier's thriving drug scene, partaking in kef, opium, and LSD, a new synthetic drug from Switzerland that he learned about from famed Beat writer William S. Burroughs. Poets Allen Ginsberg, Gregory Corso, and Peter Orlovsky also passed through Tangier; Paula once helped Ginsberg corral the other two into completing questionnaires for Sandoz (the Swiss pharmaceutical company that invented LSD) so they could receive more free drugs.

"I thought it was so stupid," she said. Her vision problems, she explained, made taking drugs too disorienting. Although her resistance caused tension in her marriage, she wasn't comfortable losing all control. "I don't even like getting drunk," she admitted. "I'm scared of it. I once had three martinis and had to go to the bathroom and hold on tight because I thought I was going to float to the ceiling."

Instead, Paula tripped out on the food. She spent hours at the open-air seafood, meat, and vegetable stalls in the city's Grand Socco, on the edge of the ancient medina. Fifty years later she could remember incredible details.

"They had everything in Tangier," she said. "They had seafood from both the Atlantic and the Mediterranean, scallops and clams that I had only read about, and this incredible calamari that I could find in New York at just this one store on Ninth Avenue. Everything was a miracle. There was no refrigeration, so everything was fresh, brought in that morning. I used to bring home chickens live! There were no cars, so everyone brought their goods in wagons. It was like turning back the centuries, it was fabulous!"

Paula didn't mind reverse time travel when it applied to food. Paula's maid showed her how to kill a chicken by tying a string around the bird's neck, the other end around a doorknob, and then slamming the door shut. She tasted her first fresh cèpes (porcini), which an old Berber woman collected from the nearby Rif mountains and sold in the market. "In New York I could only find them canned, from Germany. When I got to Tangier and saw fresh cèpes, I went berserk," she recalled. But she did not use these ingredients to cook Moroccan food. "For a long time, I could only see cooking from Dione Lucas's point of view," she said. She gleefully tackled French classics with ingredients she could never find in the States.

In the summer of 1960, Paula took her first trip around the Mediterranean—a journey that whetted her appetite for the culture. She and Michael hitchhiked across the European side, going as far north as Zaragoza in Spain, down to Bordeaux, then across Provence to Rome for the Olympics, and ending in Greece and Rhodes. Twenty years later, Paula would revisit all of these places in her books.

That fall they returned to Tangier for another academic year, and Paula began a deeper exploration of the Moroccan side of the city. She also grew closer to Jane Bowles, who spoke the best Arabic of any of the Beats in Tangier. Jane was twenty-one years older, but she took a shine to Paula. They had a certain amount in common. Both born into New York Jewish families, they were both adventurous as well as fearful. Smart and funny, they could also be tripped up by their own stubborn obsessiveness, and shared a tendency to lose themselves in their curiosities (Jane is considered a writer's writer in the way that Paula is considered a cook's cook). Jane took Paula to the *hammams* (public baths) and translated some of the conversations among the Moroccan women complaining about their husbands.

Through some of Michael's students, Paula had her first tastes of authentic Moroccan cooking. Some of the American School of Tangier's students came from Tangier's wealthiest aristocratic Moroccan families, and they regularly invited the couple to dinner for sumptuous Moroccan feasts.

"It was weird in the beginning," Paula said. "You had to learn so much. First they washed their hands communally, and then you'd eat course after course after course, all of it with your fingers."

She loved the flavors but didn't push for any recipes. Jane had told her it would be rude to ask, explaining that the best cooks were called *dadas*, descendants of African slaves who were often illiterate. Cooking was their only currency, so to ask for a recipe would be akin to stealing trade secrets. "Their knowledge was their worth," Paula said.

Paula, c. 1961

❖

Paula and Michael split up in the summer of 1961. Paula, who is adept at forgetting unhappy events, could only remember they spent the summer pursuing separate adventures. Her childhood friend Loretta recalled that this was a marital separation, after Paula discovered Michael had a brief affair with someone in Tangier. Likely confident that they would ultimately reunite, Michael went to Paris, another Beat capital, where he intended to support himself with the proceeds from selling a kilo of hash that Paula sewed into his underwear so he could smuggle it onto the plane. Paula headed to Yugoslavia for a few months. When pressed, she remembered a few romances of her own that summer ("the men are *very* good looking there," she said, implying she'd had little choice). She was quicker to recall how she finally found her *gusle* players, the blind bards of the Balkans she had read about as a child.

"I didn't get the exciting sizzle I had hoped for," she said. "They were blind, but the whole thing seemed staged." She researched her grandmother's stories and felt betrayed to discover so many were tall tales, especially the one about the men drawing strength from bears by lying down on them. She found a fortune-teller to read her coffee grounds, an old Balkan tradition. The woman told her to go easy on transatlantic flights.

"She told me I'd fly across it twenty-three times, but on the twenty-fourth time, the plane would go down." Although she had a twenty-three-flight window, Paula swore off transatlantic airlines entirely. For the next nine years, she crossed the Atlantic only by boat.

❖

That fall, Paula's tourist visa expired, so she had to leave Yugoslavia. She found she had missed Michael and felt prepared to forgive him. She rejoined him in Paris at the infamous Beat Hotel on rue Git-le-Coeur in the Latin Quarter, and they recommitted to their marriage. They stayed at the hotel for about a year; in the lobby, while Michael attended Communist Party meetings, Paula listened as American musician Mezz Mezzrow practiced the blues. She became acquainted with their neighbors, including writer James Baldwin, who asked her to look after his sister. "I took her to French class every day," Paula said.

Then Paula got pregnant. With new responsibilities, they began to leave Beat life behind. Michael got them a roomier apartment in the Fifth Arrondissement and took a prestigious job at UNESCO. She bore Nicholas in 1962 and Leila in 1963.

Life was good. She and Michael were happy, and she loved motherhood—almost more than food. They stayed in Paris for eight years, but she came away with few culinary memories. When she gave birth, she enjoyed that the nurse's aide at the *maison de naissance* (birthing center) asked whether she would prefer her artichokes

With her daughter Leila, c. 1963

roasted or sautéed. But otherwise, she immersed herself in the pleasures of parenthood, and in a part-time job sifting through the slush pile in the local office of the *Paris Review*. She visited Le Cordon Bleu only to recognize the curriculum as what Dione Lucas had already taught her. She spotted an ad for Les Trois Gourmandes cooking school, but didn't realize until years later that the "three gourmets" had been Julia Child and her Parisian coauthors, Simone Beck and Louisette

Bertholle. Their curriculum would also have been redundant. From afar, Paula watched in wonder as a culinary Francophilia swept America, sparked by the glamorous, French-speaking new First Lady, Jacqueline Kennedy, who installed a French chef at the White House, then fueled by the 1963 publication of the three gourmets' *Mastering the Art of French Cooking*.

With Michael and their children, July 1967

Several months after Leila was born, Paula began suffering terrible headaches and eye aches. She went to a doctor in Paris, who told her she was suffering from papilledema, a swelling of the optic disk, a potentially life-threatening situation. She was told that she would need to undergo exploratory brain surgery immediately, standard procedure in 1964 (MRIs didn't exist then). Fearing her daughter might be about to die, Paula's mother flew from New York to Paris that night. The next day, the doctor drilled two holes in the back of her head. When he saw her condition was harmless, he came out into the hallway and danced with her mother to celebrate the good news. About ten days later, Paula was sent home, where she swiftly recovered. But today, she wonders if that surgery played a role in her dementia. Studies show that people who experience traumatic brain injury may have an increased risk of developing dementia later in life. Her current brain scans show the operation damaged her visual cortex, which may have worsened her vision.

Paula was relieved to leave the hospital in good health. But on returning home, she found her au pair in tears. The au pair confessed that while Paula was in the hospital, she and Michael had an affair. Over the next five years, Paula's marriage crumbled. Michael's recreational drug use accelerated into addiction. He continued to have many more affairs, some with her friends, some with other au pairs. Frustrated and humiliated, Paula dealt with these developments by promptly forgetting them and hiring less attractive au pairs. She could not conceive of a life without him. In late 1967, she tried revenge, a one-night stand with a colleague of Michael's who lived on the floor below, but she hated it. She gladly agreed when Michael suggested they start over in Tangier. In January 1968, Paula moved back with the children while Michael stayed behind to join what would grow to be the Paris riots.

That May, Michael announced he had fallen in love with someone else, a Swedish artist he'd met on the Paris barricades. After Paula declined his proposal that he keep a mistress, he spent well over a year waffling over whom he wanted to be with. Paula felt acutely alone, exiled from her life, as though cast to the dark side of the moon. She seized on every distraction. She tried tennis lessons (her vision made it impossible for her to hit the ball). She took up knitting. She began moving away from the Dione Lucas orthodoxy to learn her first Moroccan recipes from a new maid she hired, Fatima ben Lahsen Riffi, a young Berber from the Rif mountains. During Eid al-Adha that spring, Fatima helped Paula buy a live lamb. Paula then taught herself how to butcher it, cribbing from the *House & Garden* cookbook, as she so memorably described in *Couscous and Other Good Food from Morocco*. Fatima also taught her the phrase "La, barak Allahu fik," which proved invaluable for navigating the markets.

It wasn't just Paula's world coming apart, however. In 1968 and 1969, she anxiously followed the headlines reporting the escalation of the Vietnam War, the assassinations of Bobby Kennedy and Martin Luther King Jr., and the riots rocking Paris, Chicago, and New York. According to Paula, in Morocco, some people even feared the coming moon walk would end the world. That's how she ended up taking her first—and last—hallucinogen, on what turned out to be an important early culinary adventure.

A British filmmaker friend arrived in Tangier to research a documentary on this phenomenon. "Moroccan Arabs had a saying that when the moon splits, the world will end," Paula said. "It's from the Koran." Some took this to mean the moon walk would bring about the apocalypse. Paula offered to join him on his journey.

They drove south out of Tangier. When they reached the edge of the Sahara, their car broke down. They spent the night at a nearby military base, where a Moroccan officer entertained himself by slipping hallucinogenic drugs into their after-dinner tea. "He must have thought we were hippies and would find it funny," she said. That night Paula saw visions of old men floating on the ceiling, an experience that did nothing to improve her feelings about drugs. "It was the stupidest hallucination. I'm sorry to disappoint you," she said.

The next morning, when two reasonable people might have hightailed it back to familiar ground, they pushed south to Gouliamime, where they witnessed an extraordinary camel market. Their car broke down again. At a gas station, a Berber shepherd invited them to his home for lunch, where his wife served bread with aged butter, the nutty Roquefort-like *smen* (recipe, page 310).

When asked to recall this period, Paula gladly shared every nuance of that *smen*. But remembering other food memories, recipes, or anything else from the dissolution of her first marriage, caused fresh pain, and not because of her dementia. "I screwed it all into a little jar and dug a hole and put it there and forgot about it." she said.

✤

In June 1969, Loretta happened to call from Brooklyn, and Paula unspooled her misery. "Michael won't make up his mind, and I don't know what to do," she told her.

"I said, 'Are you fucking crazy? Have UNESCO pack your shit up and ship it home. Put the kids with your parents and stay in my apartment,'" Loretta recalled.

Michael agreed to give Paula half his life savings, four thousand dollars, and arranged passage for her and their children back to New York. He moved with the artist to Sweden.

On the boat, Paula feigned calm for the children but felt a roiling sense of panic. She had no clear way to support herself or the kids. Her only skill was cooking, but after her Cape Cod disaster with the omelets, she felt she couldn't handle line cooking ever again. She liked the idea of working in food, but outside of cooking in a restaurant, she had no idea how to turn food into a job.

Back in the States at her now former in-laws, she and the children watched Neil Armstrong and crew make their lunar landing. The world did not end, but Paula still felt like it had.

She got a job in the typing pool of an ad agency. That fall, she and her children squeezed into a rent-controlled one-bedroom on the Upper East Side. The kids shared the bedroom, and Paula slept in a small room off the kitchen. As she stocked her pantry, she found Manhattan's grocery stores just as limited as they'd been in 1959. If anything, they were worse: the processed foods industry had made significant strides, sweetening new cereals with more sugar and inventing a way to wrap individual slices of processed cheese. The contrast with her farmers' markets in Tangier was laughable. Organic produce could only be found in "hippie health food stores," as Paula put it, and those were beyond her modest budget. No sooner had she returned to New York than she began to crave Tangier's distant flavors.

That fall the ad agency laid her off. Scrambling once again, at last a little of her moxie started to come back to her. She made a radical pledge that she kept the rest of her life: she would never again rely on anyone to support her, neither a husband nor an employer. From then on, she swore she would work only for herself. With no other alternatives to turn to, she decided to give food another shot.

International Gourmet Host

Official Newsletter of International Home Dining. Published under the auspices of Columbia House, Terre Haute, Ind., a service of CBS, Inc.

Our Editor Talks French Food with the French Ambassador's Wife

Editor PAULA NOLFERT studied at the famed Cordon Bleu and has worked with renowned gourmet chefs Diane Lucas and James Beard. Fluent in French, Spanish, Yugoslavian (and Arabic), she has traveled widely and has been a food consultant for VOGUE, Gourmet magazine, and TIME-LIFE Books.

"You can't be a good cook with only a good watch," said Madame Kosciusko-Morizet as she described her early gastronomic education to me. An acknowledged hostess of great charm, the tall distinguished wife of the French Ambassador to the United Nations entertains practically as a full-time occupation. "When I was a child in Paris, our kitchen was the most important room in the house, warm with wonderful aromas and marvelous food. In my family we were very very gourmand, eating was a part of the enjoyment of life."

The Parisian atmosphere of her New York apartment with authentic Louis XVI furniture and yellow decor is warm and inviting. There are examples of modern French art by Marc Chagall and Oliver Debré, brother of the former Prime Minister of France. The size of her dining room is impressive. The day I interviewed her its long oval table of dark mahogany was set for luncheon with organdy placemats and a charming centerpiece in the shape of an obelisk of yellow apples supported by toothpicks decorated with sprigs of field flowers.

She likes variety in her menus and often works out the timing, proportions and ingredients of new recipes with her chef by trial and error. "—but sometimes we have to give up" she said modestly. She is known as a gifted cook herself and an imaginative hostess and has created a Gallic variation of Virginian chicken stuffed with raisins and a sauce of black and green grapes. "I like to adapt recipes, even in France there is no classic one way to prepare a dish, every French home has its own recipe." When there is a pause in her formal diplomatic enter-

taining, she serves a traditionally French family dinner—*boeuf à la ficelle* for example. It is a sumptuous *pot au feu* in which a shell roast is supported by string and poached in a rich beef broth and served rare. The soup is served in consommé cups and the meat and vegetables on a large dinner plate with French mustard, *cornichons* (french pickles), burgundy wine, crusty French bread and *gros sel* (a coarse, partially refined sea salt with a light grey color highly regarded in France for its unique flavor). A small wheel of *Brie* resting on a straw mat or an assortment of cheeses follow. A light homemade sherbert ends the meal.

Another form of entertaining Madame Kosciusko-Morizet offers at her country house or away from home is a wine and cheese tasting *soirée*. "On a trip to the Congo years ago, I brought dozens of cheeses and some cold stuffed rabbit on the plane with me. We set up a barrel of wine in the dining room and everyone helped themselves." Afterwards she served a simple green salad. "Salad is a most difficult dish, the leaves must be very well dried. I use my very best towels to do the job. I lightly sprinkle on the oil and toss gently until all the leaves are well coated to avoid bruising the leaves with vinegar. No. I add the vinegar, salt and pepper. Toss well and serve immediately" she counseled.

I asked Madame Kosciusko-Morizet what was the key to successful entertaining. "A good mixture of people is most important, so I leave that to my husband. We enjoy having the people we invite to our dinner parties and our guests feel that we look forward to seeing them each time they come. The most difficult time for me is when the guests first arrive, so I start dinner very quickly and don't spend much time over drinks."

She insists that a formal French dinner needs plenty of advance planning and attention to detail—flowers, menu, guest list and wine. ("At the Elysée Palace, for example," she said, "the places must be set exactly twenty-eight inches apart.") Her menu reflects a special lightness of style and includes variations from classic French cuisine. The flowers are arranged with a thought to decor and the menu. "Ambassador Kosciusko-

Mme. Kosciusko-Morizet receives our editor in the charming room of the Ambassadorial Suite on New York's elegant East Side.

Morizet always chooses the wines, of course," she told me.

A recent dinner included *Filet de Sole Flambie au whiskey* served with a *Pouilly Fuissé*, *Canard aux poivres verts* (these are not our green bell peppers but fresh green peppercorns that are mashed with a fork and cooked into the juices from the duck) served with a red bordeaux. An assortment of 6 cheeses and a *Sorbet à l'Ananas* (Pineapples sherbert with fresh strawberries and whipped cream) served with champagne.

"I always keep my fingers crossed when I give a dinner. That's the risk with really authentic French cooking when you make everything at home and don't use starches or gelatin to hold up sauces and molds as they usually do in restaurants. Of course, my chef is very talented and can do something to repair almost any failure at the last minute."

"What would you do if something failed?" I asked.

"Well," she said, with a typically French sense of humor, "it's sometimes nice to have a failure because you chance to discover something new."

Gourmet Groups Are Fun — Why Not Form Your Own?

Why not organize a gourmet group of your own from friends, relatives, neighbors, business associates—anyone who shares your enjoyment of good food and new experiences in cooking? You'll need three or four couples interested in experimenting with new ingredients, new methods and unusual equipment and utensils.

Begin with an organizing meeting or party. Decide all the details of how to share the planning and preparing of the dinner, when and where the first one will be and how the expenses are to be shared. A membership in INTERNATIONAL HOME DINING PROGRAM will bring the complete dinner plan to you.

Division of Work and Dinner Preparation

A division of the dinner preparation might be as follows:

Host and Hostess provide the entree and beverages
Couple I prepares soup and appetizer
Couple II prepares the salad and vegetables
Couple III prepares the dessert and fish courses.

The night of the dinner, after preparing the food either at home or at the home of the hostess, each couple is responsible for the serving of the course she has prepared. Also, there is no need for the host and hostess to purchase new dishes or special serving pieces since someone in the group will probably have the necessary items. So pool resources or improvise.

This can be worked out in any way to suit your particular group. If you are a person who prefers to work in the kitchen alone, then you would

prefer to form a group with couples who wish to do likewise. However, if you feel your time is limited, but want to participate in such an endeavor, then division of work is the answer. International Home Dining makes the delegation of work simple since all recipes are on individual cards and can be easily distributed as can the special ingredients that are provided and utensils.

Larger groups could also be formed in Newcomer organizations or Women's Clubs or any similar group. Four couples then meet per house on the same night using the same menu. This program would easily be adaptable to this type of group. What a wonderful way to meet new and interesting people, and make new friends with a mutual interest.

Now, enjoy an exciting visit to a foreign land via a fabulous meal! See how quickly you will begin to incorporate your new found knowledge into your everyday meals to the utter delight of your family!

Party Boxes

NEW YORK ❖ 1969 to 1971

"For centuries the western world has depended on the east's natural abundance of rare spices and herbs. In the thirteenth century, while on his travels through the East Indies, Marco Polo wrote that 'here is the greatest abundance of spices to be found.' He gave the region its nickname of 'Spice Islands.' Indonesians have used their treasure chest of spices to refine their cuisine to one of the most delicious, interesting, albeit least known cuisines in the world."

—Paula Wolfert, *Indonesian Rice Table Buffet*,
Columbia House International Home Dining, 1971

WHEN PAULA ARRIVED AT THE PHOTO SHOOT for this chapter's recipes, she made a beeline for a table filled with dried and fresh aromatics that our editor, Andrea Nguyen, had brought from her home in Santa Cruz. Among the ingredients that Paula began examining were knobs of galangal, stalks of lemongrass, and branches of kaffir (*makrut*) lime leaves.

"Do you recognize that smell?" Andrea asked, as Paula buried her nose in the lime leaves.

"I don't remember the name, but I know I know them," Paula said. "It's just been a very long time since I smelled them."

OPPOSITE:
Newsletter from
Paula's French
party box

Paula's connection to Southeast Asian ingredients goes back to New York in 1969, when she was in a financial bind that had persuaded her to revive her dormant career in food. She could no longer call on Dione Lucas for help. Her former teacher had retired to Vermont, where she died in 1971. Paula knew not to look up James Beard, as she had burned that bridge in 1959 by turning down the Four Seasons job, but he still stood at the center of New York's small but growing food scene. For a host of reasons, that scene hadn't developed much during the ten years that Paula was away, though a somewhat greater number of Americans were interested in cooking more ambitious cuisines, and not just French. Air travel to Europe had become surprisingly affordable. Whether returning from stints with the Peace Corps or the army or from a vacation, more people were arriving home, like Paula, with a fresh curiosity for international cuisines— and fresh shock at the comparable tastelessness of American food. A small crop of new culinary productions were then in the works to cater to these curiosities. Paula wasn't yet aware of these trends, but she was perfectly positioned to take advantage of them.

She can't remember exactly what she did, but she thinks she reached out to John Clancy, the former chef from her 1959 line-cook stint on Cape Cod. In 1969, Clancy helmed the test kitchen at the biggest new international food publication, *Foods of the World*, Time-Life's landmark series. The publishers had lured in a veritable Who's Who of the food world, including Julia Child, James Beard, and M. F. K. Fisher, to serve as authors and consultants. The inaugural volume, *Provincial French Food*, had launched the year before. It weathered a scathing review from Craig Claiborne for being more Parisian than provincial and signed up half a million subscribers. In *New York* magazine, Nora Ephron had already published a takedown on the infighting the project had provoked, famously characterizing the tiny food world as "bitchy, gossipy and devious."

Paula benefitted from the smallness, however. She had briefly met the series editor, Michael Field, when he visited Tangier for research. As luck would have it, Field needed guidance with one of the odder volumes of the series, *A Quintet of Cuisines*, a catchall for a handful of countries deemed unworthy of stand-alone volumes: Switzerland, the Low Countries (Belgium and the Netherlands), Poland, Bulgaria and Romania, and North Africa. Field hired Paula as a Morocco consultant and was quickly impressed by how much she knew, not just about Morocco but the entire Mediterranean.

Through Field she got a few more small editorial gigs. But she needed more money. She had one last play. On her way back from

Tangier, she stopped in Paris and spotted a new French cooking magazine called *Cuisine A–Z* at the supermarkets. The weekly publication offered simple yet sophisticated recipes for weeknight cooking, as well as full-page color photographs of the finished dishes. Paula thought it might work in the United States, where there were few national food magazines aside from *Gourmet*, which was larded with nostalgic odes to aristocratic feasts. (The idea was prescient. From Paula's description of *Cuisine A–Z* its democratic appeal sounds somewhat like *Food & Wine*, which debuted ten years later.) It was a long shot, but maybe she could persuade someone to publish an American version in the States and hire her to help.

Ever the networker, Paula reached out to a Tangier connection who moved in elite New York media circles, Frederick Vreeland, an American diplomat to Morocco whose mother, Diana, was the legendary editor of *Vogue* and *Harper's Bazaar*. Vreeland's wife, Betty, saw merit in Paula's idea and generously pitched it to the CBS chairman, William S. Paley. Paley passed on the magazine but suggested that Paula interview at Columbia House, a subsidiary of the CBS-owned Columbia Records. The music subscription service was about to launch an epicurean program called International Home Dining. Paula was promptly hired to help run it.

A kind of Blue Apron or Sun Basket of its day, the service sent subscribers a box every month or so containing everything they'd need to throw a dinner party from a different country: an album of music from that country (of course), plus a half-dozen illustrated recipes, printed invitations, a four-page newsletter, a battle plan for the cooking, and a half-dozen harder-to-find ingredients and necessary equipment (think a basic cleaver and wok). Each box cost $9.95 plus shipping and handling, about $60.00 in today's dollars—a bargain now but a bit steep in 1969.

But what a job it was. As the series editor and organizer, Paula was paid $200 a week, plus a recipe-testing budget. It was more than enough to cover her $300 monthly rent. So that she could work from home, they offered to pay for any work use of her phone line, including long-distance calls.

Starting with the first box for a French dinner party, and with each subsequent box, Paula developed another element of what would become her visionary cookbook-writing style: unapologetically complex recipes, engaging descriptions to capture their flavors in vivid detail, and mail-order sources to bypass the limited American supply chain, so subscribers could achieve those flavors at home.

❖

Even for Paula, however, the recipes for her first French party box were—in a testament to her intense classic training—absurdly complicated. Especially the first course: *truites à la gelée de Riesling* (pictured below). The preparation involved poaching six head-on trout in a made-from-scratch court bouillon, skinning them, setting each in homemade fish aspic, then garnishing them with "flowers" of lemon peel and tomatoes (or pimiento cherry peppers) that were dipped in aspic and applied with tweezers. The trout was served with freshly made *sauce verte* (green mayonnaise).

"I made it all the time for friends in Paris," she explained.

If Paula was capable of whipping up trout set in from-scratch aspic garnished with lemon and tomato flowers for a casual lunch for friends, it suggests that all of her later books, despite their legendary rigor, were—relatively speaking—dumbed down. She never again published anything as baroque as *truites à la gelée de Riesling*.

But the dish gave her one tool she would employ often: to empower subscribers to explore new culinary ideas, Paula began her lifelong practice of sweetly if wildly understating the difficulty of her recipes. She communicated in the vernacular of the mainstream 1969 American home cook who was accustomed to processed food. "The recipe is not difficult but the glazing and decorating do take time," she wrote. "If it sounds difficult, think of it in terms of boiling a potato, making a bowl of Jell-O and decorating the Jell-O with fruit."

The recipe card for *truites à la gelée de Riesling*, from Paula's French party box

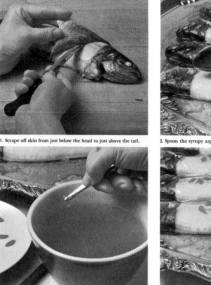

1. Scrape off skin from just below the head to just above the tail.

2. Spoon the syrupy aspic over the chilled fish.

3. Cut shapely petals from the pimiento and lemon peel.

4. Dip each petal in syrupy aspic before applying to the fish.

5. Carefully apply decoration to the trout.

6. To make *sauce verte* quickly pour in oil in a thick steady stream.

To underline just how foreign even French food remained to many Americans, Paula also felt compelled to include shallots in the box. She had difficulty sourcing them until she found a New Jersey farmer who agreed to ship shallots to the Columbia House warehouse in Terre Haute, Indiana.

❖

The second box reminded Paula that cooking could be an adventure. It focused on Chinese cuisine, which was considered very chic. To learn about the cuisine, Paula tracked down the most forward-thinking Chinese cooking instructor in New York, Grace Zia Chu. At that time, most Americans still mistook chop suey for good Chinese food. But Chu, born in Shanghai, was an early advocate for authentic regional Chinese cooking. Close to Paula's height, more reserved yet warm and funny, she became a model for the many women with whom Paula formed familial bonds while researching her cookbooks. Their intense weeks of classes involved a lot of hugging, Paula recalled fondly, which gave her a sense of belonging she hadn't felt in a long time.

Chu emboldened her to break down the sprawling cuisine with breathtaking efficiency. The resulting Chinese party box menu spanned the country: seven recipes from five regions, including a Beijing pork stir-fry with tiger lily buds and cloud ear mushrooms, Cantonese spareribs with fermented black bean sauce, and cold poached Sichuan chicken topped with tingly Sichuan peppercorns. Imagine the 1970 cook opening the box to discover those recipes along with fermented bean sauce and cloud ear mushrooms, tiger lily buds, and Sichuan peppercorns.

With each box, Paula got more creative. For the Greek party box newsletter, she found a Greek fortune-teller to share trade secrets on reading coffee grounds. To pair with the record album in the box, *The Best of Bouzouki* (a Greek mandolin-like instrument), she included dance steps to the *hasapiko*, which she learned from a friend, the young poet Daniel Halpern, who was staying on her couch after a sojourn in Tangier.

Newsletter from Paula's Chinese party box

The boxes so impressed Gael Greene, the recently hired restaurant critic for *New York* magazine, that she wrote a brief review. "It sounds like instant-gourmania for the upwardly mobile in the boondocks," she wrote. "But Columbia House's mail-order cooking adventures are fiercely authentic, exhaustingly enthusiastic and not one bit condescending."

Greene had crossed paths with Paula in Tangier while on assignment for *Cosmopolitan*. They had discovered they'd both attended Dione Lucas's cooking school but did not become friends until Paula moved back to New York. Greene soon became one of her biggest supporters.

With three boxes under her belt, at the end of 1970, Paula sashayed into a holiday party and found herself cracking up in conversation with a tall, deep-voiced filmmaker and writer named Bill. On paper, William "Bill" Bayer had a surprising amount in common with Michael Wolfert: a fellow Jewish Harvard graduate and a traveled writer, proud of his movie-star good looks. But where Michael resembled Montgomery Clift, Bill was more Gene Hackman—and taller, with broader shoulders. Bill was also younger, born in 1939. Like Michael, he had a literary pedigree; his mother, Eleanor Perry, was an Academy Award–nominated screenwriter. But Bill did not live in his mother's shadow. He had also fulfilled more of his creative ambitions than Michael, and had the élan to show for it. As a filmmaker, he'd lived in Saigon as a foreign service officer, making documentaries

Bill Bayer

and newsreels on the Vietnam War. The same year he met Paula, with encouragement from industry friends like director Brian DePalma, he directed his first feature film, *Mississippi Summer*. It was panned when it debuted the following January. But by 1970, he had already grown disillusioned with the industry, had decided to become a fiction writer, and had a book contract.

He felt drawn to Paula's strength, which belied her vulnerability. "She had children to support, and she'd made a career out of basically nothing," he recalled. "She was a powerhouse. Aggressive, but not in an off-putting way. There was something about her eyes. There was a vulnerability in them, which was at odds with her brassy personality."

Paula liked his looks (except for a short-lived mustache), his kindness, and his dark humor. At the party, Bill joked they should collaborate on a Vietnam War party box, complete with barbed wire.

They went on their first date the next day, and soon after, Bill moved in. He immediately took to her children, for their precociousness as well as their gentle natures. He also began helping her with her party boxes. Paula had always felt intimidated by Michael. But Bill drew her out. As soon as Bill started editing her newsletters, you can hear her more vividly. He even gave her the confidence to try marijuana—once, with her parents, in around 1971. "We decided we hated it," Paula said, speaking for the group.

Leila and
Nicholas, c. 1970

With Bill to help her look after Nicholas and Leila, she had time to explore new outlets. As the party boxes continued, Columbia House found it could no longer rely on American producers for the harder-to-find ingredients, so it decided to import them directly. It partnered with H. Roth & Son, an Upper East Side specialty foods store near Paula's apartment. The owner, Herman Bosboom, made Paula a convert to mail order as an alternative to limited American grocery stores, and H. Roth & Son appeared in the source lists of Paula's cookbooks well into the 1980s.

Bosboom also gave Paula her start as a cooking teacher. To help him promote the ingredients he imported for her boxes, he opened a small school across the street from his shop and hired Paula to help him find additional teachers and to teach her own classes on Saturday mornings.

Bill remembered she came home from her first class aglow. "I had them in the palm of my hand!" she told him. "I loved turning people on about what excited me," she later elaborated. She soon introduced Bosboom to an international roster of cooking experts, many of whom she met through her party boxes. In September 1971, the school was included in a roundup of New York's new cooking schools. "H. Roth, the specialty importer, runs one of the largest, most diverse cooking schools in the area," Raymond Sokolov wrote in the *New York Times*.

But it wasn't until the fifth box that Paula discovered her métier. Columbia House let her focus on a cuisine hardly anyone had heard of at that time: Indonesian. Paula had zero knowledge of the food; in her search for an Indonesian home cooking expert, an Asian art museum referred her to a batik importer named Mintari Soeharjo. The two hit it off. Madame Soeharjo invited Paula to come to an Indonesian

Gado Gado (Raw and Cooked Vegetables with a Spicy Peanut Dressing)

This is the most famous salad in Indonesia. You may use as many of the vegetables as you like, but the larger the variety the prettier the salad. You can prepare the dressing and salad in advance. Both are served at room temperature.

SALAD PLATTER OF RAW AND COOKED VEGETABLES	EQUIPMENT	WORKING TIME: 50 minutes
INGREDIENTS	Saucepan	COOKING TIME: 25 minutes
1 potato	Chopping knife	SERVES: 6-8 as part of an
2 eggs	Kettle	Indonesian buffet
½ lb. bean sprouts, fresh or canned	Colander	
1 lb. green beans	Steamer or frying basket and large	
1 lb. spinach leaves	pot with lid	
1 cup shredded lettuce or cabbage	Skillet—optional	
1 cucumber	Large bowl	
1 krupuk (fried shrimp cracker)		
Salt to taste		

OPTIONAL: cauliflower, broccoli, and bean curd cakes, fried and cubed

SPICY PEANUT DRESSING	¼ teaspoon MSG	EQUIP
INGREDIENTS	1 small piece kentjur	Chop
1 small clove garlic	1 djeroek poeroet leaf	1 qua
¼ cup chopped onion	½ teaspoon salt	Woo
2 tablespoons oil	½ teaspoon sambal ulek or red	
½ cup peanut butter	chili peppers, seeded and finely	WORK
¾ cup water	chopped, or ¼ teaspoon cayenne	COO
1 tablespoon brown sugar	pepper	MAKE
juice of ½ a lemon	¼ cup milk or cream	

Prepare the vegetables:

1 Hard boil eggs and boil the potato until tender. When cool, peel and slice. S

2 Wash and clean fresh bean sprouts thoroughly: soak in a large bowl of c the sprouts until the green husks can be easily removed. Drain in a cola sprouts soak drained sprouts in cold water overnight. Drain and sprouts, bring a kettle of water to a boil and Set aside to

---

Ketjap Benteng Manis (Javanese Sweet Soy Sauce)

A thick, sweet soy sauce that is unequaled by the American, Chinese, or Japanese variety. It is very easy to make and keeps for months at room temperature in a tightly closed jar. Use it also for marinating meat, Nasi Goreng (fried rice), and as a dip for beef kebabs.

KETJAP INGREDIENTS	1 daon salam leaf	Wooden spoon
2 cloves garlic	1 small piece laos	Strainer
2 thin blades Daon Sereh	¼ teaspoon black pepper	Bowl
¾ cup dark brown sugar		1 quart glass jar with lid
1 cup water	EQUIPMENT	
½ cup + 2 tablespoons	Heavy knife	WORKING TIME: 10 minutes
dark molasses	1 quart enameled or stainless	COOKING TIME: 15 minutes
⅔ cup Japanese soy sauce	steel saucepan	MAKES: 1¾ cups sauce

1 Give a good whack to the garlic cloves with the side of a heavy knife and peel off their skins. Twist the sereh blades to break their stiffness and tie into a knot. Set aside.

2 Over moderate heat, combine sugar and water in a saucepan and stir until the sugar dissolves. Cook for five minutes.

3 Lower heat and add other ingredients. Simmer for ten minutes. Remove from heat and strain liquid into a bowl. Cool.

4 When cool, pour into a glass jar and cover tightly.

Saté Bumbu (Skewered Beef)

Delicious, slightly hot, bite-sized bits of skewered beef flavored with spices and Ketjap Benteng Manis. In Indonesia you can buy Satés from street vendors as a snack at any time of the day or night. They make marvelous cocktail party fare.

INGREDIENTS	BUMBU	EQUIPMENT
1¼ lb. sirloin, trimmed of	¾ to 1 teaspoon sambal ulek or	Heavy knife
fat and boned	red chili pepper, seeded and	Mortar and pestle
1 tablespoon vegetable oil	finely chopped or ¼ teaspoon	Mixing bowl
1 small piece laos	cayenne pepper	"Wadjen" or 10" skillet
1 Daon salam leaf	2 cloves garlic	Wooden spoon
1 tablespoon Ketjap	3 macadamia or "kemiri" nuts	12 bamboo skewers
Benteng Manis	½ teaspoon ground coriander	Aluminum foil—optional
¼ teaspoon MSG	1 teaspoon salt	Broiler, charcoal grill or hibachi
	½ teaspoon brown sugar	
		WORKING TIME: 10 minutes
		COOKING TIME: 10 minutes
		GRILLING TIME: 1 minute
		SERVES: 6

The day before:

Soak the bamboo skewers in water overnight to avoid burning them when exposed to heat.

Early in the day:

Cut the sirloin into 36 bite-sized cubes. Set aside.

Make the bumbu (spice mixture): Peel the garlic by giving it a good whack with the side of a heavy knife. Slip off the peel. Place the garlic, pepper, nuts, salt, sugar and coriander in a mortar. Grind the bumbu with a pestle until it forms a smooth paste and all the ingredients are well combined.

In a "wadjen" or skillet heat 1 tablespoon oil over moderate heat. Add the bumbu and fry for one minute, breaking and separating the paste with a wooden spoon. Add the meat, laos, salam leaf, ketjap and MSG, and stir and fry the meat for about 3 minutes or until meat is brown. Set aside for one hour, tossing the meat in the spicy sauce occasionally.

Remove bamboo skewers from water. Thread the meat on skewers and spoon sauce over the meat. If you neglected to soak the skewers: cover the exposed bamboo with aluminum foil. Cover the satés to keep them moist. Refrigerate until grilling time.

Just before serving:

Preheat the broiler to its highest point and grill 4-5 inches from heat for one minute or until sizzling. Turn meat over and grill other side. Remove foil from skewers (if you have used it) and serve at once.

0 minutes before serving time, light a charcoal grill or hibachi. When coals are ready, grill the beef, d serve at once.

Sambal Ulek (Red Chili Condiment)

An explosive chili paste for "spice enthusiasts." You can make your own with fresh chili peppers or with dried red (Italian style) peppers. After adding sambal ulek, if your food is too hot for your taste, add a little sugar, water, milk or santen, or use more rice to soften its potent blow.

INGREDIENTS	1 tablespoon vinegar, lime or	WORKING TIME: 5 minutes
8 red chili peppers (fresh),	lemon juice	MAKES: ⅓ cup
chopped	¼ teaspoon sugar	NOTE: (1 teaspoon sambal ulek
or		equals 2 hot chilies)
⅓ cup Italian red peppers, dried	EQUIPMENT	
¼ teaspoon salt	Saucepan	
⅓ cup water	Mortar and pestle, or an electric	
	blender	
	1 small jar with lid	

1 Fresh chili peppers—in a mortar and pestle crush the fresh chilies mixing in salt and vinegar, lime or lemon juice and sugar. Add water by the teaspoonfuls until you have a smooth mixture. Place in a small jar with a lid and refrigerate until ready to use.

2 Dried chili peppers—Boil ⅓ cup water with ¼ cup Italian-style dried red peppers for three minutes. Spoon the water and peppers into a mortar. Add salt and vinegar, lime or lemon and sugar and grind with a pestle until a paste. If using an electric blender: Double recipe and blend at high speed for 15 seconds. Turn off the machine and scrape down the peppers that cling to the sides of the jar. Repeat blending until the chilies form a paste. Spoon the mixture into a small jar and refrigerate covered. This sambal will keep for a few weeks.

Sambal Goreng Udang (Fried Spiced Shrimps)

INGREDIENTS	1 slice laos	EQUIPMENT
1 lb. fresh medium sized shrimps	1 Daon salam leaf	Paring knife
2 cloves garlic	1 teaspoon salt	Chopping knife
½ medium onion	1 teaspoon brown sugar	"Wadjen" or 10" skillet
1 medium tomato	½ cup santen (see recipe	Wooden spoon
2 tablespoons oil	card #4)	
1 teaspoon sambal ulek, or finely	juice of half a lemon	WORKING TIME: 25 minutes
chopped and seeded red chili		COOKING TIME: 10 minutes
peppers, or ¼-½ teaspoon		SERVES: 6 as a side dish for an
cayenne pepper		Indonesian buffet

1 Shell and devein the shrimps: use your two thumbs to break apart the under shell of the shrimp. Separate and lift off the shell. At the tail end gently pull off the two wings. With a paring knife make a slit along the outside curve and rinse out the black or white intestinal vein (it's not always there) under cool running water. Refrigerate shrimp until ready to use.

2 With the side of a chopping knife, strike the garlic and peel. Mince very fine. Slice the onion into thin shreds. Cut the tomato in half and squeeze to remove seeds. Cut the pulp into small chunks.

3 Heat 2 tablespoons oil in the "wadjen" or skillet over moderate heat. Saute onions and garlic for five minutes without burning, stirring frequently. Add the sambal ulek, laos, daon salam leaf and stir and fry for one minute.

4 Add the shrimps and tomato, salt and sugar. Pour in the santen, raise heat and bring to a boil. Lower heat to medium and simmer until the shrimps turn pink, stirring constantly. Stir in the lemon juice and mix well. Serve hot.

5 This may be prepared earlier in the day. Cool, then cover tightly with plastic wrap and refrigerate. Reheat gently to a simmer without further cooking before serving.

Krupuk (Shrimp Crackers)

INGREDIENTS	EQUIPMENT	FRYING TIME: 5 minutes
1 package krupuk	"Wadjen" or frying skillet	
1½-2 cups vegetable oil	Slotted spoon	
(If the crackers are moist, dry	Air-tight canister	
in a low oven before frying;	Fat thermometer—optional	
otherwise, they will not swell	owels	
and will remain hard)		

1 Heat the oil to 375° on a fat the bread dropped in hot oil turns gol

2 Drop the crackers into the hot oi few seconds will begin to swell, ri with a slotted spoon and push it let fry for five seconds longer. Do

3 Drain on paper towels and store onion shreds and fish.

community center in Elmhurst, Queens, to watch the preparation of *slametan*, a Javanese wedding feast.

There, she found a dozen Javanese women sitting on the floor grinding spice pastes called *bumbus* on wide, shallow stone mortars (*cobeks*) with right-angled pestles. The room was filled with the powerful scents of herbs and spices she'd never experienced before: tamarind, shrimp paste, lemongrass, kaffir (*makrut*) lime leaves. She was seized by a deep curiosity but didn't stand in a corner with a notepad observing. Instead, she got down on the floor and persuaded someone to show her how to use a *cobek* to make some of the *bumbus* herself.

"I was interested in doing it the way they do it so I could feel it, so I could understand it!" Paula said. "I wanted to *breathe in* what they were doing."

Still, for all the intense aromas, she did not lose herself in them. She still needed precise recipes. Since no one was using measuring spoons, she took out her own set. She went around the room cheerfully measuring everyone's pinches and handfuls.

Her immersive approach showed up in her writing. The newsletter was one big *bumbu*, a heady, complex spice paste focused on the feast and the flavors of the archipelago: "The sophisticated cuisine of Central Java depends upon a skillful blending of sweet, sour and hot chili spices; in Bali the emphasis is on artistic presentation of food with sharp, strong flavors; Sumatran cooking is famous for its explosive, spicy quality."

Determined to help subscribers achieve these flavors at home, she suggested they grow their own cilantro (coriander) and harvest the seeds, both then nonexistent in American supermarkets. "Coriander seeds are pungent and aromatic," she wrote. "When they are ground, they release a sweet aroma, and their oil provides one of the two flavorings used in the production of gin! You can plant the seeds for they grow very easily into the leaf herb called Chinese parsley, or cilantro, which is wonderful in soups, salads and stews."

Paula included recipes for a bright, lemongrass beef *satay* (recipe, page 72) and a rich peanut sauce (recipe, page 75). She also slipped in a step-by-step method for making coconut milk and from-scratch directions for *ketjap manis* (sweet soy sauce) and *sambal oelek* (chile paste). With importing help from Bosboom and Madame Soeharjo, she was able to send subscribers fresh kaffir (*makrut*) lime leaves, lemongrass stalks, and *daun salam* leaves, a bay-like herb with a bitter-almond flavor that's still rare in the United States today.

After the success of the Indonesian box, Paula started a box for the cuisine that would define her: Moroccan. To find a Moroccan cooking teacher, Paula called the Moroccan consulate. The consul

OPPOSITE:
Recipe cards
from Paula's
Indonesia
party box

general himself, Abdeslam Jaidi, insisted his mother was one of the best cooks in the country. Paula was skeptical, but it turned out the Moroccan king, Mohammed V, was fond of her *bastilla*, a flaky, sweet-savory pastry layered with braised pigeon, eggs, and a mixture of ground almonds, confectioners' sugar, and cinnamon. The only problem was that his mother lived in Rabat. Paula explained she needed someone local.

While she continued her search for a Moroccan expert, she started researching a Mexican party box. In an unlikely encounter, she took a Mexican cooking class with another future food legend who would become an important role model. Diana Kennedy is arguably the Paula Wolfert of Mexican food, an expert on the country's regional cuisines and perhaps even more of a stickler about her recipes. When they met, Kennedy was drafting her 1972 landmark, *The Cuisines of Mexico*. Now ninety-one, Kennedy still lives in Mexico and remembers their meeting vividly. In a phone conversation, in her charming British accent, she explained, "I made a flan, and made the great mistake of testing it with a knife. Paula nearly exploded. She said, 'Oh my God, you don't do that! You use a needle!' Obviously she's absolutely right. I picked up the nearest instrument, as I am wont to do. But it wasn't good enough for Paula!" With their shared rigor, they became fast friends.

But that fall, before Paula could finish either the Mexican or the Moroccan party boxes, Columbia House shut down the program. Problems had come up with the sourcing: in the unrefrigerated Columbia House warehouse, prompted by the heat of the Terre Haute summer, the shallots had sprouted and the Indonesian spices had turned out to have bugs. It's also possible the uncompromising boxes failed to recruit repeat customers. The economy stumbled as well, and her cooking school at H. Roth & Sons struggled to find students in the downturn.

To make up some of the shortfall, Paula landed her first gig as a restaurant consultant, at the Rainbow Room, the landmark Rockefeller Center rooftop restaurant. There, the restaurateur Tony May ran an international dinner series he called Fortnights, perhaps the first guest chef appearances to take place in New York, what are now known as pop-ups. For these Fortnights, May flew in Mediterranean chefs to cook for two weeks at a time. He hired Paula to help him research and organize the dinners; she proudly boasts they brought the first women cooks from Puglia to New York to introduce handmade *orecchiette* pasta. In Paula, May found a kindred spirit also ahead of their times. "Back then, no one knew how even to pronounce Italian—they called it eye-talian," he said. "We were both working toward the future, if you will."

But May could only afford to pay her a hundred dollars a week out of petty cash. Without her Columbia House job, Paula was essentially broke—for the third time since leaving Tangier, she faced the bleak prospect of starting over from scratch yet again. "What am I going to do?" she lamented to Bill.

"I said, 'Write a Moroccan cookbook! You're always talking about it! I'll help you!'" he recalled. Over a weekend, Bill helped her draft a book proposal. Meanwhile, Paula shared her plan with Kennedy, who offered to put in a good word with her editor at Harper & Row, Fran McCullough, who recalls Kennedy saying, "'Dearie, I think I have a student who is the real thing, and she wants to write a book about Morocco.'"

McCullough had an unusually open mind about cookbooks; her sum experience then consisted only of Kennedy's debut. McCullough came to Harper & Row as a literary editor, best known for her work with poet Sylvia Plath. (McCullough saw similarities, she later said, between Paula's marriage to Bill and Plath's to poet Ted Hughes, in the ways they urged each other to strive for something timeless in their work, to think big.)

"I didn't know anything about Moroccan food," McCullough said. "I looked in the New York phone directory and saw there was one Moroccan restaurant, and I thought, 'Oh this isn't good.' But it was all so exciting and wonderful and mysterious. And I trusted Diana implicitly." Harper & Row bought the book for thirty-five hundred dollars (roughly twenty thousand dollars in today's currency). It also commissioned Bill to take the book's photographs.

Paula soon returned to Rabat for a culinary homecoming.

Indonesian Party Box

❖ ✻ ❖

Paula is not known for her expertise on Southeast Asian food. But she mastered Indonesian cooking in 1971 while researching a Javanese feast for one of her favorite Columbia House party boxes. The party box menu included seven rigorously authentic Javanese recipes, including homemade versions of the condiments *ketjap manis* and *sambal oelek*. She filled the boxes with hard-to-find ingredients such as shrimp crackers, galangal, kaffir (*makrut*) lime leaves, daun salam leaves, and candlenuts (pictured, at left) to help subscribers create the flavors at home. Here are two of the box's most accessible recipes, a beef *satay* and a peanut sauce for dipping.

Indonesian Beef Satay

Indonesian Peanut Sauce

Indonesian Beef Satay

Paula has a lifelong love of skewered meats, particularly Mediterranean versions like kebabs and kibbe, and this *satay* fits right in. Way ahead of its time, her Indonesian party box included fresh lemongrass and kaffir (*makrut*) lime leaves for subscribers to use in the recipes. But writing for a 1971 audience, she applied them sparingly. Here, Andrea Nguyen updates Paula's recipe, increasing the aromatics.

TO MARINATE

2 tablespoons coarsely chopped fresh lemongrass (from 1 medium-small stalk; bottom bulb portion only, with tough outer leaves removed)

1 tablespoon packed dark brown sugar

2 small shallots, coarsely chopped

2 garlic cloves, coarsely chopped

Chubby ½-inch (1.25-cm) piece fresh ginger, peeled and coarsely chopped

2 tablespoons soy sauce, regular or gluten-free

1 tablespoon rice vinegar

1 tablespoon neutral oil, such as peanut or safflower

1½ teaspoons ground coriander

¾ to 1 teaspoon cayenne pepper

TO COOK AND SERVE

Generous 1 pound (450 g) top sirloin

About 2 tablespoons neutral oil, such as peanut or safflower

1 cup (240 ml) Indonesian Peanut Sauce (page 75)

Sliced Fresno or jalapeño chile, for serving (optional)

Makes 8 to 10 skewers; serves 4

⏱ The beef marinates for 1 to 2 hours.

In a shallow dish, soak 8 to 10 wood or bamboo skewers in water to cover for 1 to 2 hours.

Meanwhile, to make the marinade, in a mini food processor, combine the lemongrass and sugar and process until a paste forms. Add the shallots, garlic, ginger, soy sauce, vinegar, oil, coriander, and cayenne (use the larger amount if you like heat) and process until an oatmeal-like texture forms. Transfer to a shallow bowl. Alternatively, in a mortar with a pestle, crush together the lemongrass and sugar until a paste forms. Add the shallot, garlic, ginger, coriander, and cayenne and continue to work the ingredients together to form a rough paste. Transfer to a shallow dish and stir in the soy sauce, vinegar, and oil.

Trim off any gristle from the beef, then cut into ¾-inch (2-cm) cubes. Add the beef to the marinade and mix to coat well. Thread

recipe continues →

4 or 5 cubes onto each skewer. Set aside at room temperature to marinate for 1 to 2 hours.

Light a medium-high fire in a charcoal or gas grill. Arrange the skewers directly over the fire and grill, turning the skewers a few times and basting as needed with the oil, until the beef is lightly charred all over but still medium within, about 7 minutes. Serve at once with the peanut sauce and chile (if using).

Indonesian Peanut Sauce

This subtly spicy sauce makes a great dip for beef *satay* (page 72). It doubles as a dressing for *gado-gado*, the Indonesian composed salad of raw and cooked vegetables, hard-cooked eggs, tofu, and shrimp chips.

⅓ cup (75 g) unsalted creamy peanut butter

¾ cup (180 ml) water

1 teaspoon minced fresh lemongrass (from bottom bulb portion only, with tough outer leaves removed)

¼ teaspoon flaky sea salt

2 tablespoons neutral oil, such as peanut or safflower

¼ cup (40 g) chopped shallot

½ teaspoon minced garlic (from 1 small clove)

1 tablespoon packed brown sugar

Juice of ½ lemon

½-inch (1.25-cm) piece fresh galangal or ginger

1 fresh kaffir (makrut) lime leaf

¼ teaspoon cayenne pepper

¼ cup (60 ml) coconut milk

In a small bowl, stir together the peanut butter and water, mixing well. Set aside. Using a mortar and pestle, the back of a knife and a cutting board, or a mini food processor, crush the lemongrass with the salt until a coarse paste forms. Set aside.

In a small saucepan, heat the oil over low heat. Add the shallot and garlic and cook, stirring often, until softened and translucent but not brown, about 10 minutes. Add the peanut butter mixture, raise the heat to medium-high, and bring to a boil, stirring constantly to prevent scorching. Add the brown sugar, lemon juice, galangal, lime leaf, and cayenne and stir to combine.

Turn down the heat to medium-low and simmer, stirring frequently, for 10 minutes to infuse the flavors. Discard the galangal and the lime leaf. Stir in the coconut milk and lemongrass paste. Remove from heat and let cool completely (the flavor builds as the sauce rests). Taste and adjust the seasoning with more salt and cayenne if needed. Serve at room temperature or transfer to a tightly capped jar and refrigerate for up to 1 week.

Makes 1 cup (240 ml)

🕐 The sauce can be served right away or refrigerated for up to 1 week.

Madame Couscous

MOROCCO AND NEW YORK
✣ 1972 to 1976

"To my mind four things are necessary before a nation can develop a great cuisine. The first is an abundance of ingredients—a rich land. The second is a variety of cultural influences; the history of a nation, including its domination by foreign invaders, and the culinary secrets it has brought back from its own imperialist adventures. Third, a great civilization—if a country has not had its day in the sun, its cuisine will probably not be great; great food and a great civilization go together. Last, the existence of a refined palace life—without royal kitchens, without a Versailles or a Forbidden City in Peking, without, in short, the demands of a cultivated court—the imagination of a nation's cooks will not be challenged."

—Paula Wolfert, in *Couscous and Other Good Food from Morocco*

IT'S HARD TO CALCULATE THE IMPACT OF Paula's first cookbook because its reach is so vast. The first comprehensive English-language Moroccan cookbook in the United States, the United Kingdom, and Morocco, it introduced the country and culture to many Americans, and it remains an indispensable reference on the cuisine, even for Moroccans. In San Francisco, Mourad Lahlou, one of the best Moroccan chefs in or out of Morocco, admits that he's used the work as a cheat sheet. He grew up in a traditional Moroccan household where men weren't allowed in the kitchen. So as an adult, he had to teach himself the cuisine, working largely from memory.

OPPOSITE:
With Khadija
Jaidi outside
Rabat, c. 1972

Recreating the food of your birthplace is challenging when you're oceans away from it. After Mourad met Paula at his pioneering Moroccan restaurant, Aziza, he dove into *Couscous*.

"If I wanted to know how to make aged butter or preserved beef or a tagine, instead of calling someone in Morocco or trying to remember what I saw my family do in my childhood, I could just go to her cookbook," he told me. "Because she did the research, she got the recipes from people who really knew what they were doing."

Given the work's scope, it's astonishing how quickly Paula wrote it. Unlike her next eight books, which each took on average five years to complete, Paula wrote *Couscous* in about eighteen months. To gather materials for the book, she made three trips from New York to Morocco between 1971 and 1972, each of which lasted one to three weeks and all of which were arranged by the consul general, Abdeslam Jaidi, through the Moroccan government. With a head start from having lived in Morocco for a total of three years, she was able to research most of the recipes at breakneck speed, inside of six weeks. Retrieving her memories from that compressed period felt akin to reverse engineering the spice combinations in a Moroccan couscous. Even when we established the chronology, she kept convincing herself (and me) that key events had happened in a different order.

❖

The first trip was fast and furious, lasting ten days. They came to call it The Golf Trip; in late December 1971, shortly after Paula signed her book contract, Jaidi and his wife, Janet, finagled a deal to fly Bill and Paula on a chartered jet with a group of US professional golfers who were attending the Moroccan king's inaugural golf tournament (now called the Trophy Hassan II). Incredibly, it was Paula's first flight across the Atlantic. She had not been willing to risk airplane travel after the Balkan fortune-teller had cautioned her that her twenty-fourth transatlantic flight would crash.

Relieved when they landed safely, she and Bill abandoned the golfers for a road trip to Marrakech, Essaouira, Tangier, Tétouan, Fez, and then into the Berber countryside and up into the Atlas Mountains that form Morocco's spine. The road trip gave Paula a better grasp of the country's geography, allowed Bill to take his first photographs, and inspired Paula to dream of returning to Tangier with her family for good. In Tangier, Paula introduced Bill to her old friend Paul Bowles, in an effort to sell him on the idea of moving back there, at least for one year. She appealed to Bill's parsimonious side, pointing out how affordable it would be to rent a villa and hire servants. She also urged him to research a novel about Isabelle Eberhardt, a Swiss adventurer who, beginning in the late nineteenth century, spent nearly a decade in North Africa.

"I identified with her because she was another Jewish girl in love with the Arab world," Paula explained of her idol. "Except she converted to Islam and had to disguise herself as a man to get around Algeria and Tunisia in the early 1900s, which was very hard to do."

❖

But it was the next trip, in the spring of 1972, that proved pivotal. Traveling solo to the outskirts of the coastal city of Rabat, Paula finally got to meet the consul general's mother, Madame Khadija Jaidi, to study with her. In three short weeks, Paula received the equivalent of a Grande Diplôme in Moroccan cooking.

Madame Jaidi lived in the Souissi suburb of Rabat, in a rambling two-story home set in a small, bucolic compound complete with an orange grove. At this charming homestead, affectionately called The Farm by her family, several servants helped her cook sumptuous midday feasts for a rotating cast of visitors.

All of her life, Jaidi had access to some of the best food in Morocco. Her background is a bit of a mystery: For years, Paula remained under the impression that Madame Jaidi had served as a *dada*, or servant cook, to the Moroccan royal family, rising to manage the king's kitchens in his Rabat palace. But when I checked this with the Jaidi family, I was told that she had never cooked in the palaces but had instead been born into the royal family's inner circle, and that the king had appointed her father to be the pasha (mayor) of Mogador (now called Essaouira). Growing up in the quarters surrounding the Rabat royal palace, she may have learned to cook from the *dadas* there.

Like Paula, Madame Jaidi could maneuver in worlds both high and low. She was quirky, too. Although wealthy, she dressed in Berber peasant clothes. In photographs, she looks like a farm woman from Biblical times, with an ample bosom and weathered hands.

When Paula unpacked her belongings, she discovered to her chagrin that she had forgotten an alarm clock. As she wrote in *Couscous*, "So much of the important kitchen work is done early in the morning and I didn't want to miss a thing." But she quickly discovered she didn't need one: at sunrise the next morning, she awakened to the rhythmic clanking of kitchen workers grinding spices in brass mortars and pestles for the day's meals.

Each morning at seven o'clock, she joined Madame Jaidi in her traditional Moroccan kitchen to prepare lunch, the main meal of the day. It's hard to imagine a more picturesque setting: they worked outdoors in the leafy shade of the orange trees, protected from rain by a simple wooden shelter, sitting on wooden orange crates draped with ornate Moroccan rugs, their heads tilted toward each other. Madame Jaidi cooked on charcoal braziers and propane-fueled burners, and a few assistants helped her prepare the ingredients. For five hours they all worked together, talking quietly, surrounded by the enticing scents of charcoal smoke, fresh spices, and breezes off the Atlantic coast. Lunch started at two o'clock, followed by an afternoon nap. At night, Jaidi and Paula retired indoors to watch television, usually the Moroccan news.

A precise and exacting cook, Madame Jaidi had a repertoire of forty to fifty traditional dishes that she had perfected over countless repetitions.

"I would take a pinch out of her hand and measure it, and every time it was always the same. She would slice meat; it was always five ounces on the scale," said Paula. Jaidi was best known for her *bastilla*, a sweet-savory pie made with flaky Moroccan *warka* dough and a rich filling of braised pigeon and almonds. She would peel and crush the almonds by hand, "which takes hours!" Paula said. "Nothing was done the easy way."

Jaidi informed and inspired many of the salads and spreads in *Couscous*, including the herb jam (recipe, page 90) for which Paula is still known. Under Jaidi's tutelage, Paula learned how to prepare

Paula at a Moroccan market, wearing the djellaba commissioned for her by Madame Jaidi

and finesse excellent tagines, the Moroccan stews cooked in cone-shaped pots of the same name. As with a classic French sauce, creating a certain intensity was key. If the meat needed extra browning, Jaidi glazed it under a clay dish stacked with hot coals. Jaidi taught Paula how tagines had an intense, slowly reduced sauce, much more concentrated than the light broth required for couscous, which was often served after the tagine, to conclude the meal. As they steamed the couscous over the single propane burner, Jaidi showed Paula how the grains expanded not while they were steaming but rather while they cooled.

In the kitchen and in the nearby outdoor food markets, Jaidi also introduced Paula to nuances in Moroccan ingredients. "Even though I was aware of Moroccan spices, she was *very* particular," Paula recalled. Jaidi introduced her to four kinds of ginger and to two kinds of cinnamon: sweeter Ceylon (*Cinnamomum verum*), called *dar el-cini* in Morocco, used in desserts, and the more assertive

Vietnamese cinnamon (*C. loureiroi*), known as *karfa*, used in savory dishes. Jaidi also familiarized Paula with the subtleties in the flavors of Moroccan honeys. To ensure that they could easily move through marketplaces, Jaidi outfitted Paula with a custom-made Berber *djellaba*, the hooded robe she wears on the author photo on the back jacket for *Couscous*.

Paula felt more at ease with kind, patient Madame Jaidi than she ever had with gossipy James Beard or brusque Dione Lucas. In our interviews, Paula spoke of Jaidi with the same tenderness with which she recalled her grandmother.

"She was so good," Paula said. "She was what a mother should be. Just love. And smothering you with it but in a nice way. She never spoke, she just hugged."

The traditional Moroccan kitchen also felt surprisingly comfortable and familiar. Paula's apprehension about large knives was rendered moot because Moroccan cooks rarely used them. If a vegetable needed cutting, Madame Jaidi used scissors or a small paring knife; she deployed a heavy cleaver only to chop large cuts of meat. Spices were toasted and pounded daily in a heavy *brass* mortar, "not wood, since saffron and garlic will soon leave their traces," Paula wrote. She noticed that certain implements brought unexpected new flavors to familiar foods. When pounded in a mortar with a pestle, parsley and cilantro tasted sweeter and more vibrant. When grated instead of chopped, onions took on a wonderful creaminess and tomatoes an almost velvety texture.

If Jaidi didn't know how to prepare a dish, she took Paula to meet the best cook who did. In *Couscous*, Paula tells the wonderful story of meeting Jaidi's best friend, Rakia, a master at *djej mefenned*, a savory, richly spiced dish that requires swirling a whole (not cut up) chicken in hot fat while basting it with beaten eggs. Rakia did this while she chain-smoked, "cracked jokes . . . sang and belly-danced around the kitchen," Paula wrote. It was perhaps the only dish Paula failed to replicate back home, though she nearly drove herself mad trying.

Paula also persuaded Jaidi to indulge her curiosities. Jaidi never made the paper-thin pastry leaves for her *bastilla*, always buying them from specialists. Because Paula wanted to include the tricky pastry recipe in the book, they found a bakery to teach Paula how to make it.

When lunch was served, Jaidi would withdraw to rest but had always invited a new authority to dine and share his or her knowledge with Paula. "She'd invite the president of some company and make the ultimate couscous," Paula gleefully recalled. "I was so lucky, I can't even tell you."

The two women formed a bond that endured until Jaidi's passing years later. In *Couscous*, Paula gave her prominent mention in her preface and text, and opened the Savory Pastries chapter with a photograph of her seated before a magnificent *bastilla*. In 2011, Paula published an update to *Couscous* called *The Food of Morocco* and dedicated it "to the memory of my mentor and friend Khadija Jaidi."

❖

After this three-week immersion, in late spring of 1972 Paula returned to New York, buzzing. She had only six months to adapt her recipes for American kitchens before she and Bill returned to Morocco to obtain additional photographs and research materials— and, she hoped, to move to Tangier for good. In New York, through old Tangier connections, she found a private Moroccan chef, a man named Omar Kadir, to help her round out the last of the book's recipes. He introduced her to a Moroccan woman who taught her *rghaif*, complex Moroccan pastries, and he shared his own couscous, an early favorite in the book.

Writing up the recipes, Paula had to invent a new vocabulary to capture certain Moroccan cooking methods. For example, after much observation, she settled on *rake* to describe the action of running one's fingers through steamed couscous (recipe, page 104).

But when she began testing her recipes, she faced her first roadblock: American ingredients. She was prepared to sacrifice clay tagines for metal pots but didn't want to compromise on quality produce. "I wanted the vegetables to taste right!" she said. She avoided New York supermarkets and shopped at The Good Earth, a health food store near her home. She learned its produce delivery schedule and ordered in advance. In *Couscous*, she urged readers to "turn the markets of your town into souks," to treat food shopping like an adventure. Madame Jaidi's four kinds of ginger and two kinds of cinnamon were unavailable or hard to source, but they were listed in the book, just in case they became more widely available in future years (with the same hope, Paula included salad recipes that called for arugula— and we know how that turned out). To parse out the components of the legendary Moroccan spice blend *ras el hanout*, Paula brought a sample she had purchased in Fez to Herman Bosboom, the importer who had helped her with the Columbia House party boxes. Together they identified twenty-six ingredients, which she listed in the book, from Spanish fly to grains of paradise and nigella seeds. Bosboom in turn introduced her to a scientist at the Bronx Zoo, who helped her list their botanical names.

Paula spent long days at the main branch of the New York Public Library on Forty-Second Street, perusing works of history and literature by James Edward Budgett Meakin, Herodotus, and Edith Wharton to paint a rich portrait of the country and its culture. From her research and conversations with Bill, she devised the four prerequisites for a great national cuisine quoted at the top of this chapter.

To write the book, for inspiration Paula looked to her heroes, authors of other well-researched, narrative-style cookbooks, such as Diana Kennedy, Claudia Roden, and Elizabeth David. That summer, she and Bill holed up at Bill's father's house in Duxbury, Massachusetts, while her children went to camp and his father vacationed on Martha's Vineyard. Sitting at facing desks, they sorted some of Paula's notes into the book's massive forty-five-page introduction. They organized the rest into chapter openings and recipe headnotes. The couple also combed the stacks of Harvard's Widener Library, running into historian Thomas Glick (a childhood friend of Bill's), who pulled rare books on Moorish and Spanish history to aid their research.

In spare moments, they organized their move to Tangier. Bill agreed to live there for at least one year. Paula enrolled the children at the American School of Tangier in the fourth and sixth grades—on scholarship now because the school was running low on American kids. They found an inexpensive villa to rent near Paula's old neighborhood.

❖

The family packed everything up and flew to Tangier that fall. The kids stayed in their school's boarding rooms for three weeks while Paula and Bill conducted a final fast-paced research trip, arranged by Abdeslam Jaidi's contacts at the Ministry of Tourism, to round out the book: Paula to deepen her knowledge of regional specialties and Bill to take more shots of food and the countryside. They came to call it The Caid Trip: at each stop, they met with local officials with romantic titles like his excellency, pasha, or *caid* (administrator), all of whom she would later acknowledge in the book's preface.

"In every town, the mayor, or whoever was in charge, had to find me the best cook to teach me the local dish," Paula said. "I thought that was how you write cookbooks! I had no idea you really had to work."

LEFT TO RIGHT: Leila, Bill, Paula, and Nicholas in their home in Tangier

Some visits went better than others. In one coastal town, one cook's pièce de résistance, a fish preparation, turned out to be "gooey and disgusting," Paula recalled. On the other hand, in Marrakech, though she had only one night there, her hosts not only found her a man to make the city's iconic lamb dish, *tangia*, but the same cook then took Paula on a thrilling late-night dash through the souks to buy the ingredients and then to a hammam, where they paid to have the lamb buried overnight in the coals used to heat the baths. The next morning, city authorities closed down the Jardin Majorelle so she and Bill could enjoy *tangia* as it was meant to be eaten: out of doors. "This would be like the mayor of New York closing down Central Park," Bill said, still astonished at the gesture decades later.

❧

That winter, though Paula and Bill were full-time Tangier residents, Bill made a quick visit to New York for work. At the Harper & Row offices, he turned in his photographs and looked over the copyedited manuscript with their editor, Fran McCullough. The pages were covered in red ink where the copyeditor had tried to rein in Paula. Paula was so new to writing recipes—and so excited about her finds—that her recipe methods shared too many details about exactly how to cook each dish. Bill knew Paula would be overwhelmed by all of the red ink. But time was running out. To help Paula sift through the many edits, Bill urged McCullough to fly to Tangier to go over the manuscript with Paula in person.

"Bill must have been very persuasive, because I went upstairs and managed to talk my bosses into sending me to Morocco, which is something [editors] could never, ever do," McCullough said. Then, as now, publishing budgets did not allow for such boondoggles.

It turned out to be the trip of a lifetime. "It was like going down the rabbit hole," McCullough said of her many exotic Tangier experiences, big and small. "When I walked into the house for the first time, Paula's maid had made this wonderful small couscous that Paula had never eaten before. There was a bowl of clementines on the table—this was before clementines came to America—and I was just stunned by these amazing little jewel-like fruits." (The couscous went into the book as Small Family Couscous.) Paula also took McCullough to meet Paul Bowles and other writers, and McCullough went on to edit Millicent Dillon's *A Little Original Sin*, a biography of Jane Bowles.

For a week, they worked late into the night, rewriting large sections of the book. "I was very jet-lagged, but Paula would get upset that I wasn't up early to begin again with laser-like focus," McCullough remembered, with a mixture of fondness and awe at

Paula's unflagging energy and dedication. With McCullough's help, Paula accepted the copyedits. To promote the book by giving it some edgy buzz, McCullough, inspired by the recipe for pot brownies in the 1954 *Alice B. Toklas Cook Book*, convinced Paula to overcome her marijuana aversion and include a recipe for *majoun*, a kef candy demonstrated to her by Mohammed Mrabet, a friend of Paul Bowles.

❖

Although *Couscous* would ultimately become one of Paula's best-selling titles, when it launched in the fall of 1973, as Paula put it, "it died on arrival."

"It just seemed to make no impression on anyone at all," McCullough recalled, "except for a few people who immediately saw that there was new serious cookbook publishing going on."

A few publications like *New York* magazine and the *New York Times* were positive. The most prescient review appeared in the Midwest. "It is a book so comprehensive that it makes one long for a series by Ms. Wolfert from each culture area around the globe," wrote the reviewer in the *Minnesota Daily*.

The work connected with forward-thinking chefs and home cooks. "Her Moroccan cookbook was really important for me, and for I think a lot of people of my generation," said food writer Ruth Reichl. "I was in Berkeley with this collective restaurant [The Swallow]. We did a lot of catering. And we made the *bastilla* endlessly. And made *warka* by hand."

Berkeley restaurateur Alice Waters, who had opened Chez Panisse only two years earlier, also embraced the book early. "We've been steaming our own couscous ever since," she said.

But in its earliest years, *Couscous* found few buyers outside the small food world. The title didn't help, despite Paula's assurances that everyone would know what couscous was. At a bookseller's meeting to promote it, McCullough remembered that "every single bookseller who came by said, 'what's cowse-cowse?'"

In hopes of stirring up interest, McCullough sent a copy to Julia Child, though Child and Paula had never met. In a letter to McCullough on L'École des Trois Gourmandes stationery, Child typed, "I think it is an excellent book, the first one I've seen that really explains how to go about things—I am

Julia Child's letter of encouragement

Madame Couscous 85

making couscous right now, and am just letting it dry under a damp towel, waiting for its final steaming." She suggested bringing Paula to America to merchandise the book. In the margin, she handwrote, "[The couscous] was lovely—light, fluffy, perfect!"

But interest in the book remained so low that Harper & Row couldn't justify financing a book tour. When it was finally time for a second printing years later, the publisher cut costs by pulling all of Bill's color photographs. Although Paula was disappointed by the book's low sales, she was not devastated. For all of her hard work, she surprisingly did not yet identify herself as a cookbook author. When she received her first copy of the book in Tangier and her mailman addressed her as Madame Couscous, she jumped up and down with delight. But she didn't see *Couscous* as her own. "I was building on a career. I just didn't quite know what that career was yet."

❖

Tangier became home for the next three years, some of the happiest of their lives. They bought a house called Villa Melusine in Tangier's Nouvelle Montagne (New Mountain), a hillside suburb west of the city, with views of the city and the Rif mountains beyond. Paula reunited with Fatima, her beloved maid from her second Tangier stint in 1968. Fatima moved in above the garage with her new husband, Ahmed, whom Paula and Bill hired to be their gardener and butler. Paula's children, Nicholas and Leila, were now teenagers; when they repeated the Tanjaoui curse words they picked up from their new friends in the neighborhood and at school, Fatima covered her ears.

With her fertile Tangier garden, horticulture replaced food as Paula's primary obsession. A neighbor, an eccentric old Englishman, taught her how to crossbreed day lilies, and she cultivated fruit trees in her hillside orchard, teaching herself to make jam from their bounty.

Having persuaded Bill to write that novel about Swiss adventurer Isabelle Eberhardt, Paula helped him retrace Eberhardt's steps across Tunisia and Algeria; in 1976, he published *Visions of Isabelle*. Paula drifted back to classic French cooking, translating Louisette Bertholle's *Secrets of the Great French Restaurants*. Tangier's population shifted to include more

Paula's Tangier home

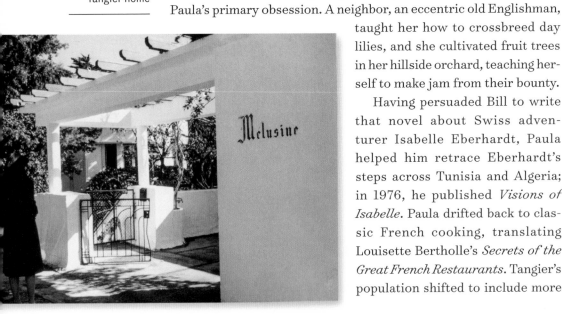

people from Lebanon, Egypt, Syria, and Israel, along with Italy, France, Spain, and Portugal. Through a wider circle of friends, Paula soon collected enough recipes for a second cookbook she called *Mediterranean Cooking*. Always focused on flavor first, she became fascinated by the ways each country extracted unique tastes cooking the same shared Mediterranean pantry. She organized the recipes not by country but by ingredient, by taste. For example, a chapter on garlic and olive oil included recipes for Spanish *gambas al ajillo* (shrimp in garlic sauce) and the French fish soup bouillabaisse. Another chapter focused on the nightshades (eggplants, peppers, and tomatoes) and included recipes for Yugoslavian *ajvar* and Turkish *hungar begendi* (eggplant cream).

McCullough wanted it for Harper & Row, but because of the poor sales of *Couscous*, she couldn't afford to match the offer of seven thousand dollars from Quadrangle Books, an imprint of the *New York Times*. The book was well received in food circles, not least for its innovative organizational structure. But it lacked the depth of Paula's other books because its recipes were acquired in Tangier living rooms. Its restrained politesse felt almost shallow compared to the adventure and immersion of *Couscous*. It remains a sentimental favorite, more for reading than for cooking, since she published improved versions of almost all of the recipes in later books (including a reissue of *Mediterranean Cooking* itself in 1994).

Fatima ben Lahsen Riffi, Paula's housekeeper and cooking tutor, with her husband, Ahmed, in Paula's garden in Tangier

By 1976, Bill had persuaded Paula to return to New York. Tangier had become expensive, and her children needed to attend good high schools. But she resisted until her hand was forced with the publication of *Tangier*, a mystery novel by Bill populated with characters who were such thinly veiled versions of people they knew that Paula feared they had offended everyone beyond repair. The Western Sahara War had broken out as well, which contributed to her willingness to leave. For the second time in her life, Paula returned to New York from Tangier full of trepidation, for she had no idea what she was going to do.

A Moroccan Feast

✢ ✤ ✢

These dishes can all stand deliciously on their own. But together they form a traditional Moroccan meal, which typically consists of a first course of four or more salads and spreads (a bit like Italian antipasti or Middle Eastern mezes), followed by a tagine, then a couscous, and finally a dessert.

In *Couscous* Paula wrote, "I find that Moroccan food always tastes better when eaten Moroccan style—the contact between the fingers and a hot *tagine* . . . always adds to the pleasure." For a true Moroccan experience, enjoy the meal on a low table, on pillows instead of chairs. Instead of transferring the dishes to individual plates, serve the foods out of their cooking vessels or from a platter. Instead of silverware, let guests pinch the foods with flatbreads or with the thumb and first two fingers of their right hands. Encourage them as Paula did in the book, quoting a work on Moroccan culture, "To eat with one finger is a sign of hatred; to eat with two shows pride; to eat with three accords with the Prophet; to eat with four or five is a sign of gluttony."

SPREADS AND SALADS

Wild Greens Jam

Moroccan Salsa

Eggplant Zaalouk

Grated Cucumber Salad with Oregano

TAGINE

Chicken M'Chermel

COUSCOUS

Berber Couscous for Spring

Steamed Couscous

Hand-Rolled Couscous

DESSERT

Poached Pears with Dried Fruits

Wild Greens Jam

Also known as Paula Wolfert's herb jam, this savory, creamy spread has acquired a cult following. A mix of greens are steamed until buttery soft, then cooked again in Moroccan spices and massaged with plenty of olive oil.

This version has been tweaked to play up Paula's favorite component, the peppery yet sweet—and incredibly nutritious—wild greens. She first learned about purslane and mallow from cooks in Morocco, then championed them her entire career, culminating with her book *Mediterranean Grains and Greens* (see the chapter starting on page 213 for more). But they're not required. Feel free to swap in more of your favorite store-bought greens or even replace some or all of the cultivated and wild greens with up to 16 ounces (450 g) defrosted frozen spinach. Whether wild or cultivated, the cooked greens taste almost like pâté, brightened with garnishes of preserved lemons and black olives. Enjoy them with a spoon, on a cracker, or served alongside grilled fish, meat, or tofu.

---

12 ounces (350 g) young cultivated greens, such as spinach, Swiss chard, arugula, or beet, or a mixture, stemmed and coarsely chopped

4 ounces (115 g) wild greens, such as purslane, mallow, or nettles, or a mixture, stemmed and coarsely chopped

1 cup (40 g) coarsely chopped fresh flat-leaf parsley leaves

3 garlic cloves, unpeeled

½ cup (20 g) fresh cilantro leaves, chopped

¼ teaspoon flaky sea salt

4 to 5 tablespoons (60 to 75 ml) extra-virgin olive oil, or more if needed

¼ teaspoon sweet smoked paprika (pimentón de la Vera dulce)

¼ teaspoon ground toasted cumin, preferably Moroccan

Pinch of cayenne pepper

Juice of ½ lemon

½ preserved lemon (page 306), pulp discarded and rind rinsed and slivered

12 oil-cured black olives, preferably Moroccan, rinsed (see note)

Flatbread or crackers, for serving (optional)

Serves 4 to 6 as part of a traditional salad course

🥄 The salad is refrigerated for at least 1 hour or up to 4 days (its flavor improves daily).

Fit a large pot with a steamer basket, add water to the pot to just below the base of the basket, and bring the water to a boil over high heat. In batches, add the cultivated and wild greens, parsley, and garlic cloves. As soon as a batch just softens, push it aside with tongs or a spoon and add more. (Paula uses this method to cook an enormous amount of leafy greens efficiently and evenly.) Once all of the greens are added, let them steam until the garlic is soft and the greens are very tender. The total cooking time is 10 to 15 minutes, depending on the type of greens.

Remove the pot from the heat. Remove the steamer basket from the pot and let the contents of the basket cool. Retrieve the garlic, peel the cloves, and set aside. Squeeze the greens dry in a kitchen towel and chop finely. Using a mortar and pestle, the back of a knife and a cutting board, or a mini food processor, crush together the steamed garlic, cilantro, and salt until a paste forms.

In a 10-inch (25-cm) frying pan, preferably earthenware (stainless steel or enameled cast iron are also fine), heat 2 tablespoons of the olive oil over medium-low heat. Add the garlic paste, paprika, cumin, and cayenne and cook, stirring, until fragrant, about 30 seconds. Add the chopped greens and cook, mashing and stirring with the back of a spoon or fork, until all of the liquid has evaporated, 10 to 15 minutes. Transfer to a bowl and let cool to room temperature.

Stir the lemon juice into the cooled greens. Mash in enough additional oil until the mixture is creamy and smooth (about 2 tablespoons, or more to taste). Cover and refrigerate for at least 1 hour or up to 4 days.

Just before serving, taste and adjust the seasoning with more salt, cumin, and/or lemon juice if needed. Serve in its dish or shape into a round on a platter. Garnish with the preserved lemon slivers and black olives. Offer with flatbread, if desired, and invite guests to scoop up the jam.

NOTE Rinse the olives with cool water, then taste for saltiness and bitterness. If they are too salty, soak them in lukewarm water to cover for 30 minutes to 1 hour; drain and rinse well. Repeat as necessary. If they are too bitter, place them in a small saucepan, cover with water, and bring to a boil; drain and rinse well. Repeat as necessary.

CLOCKWISE FROM LEFT:
Eggplant Zaalouk (page 95),
Grated Cucumber Salad with
Oregano (page 97), Wild Greens
Jam (page 90), Moroccan
Salsa (page 94)

Moroccan Salsa

In Tangier in the 1970s, Paula loved cooking alongside Fatima ben Lahsen Riffi, her friend and housekeeper in Tangier. Born in the nearby Rif mountains, Fatima showed Paula how to navigate Moroccan markets, helped her butcher whole animals, and taught her appealing, simple recipes from the countryside like this light, refreshing salsa-style salad. (When Andrea and I cooked it for her, Paula exclaimed, "Oh, I feel Fatima is here!")

Because Paula learned to make this dish after *Couscous* appeared, she first published it in *Paula Wolfert's World of Food*. She originally called for peeling the tomatoes because American supermarket tomatoes then had such thick skins. But peak summer tomatoes don't need peeling. For added color, use a mix of heirloom tomatoes like Green Zebras and yellow Brandywines. You can roast your own bell peppers (see Ajvar recipe, page 20) or use store-bought. Serve the salsa on its own or anywhere you would serve Mexican salsa. It's also great on a sandwich.

---

3 tablespoons (45 ml) fruity extra-virgin olive oil

Juice of ½ lemon, or to taste

½ teaspoon ground toasted cumin, preferably Moroccan

½ teaspoon flaky sea salt

Pinch of sweet smoked paprika (pimentón de la Vera dulce)

Pinch of cayenne pepper

1 pound tomatoes, halved, seeded, and cut into ¾-inch (2 cm) chunks

¾ cup (145 g) peeled and diced roasted red bell pepper

3 tablespoons (30 g) finely chopped red onion, rinsed, drained, and squeezed dry in paper towels

1 preserved lemon (page 306), pulp discarded and rind rinsed and minced

Serves 4 to 6 as part of a traditional salad course

In a serving dish, whisk together the olive oil, lemon juice, cumin, salt, paprika, and cayenne. Add the tomatoes, roasted pepper, and onion and toss to coat. This salsa can be served right away but tastes best if covered and refrigerated until well chilled, about 30 minutes. Just before serving, stir in the preserved lemon.

Eggplant Zaalouk

A kind of Moroccan baba ghanoush with tomatoes instead of tahini, this smoky eggplant spread is among Paula's favorite Moroccan "salads," and she has published several versions over the years. In *Couscous* she wrote, "You can play around with this recipe, using whatever you happen to have on hand." Red bell peppers can be cooked along with the eggplant, or fried zucchini coins can be stirred in with the tomatoes. If you favor garlic, use the full amount.

---

2 eggplants, (about 12 ounces | 350 g each; see note, page 23)

2 or 3 garlic cloves, peeled

1 teaspoon flaky sea salt

5½ tablespoons (80 ml) extra-virgin olive oil

12 ounces (350 g) red tomatoes, peeled, halved, seeded, and finely chopped, or 1½ cups (270 g) drained chopped canned tomatoes

¾ teaspoon ground toasted cumin, preferably Moroccan

½ teaspoon sweet smoked paprika (pimentón de la Vera dulce)

Pinch of cayenne pepper

2 tablespoons finely chopped fresh cilantro

Juice of ½ lemon

Light a medium-low fire in a charcoal or gas grill, or position an oven rack 7 to 8 inches (17.5 to 20 cm) from the heating element and preheat the broiler. If you are grilling, slowly grill the eggplants, turning them as needed, until the skin is blackened on all sides and the flesh is softened to the point of collapse, 20 to 30 minutes. If you are broiling, halve each eggplant lengthwise, arrange them cut side down on a foil-lined sheet pan, and broil until the skin is blackened and the flesh is tender, about 20 minutes.

Transfer the eggplants to a colander set in the sink and let cool slightly. Using a spoon, scoop out the flesh from the skin, discard the skin and any large seed pockets, and let the flesh drain in the colander. Squeeze the flesh gently to remove any bitter juices.

Meanwhile, using a mortar and pestle, the back of a knife and a cutting board, or a mini food processor, crush the garlic with ½ teaspoon of the salt until a coarse paste forms. In a frying pan, preferably earthenware (stainless steel and enameled cast-iron also work), heat 3 tablespoons (45 ml) of the olive oil over medium heat. Add the tomatoes, garlic paste, cumin, paprika, cayenne, and the remaining ½ teaspoon salt. Cook, stirring occasionally,

Serves 4 to 6 as part of a traditional salad course

The spread improves with time, so make it a day ahead if you can. It can be refrigerated for up to 4 days.

recipe continues →

until the tomatoes have thickened and most of the moisture has evaporated, about 20 minutes.

Add the eggplant to the frying pan, crushing any lumps with the back of a spoon or fork. Stir in the cilantro and continue cooking, stirring often, until the mixture is thick but not dry, 10 to 15 minutes longer. Transfer to a serving bowl. Fold in the lemon juice and the remaining 2½ tablespoons olive oil. Taste and adjust the seasoning with more salt if needed. Let cool before serving.

Grated Cucumber Salad with Oregano

While researching her first cookbook in the early 1970s, Paula was delighted by the lack of chef's knives in traditional Moroccan kitchens. Instead of chopping vegetables, cooks often grated them to unusual textural effect. In this salad, cucumbers take on an unexpected lightness, even silkiness, when grated and squeezed dry. If you can find them, use fresh *za'atar* (a thyme-like herb used in the dried spice blend of the same name), and curved Armenian cucumbers, known as *feggous* in Morocco, which have a denser flesh and smaller seeds than most other cucumbers.

---

2 pounds (900 g) cucumbers, peeled, halved lengthwise, and seeded

1 tablespoon extra-virgin olive oil

2 teaspoons fresh lemon juice or unfiltered cider vinegar

1 tablespoon sugar or honey (optional)

Pinch of flaky sea salt

1 scant tablespoon fresh oregano, za'atar, or marjoram leaves, or a mixture, chopped

12 to 15 oil-cured black olives, preferably Moroccan, pitted and rinsed (see note, page 91)

Using the large holes of a box grater or the grater attachment of a food processor, grate the cucumbers. Wrap the grated cucumbers in a kitchen towel and squeeze dry.

In a serving dish, stir together the olive oil, lemon juice, sugar (if using), and salt. Add the cucumber and toss well. Sprinkle with the oregano, garnish with the olives, and serve right away or slightly chilled.

Serves 4 to 6 as part of a traditional salad course

⏱ This salad does not improve with time and should be prepared shortly before serving.

Chicken M'Chermel

Gingery, lemony, peppery, sweet yet savory—this tagine is one of Paula's favorite examples of the classic Moroccan combination of chicken with preserved lemons and olives. It is also a beautiful example of the subtlety and intensity of the best Moroccan tagines, which is why she included a version of it in the proposal for her first Moroccan cookbook.

This recipe will work equally well in either a traditional Moroccan clay tagine on the stove top or, because a clay tagine acts like stove-top oven, in a metal casserole (stainless steel or enameled cast iron will work) in the oven. In addition to a generous heaping of green olives and plenty of onion (here blitzed in a food processor), the dish has a secret enriching ingredient, chicken livers. "They're used the way French cooks use foie gras, as a thickener for the sauce," Paula says. Tagines are traditionally eaten with the first three fingers of the right hand, sometimes with flatbread to help grab onto the meat, though silverware can be used.

¼ cup (60 ml) extra-virgin olive oil

2 garlic cloves, thinly sliced

1 teaspoon ground ginger

1 teaspoon sweet smoked paprika (pimentón de la Vera dulce)

¼ teaspoon ground toasted cumin, preferably Moroccan

¼ teaspoon freshly ground black pepper

Flaky sea salt

6 or 8 skin-on, bone-in whole chicken legs (4 pounds | 1.8 kg total), preferably organic and air-chilled, cut into thighs and drumsticks

1 to 2 chicken livers (2 ounces | 60 g total)

3 large red onions (1½ pounds | 675 g total)

½ cup (120 ml) water

¼ cup (10 g) chopped fresh cilantro

¼ cup (10 g) chopped fresh flat-leaf parsley, plus more for garnish

2 tablespoons saffron water (page 308)

¼ teaspoon ground turmeric

1½ cups (180 g) pitted Picholine olives, rinsed (see note on page 91) and at room temperature

2 preserved lemons (page 306), quartered and rinsed of excess salt (see note)

⅓ cup (80 ml) lemon juice (from about 2 lemons)

6 to 8 flatbreads, such as pita or naan, warmed, for serving (optional)

Serves 6 to 8

🕐 The chicken marinates overnight.

The day before serving, in a large bowl, stir together the olive oil, garlic, ginger, paprika, cumin, black pepper, and 1 teaspoon salt. Pat the chicken pieces dry with paper towels. Slide your fingers under the skin to loosen it from the flesh, taking care not to tear the skin or to remove it entirely. Add the chicken pieces and livers to the marinade and rub them all over, working the mixture under and over the chicken skin. Cover and refrigerate overnight.

The next day, if you are using a metal casserole, preheat the oven to 325°F (160°C). If you are using a tagine, you will not need the oven. Cut the onion into 1-inch chunks and pulse in batches in the processor to finely chop (avoid a pureed texture). Set a large sieve in the sink and line a large bowl with a kitchen towel. Transfer the onions to the sieve and rinse under cool running water. Transfer the rinsed onions to the prepared bowl and squeeze dry with the towel.

In a tagine 12 inches (30 cm) wide and 2½ inches (6.25 cm) deep, or a 6- to 8-quart (6- to 8-l) heavy stainless-steel or enameled cast-iron casserole, combine the water, cilantro, parsley, saffron water, turmeric, and about one-fifth of the onion. Add the chicken, livers, and their marinade and stir to coat.

If using a tagine, cover and set it on a heat diffuser over medium-low heat. If using a casserole, place a piece of crumpled parchment on top of the chicken, cover with a lid, then transfer to the oven. Whether in the tagine on the stove top or in the casserole in the oven, cook the chicken for 50 minutes. As the chicken pieces cook, gently turn them and the livers often in the sauce, being careful not to tear the chicken skin or let the sauce rise above a simmer.

Use a slotted spoon or tongs to transfer the livers to a small bowl or mini food processor. Mash or process them to a coarse paste, then return to the tagine or casserole with the remaining onions. Return the covered tagine to a simmer on the stove top or the covered casserole to the oven and continue cooking, stirring occasionally, until the chicken is very tender and the flesh falls easily from the bone, or an instant-read thermometer inserted near (but not touching) the bone registers between 185° and 195°F (85° and 90°C), 1½ to 2 hours longer on the stove top or about 1 hour longer in the oven. The thighs may cook more quickly than the legs; if that happens, submerge the legs in the sauce and stack the thighs on top to keep them warm in the steam.

Transfer the chicken pieces to a sheet pan and cover to keep warm. The sauce should measure about 1½ cups (360 ml) and be thick enough that a wooden spoon pulled across the bottom of the cooking vessel leaves a trail. If the sauce is too thin, simmer over medium heat until reduced to about 1½ cups (360 ml). Stir in the chicken, olives, preserved lemons, and lemon juice. Taste and adjust the seasoning with salt and lemon juice if needed.

recipe continues →

Position an oven rack 7 to 8 inches (17.5 to 20 cm) from the heating element and preheat the boiler. Place the tagine or casserole under the broiler and broil until the chicken and sauce are golden brown, about 4 minutes. Serve the chicken in the tagine or casserole, or on individual plates. Garnish with fresh parsley and accompany with flatbread, if desired.

NOTE The preserved lemon quarters can be served whole or coarsely chopped, with or without their pulp. The pulp will impart a more intense flavor to the sauce. While the rinds are easier to eat if coarsely chopped, it is more traditional to serve the lemon quarters whole and let guests pull them apart into smaller pieces using their fingers or flatbread.

Berber Couscous for Spring

This fragrant, soulful masterpiece is an ideal project for people who like to play with their food. It is best to tackle the cooking with at least one other friend. The process can be even more relaxing if spread out over two days.

"This is the kind of couscous you will find in small villages in the foothills of the Middle Atlas Mountains, and it is extraordinary," Paula wrote in 1973. In an early call for seasonal cooking, she continued, "It is served in the spring, when everything that grows is fresh and young and tender, and it has a miraculous clean taste. Everything in it should be as fresh as possible, except of course the *smen*," or aged butter (which is optional but another fun experiment). Be sure to use the full amount of black pepper, which tastes floral in the creamy broth.

---

2 tablespoons unsalted butter, preferably clarified

1 large yellow onion (about 14 ounces | 400 g), thinly sliced

Herb bouquet of 8 sprigs each fresh flat-leaf parsley and cilantro, tied together with kitchen string

1 (3-inch | 7.5-cm) cinnamon stick

1 tablespoon saffron water (page 308)

1½ teaspoons flaky sea salt

1½ teaspoons freshly ground black pepper

6 cups (1.5 l) water

8 to 10 bone-in, skin-on chicken thighs (3 pounds | 1.4 kg total)

2 large tomatoes (about 1 pound | 450 g total), halved and seeded

8 to 10 white pearl onions, peeled

1 pound (450 g) small white turnips or radishes, or a combination, trimmed

¼ cup (40 g) golden raisins

1½ pounds (675 g) small zucchini, trimmed and halved lengthwise

2 cups (340 g) peeled fava beans (from 4 pounds | 1.8 kg unshelled), lima beans, or peas

1 cup (240 ml) heavy cream

1 serrano chile, stemmed, halved, and seeded (optional)

3 tablespoons (45 ml) olive oil

Steamed Couscous (page 104), steamed and raked 2 or 3 times

2 to 3 tablespoons (30 to 45 g) smen (page 310) or unsalted butter, preferably clarified

In a 6- to 8-quart (6- to 8-l) enameled cast-iron casserole or Dutch oven, melt the butter over medium heat. Stir in the onion, herb bouquet, cinnamon stick, saffron water, salt, and pepper. Cover and cook, stirring occasionally, until the onion is softened, about 5 minutes. Uncover and cook, stirring a few times, until the onion turns golden, about 5 minutes longer.

Pour in the water and bring to a simmer. Add the chicken thighs, cover, turn down the heat to low, and simmer for 45 minutes. Transfer the chicken to a platter and tent with foil to keep warm.

Serves 8 to 10

Allow at least 1 full day to cook this. Make sure the steamed couscous is ready for its final steaming.

recipe continues →

Reserve the broth. (The dish can be prepared up to this point up to 1 day in advance. Cover and refrigerate the chicken and broth separately overnight.)

Using the large holes of a box grater, and with the cut side against the grater, grate the tomato halves and discard the skins.

At least 1 hour before serving, skim off the fat from the surface of the broth and bring the broth to a simmer over medium heat. Add the pearl onions, turnips, and raisins, and when the broth returns to a simmer, turn down the heat to medium-low, cover partially, and simmer until the vegetables are just tender, about 20 minutes. Add the zucchini and continue cooking until the zucchini are just tender, about 10 minutes. Add the grated tomatoes, favas, cream, and the chile, if using. Simmer until all the vegetables are very tender, about 10 minutes longer. Remove from the heat, taste, and adjust the seasoning with salt if needed. Scoop out 1⅓ cups (330 ml) of the broth and set aside for mixing with the couscous. Cover the pot partially to keep the vegetables and the remaining broth warm. Reheat gently until hot just before spooning it over the chicken.

In a 12-inch (30-cm) frying pan, heat the oil over medium-high heat. Add the chicken thighs, cover partially, and cook, turning once, until well browned, about 8 minutes. Transfer the chicken to a plate.

Meanwhile, return the water to a boil over high heat for the final steaming of the couscous. Line the steamer basket with muslin or cheesecloth. Add the steamed couscous to the basket and steam, uncovered, for 10 minutes.

Transfer the couscous to your widest serving dish. Using a wire whisk, gently coat the couscous grains with the smen. Gradually sprinkle with the reserved 1⅓ cups (330 ml) broth if using hand-rolled couscous or 1 cup (240 ml) if using instant couscous. Rake the grains with your whisk and your fingers. Let stand for 10 minutes to allow the couscous to swell and absorb the broth. Gently mound the couscous and form a well in the center. Nestle the chicken in the well, top with the vegetables, and spoon on a little more broth. Serve the remaining broth on the side, as Paula writes, "for those who like their couscous very moist."

Steamed Couscous

"If I could teach people one thing, it's to know the magic of steamed couscous," Paula told me. "If I could teach them two, it would be to roll their own," she added (recipe follows, page 109). Most of us cook couscous like rice, simmering it in water or broth. But steaming it triples its volume, rendering it lighter, fluffier, and, Paula insists, easier to digest.

In Morocco, couscous is typically steamed three to seven times before serving. What might be the most magical part of this kitchen ritual is that the couscous does not swell as it steams but rather when it is resting on a wide platter between steamings, after it has been *raked* with milk or water. Nothing but a slow hydration process, raking works best on a large platter made of unglazed clay, a material that helps absorb moisture. Paula suggests using an Italian-made clay pot liner, about 18 inches (45 cm) in diameter, sold at many garden stores. Any wide plate will do, however. Traditionally couscous is raked with water, but from a Moroccan friend Paula discovered that raking it with milk "really makes it 'sing.'"

Hand-Rolled Couscous (page 109), or 1½ pounds (675 g) 100 percent semolina instant couscous

2 tablespoons smen (page 310) or unsalted butter, preferably clarified, cut into ¼-inch (6-mm) cubes and at room temperature

1½ cups (360 ml) whole milk, at room temperature

½ cup (120 ml) room temperature water, plus ¼ to ½ cup (60 to 120 ml) if using hand-rolled couscous

Serves 8 to 10

🕐 The steamed couscous can be held several hours before serving.

Pour water into the bottom of couscousière or into a large pot fitted with a flat-bottomed steamer basket to within 1 to 2 inches (2.5 to 5 cm) of the base of the top tier of the couscousière or the steamer basket, then remove the top tier or basket. Bring the water to a boil over high heat. (Paula also suggests tossing a penny into the pot; when it stops clicking, it's time to add more water.)

If using instant couscous, put the couscous in a large bowl, add 2 cups (480 ml) water, stir, and let stand for 1 minute. Drain and transfer the moistened couscous to a wide platter, preferably an unglazed earthenware platter 18 inches (45 cm) in diameter. With dampened hands, lift up the moistened grains, rub them gently between your palms, and let them fall back onto the platter to break up any lumps. Repeat once or twice as needed to remove

recipe continues →

any remaining lumps. If using hand-rolled couscous, it is ready for steaming once it has been shaped on the earthenware plate.

Whether using homemade or store-bought instant couscous, follow these steps to steam it to plump perfection.

FIRST STEAMING AND RAKING

Line the inside of the top tier of the couscousière or the steamer basket with muslin or cheesecloth, extending the four corners of the cloth over the sides of the steamer, being careful not to let it get near any flame. Fit the steamer basket snugly over the boiling water. If you see steam escaping along the sides, seal the seam with a long strip of foil or a dampened kitchen towel.

Add the couscous to the cloth-lined couscousière tier or steamer basket and steam, keeping the water at a steady boil, uncovered, for 20 minutes.

Gather up the cheesecloth, then dump the couscous onto the platter, shaking out the cheesecloth. Using a wire whisk, spread out the grains. Scatter the cubes of smen over the couscous and, using the whisk, gently toss the hot grains to coat them evenly with the smen. Working in batches of several tablespoons at a time, sprinkle the milk over the couscous and, using the whisk, your fingers, or a combination, rake the milk into the grains, lifting and stirring them gently to break up any lumps after each addition. When all of the milk has been incorporated, smooth out the grains into a thin layer and let stand for 10 minutes. The couscous will begin to swell.

SECOND STEAMING AND RAKING

Return the cheesecloth to the couscousière tier or steamer basket. Add the couscous and steam at a steady boil, uncovered, for another 20 minutes.

Regather the cheesecloth, return the couscous to the platter, and spread out again with the whisk. Working in batches of a few tablespoons at a time, sprinkle the ½ cup (120 ml) water over the couscous and, using the whisk, your fingers, or a combination, rake the water into the grains, lifting and stirring them gently to break up any lumps after each addition. When all of the water has been incorporated, smooth out the grains into a thin layer and let stand for another 10 minutes. The couscous will continue to swell.

If using hand-rolled couscous, repeat the steps for the second steaming and raking with the ¼ to ½ cup (60 to 120 ml) water, adding as much as needed for the grains to plump nicely. If the grains still appear tight, you can steam and rake hand-rolled couscous up to four more times, or for a total of seven times.

THIRD STEAMING (for hand-rolled couscous only)

When the couscous has plumped to your satisfaction, serve at once. Or if you are preparing the couscous in advance, cover the grains loosely with a damp kitchen towel and remove the couscousière or pot from the heat, reserving the water in the bottom. The couscous will hold for several hours. To serve the couscous on its own, return the water in the bottom of the couscousière or pot to a boil and steam the couscous for 10 more minutes before serving. To incorporate the couscous into a recipe such as Berber Couscous for Spring (page 101), follow the instructions in the recipe for the final steaming.

Hand-Rolled Couscous

Hand-rolling couscous offers one of life's rare chances to pretend to be an oyster creating a pearl. Couscous consists of coarsely ground semolina grains that are moistened with water and then coated with several layers of finely ground semolina—like pearls seeded by a grain of sand. The ideal rolling surface is the same as for raking steamed couscous: an unglazed earthenware platter 18 inches (45 cm) in diameter (see headnote on page 104); an earthenware cazuela also works. Purchase the two kinds of semolina at a good Middle Eastern market or online.

Pinch of flaky sea salt

½ cup (120 ml) cool tap water

1 cup (about 160 g) coarse semolina

1 cup (about 160 g) fine semolina

In a small bowl, dissolve the salt in the water. Spread the coarse semolina in a thin layer on an unglazed earthenware platter 18 inches (45 cm) in diameter or other wide plate. Sprinkle the coarse semolina with 1 to 2 tablespoons of the cold salted water and, at the same time, rotate the palm and fingers of one hand in a circular direction over the moistened grains to create tiny spheres.

After several rotations, alternately sprinkle the fine semolina and the salted water over the spheres, adding only a few tablespoons of each at time and continuing to rotate your hand. With each new layer the spheres will begin to form couscous grains.

When all the water and the fine semolina have been incorporated, transfer the couscous to a fine-mesh sieve to shake off any excess flour. For steaming instructions, see page 104.

Makes about 3½ cups (14½ ounces | 415 g)

Hand-rolled couscous that has not been steamed does not hold well, so plan to steam it right away.

Poached Pears with Dried Fruits

When I traveled to Marrakech to meet up with Paula in 2008, she was delayed in Fez on the first night and asked me to visit the celebrated Le Tobsil restaurant on her behalf. How I loved playing Paula Wolfert for the night, visiting the kitchen and asking to meet the chef, Fatima Mountassamin, so that I might write down her technique for this recipe that Paula later shared in *The Food of Morocco*. But over the next week, I realized that my shy effort paled next to Paula's bold, immersive approach, her ability to bond with cooks in the field like family. That said, these simple poached fruits are a lovely way to end a traditional Moroccan meal. Offer with butter cookies for extra flair.

---

3 cups (720 ml) water

⅓ cup (80 ml) honey

½ navel orange with rind, sliced ½ inch (1.25 cm) thick

1 (3-inch | 7.5-cm) cinnamon stick

2 bay leaves, cut in half

1 whole clove

6 large Bartlett pears with stems, peeled

½ cup (75 g) dried fruits, such as pitted prunes, apricots, golden raisins, or a mixture

Butter cookies (such as Greek Butter-Almond Cookies with Ouzo, page 175), for serving (optional)

Serves 6

🕑 The pears can be poached and refrigerated in their poaching liquid for up to 1 day. Rewarm gently before serving.

In a large pot, combine the water, honey, orange slices, cinnamon stick, bay leaves, and clove and bring to a boil over medium-high heat, stirring to dissolve the honey. Add the pears and dried fruits, then cover with a crumpled sheet of parchment paper, gently pressing down to ensure the pears are submerged. Turn down the heat to medium, and simmer the pears, turning them often, until they are tender, 15 to 25 minutes, depending on their size and ripeness.

Using a slotted spoon, transfer the pears and dried fruits to a shallow serving bowl or platter. Raise the heat to high and boil the poaching liquid until reduced to 1 cup (240 ml), about 15 minutes. Strain the syrup through a fine-mesh sieve, then pour over the pears.

Serve warm or at room temperature with the cookies (if using) alongside.

A Big and
Empty Place

NEW YORK AND FRANCE
❖ 1976 to 1983

"I come from the Southwest, which is a big and empty
place—very few people and lots of land. And we're not
on the main route to anywhere. What most people, and
this includes the French, know about my region is that
it's the land of Armagnac and foie gras. So we have a long
way to go to make our regional cooking better known."

—André Daguin in an interview by Paula Wolfert,
Bon Appétit, June 1979

IF PAULA'S MEMORIES of her first marriage were buried in the dark
and her recollections of *Couscous* dimly lit by a kind of sunrise, the
time she spent on *The Cooking of South-West France* sparkled in
the glorious morning sun. She confidently recalled her numerous
research trips to France, nineteen magazine articles, and countless
teaching tours from that period. Unlike *Couscous*, which she pulled
off in eighteen months, she invested five years writing *South-West
France*, from 1978 to 1983. This chapter only confounds because
there are too many good stories to tell. It seems impossible that one
person lived through all of them.

The fact that one cookbook writer contributed two such dispa-
rate books, *Couscous* and *South-West France*, to the American canon
seems equally improbable. Where *Couscous* brought Moroccan classics to the English-speaking world, *South-West France* celebrated
avant-garde innovations alongside such lesser-known regional

OPPOSITE:
Paula in the
kitchen with
André Daguin

French staples as duck confit and cassoulet. Among food insiders, the latter volume established Paula as a culinary legend.

South-West France acquired a cult following among a certain type of home cook willing to chase down rare Tarbais beans for a proper cassoulet. More important, a new generation of chefs admired her book for its rare depth and scholarly approach. (In the late 1970s and early 1980s, the career of chef gained more respect. In 1977, the US Department of Labor reclassified the post as "professional" rather than "domestic.") Many of these young chefs had trained in classic French technique and found the subject relatable. Indeed, French food was so dominant in the United States when Paula's book appeared that it felt to many chefs like another "room in the attic," as Alice Waters put it—like one of those dreams in which you find a wing of your house that you never knew existed but that somehow feels familiar, as though it's been there all along.

When the book was released in 1983, it also legitimized a nascent restaurant trend in regional cooking. "The byword of the food scene these days is regional, and the trend is by no means confined to these shores," wrote Donna Warner in a 1984 review of the book in *Metropolitan Home*. "Just as black-eye peas and Smithfield ham have shaken up dandified American palates, so has the robust 'peasant cooking' of Southwest France redefined the haute sensibilities of French cuisine." One regional pioneer, groundbreaking Florida chef Norman Van Aken, dedicated two full pages to *South-West France* in his memoir, describing how he cooked through the book in the winter of 1985 with his young line cook, rising star Charlie Trotter. "Perhaps more than any other cookbook at that time it was Paula Wolfert's *The Cooking of South-West France* that caused us the most study," he wrote. "The book was dense with information and we pored over it like Talmudic scholars."

The book even presaged a 2000s movement in nose-to-tail and root-to-stalk cooking championed by London chef Fergus Henderson, who chose Paula's cassoulet as his favorite recipe of all time in 2006.

So how did Paula get from Morocco to Gascony, from the classic to the cutting edge? She didn't do it overnight. She could not have gained the necessary access to the best southwestern French kitchens as a mere Moroccan cooking expert from Brooklyn—even one with her considerable charms. She first needed to become a professional food writer, with a major platform from which she could promote those French chefs in the United States. She would also need to reacclimate to restaurant kitchens after twenty years away—and deal with her aversion to chef's knives.

From 1976 to 1978, Paula underwent a Paula-esque culinary boot camp—unplanned, immersive, and wildly adventuresome—to establish herself as an internationally regarded restaurant consultant, food reporter, and cooking teacher. It all started in the Philippines.

❖

When Paula and Bill moved back to New York from Tangier in the summer of 1976, Paula tried to calm her fears about her uncertain future by keeping a beatnik mind, open to opportunity. The food scene was improving, especially when New York's first "Greenmarket" opened that year—a place she could buy food directly from farmers, as in Tangier. She and Bill quickly reconnected with *New York* magazine critic Gael Greene, who made them a regular part of her reviewing nights out. Through Greene, they experienced the city's exciting, growing restaurant scene.

Although most observers did not recognize it at the time, the country stood at the cusp of a food revolution—of a nationwide explosion of interest in cooking, marked by a flood of new restaurants, cookbooks, cooking schools, even new American wines. In 1976, New York's restaurant scene had grown, but the city was very much in thrall to nouvelle cuisine, a French trend in elemental cooking and lightened sauces like beurre blanc that Paula found ridiculous. She viewed the Gallic import as novelty for novelty's sake, as a movement devoid of tradition or much flavor. But she knew that if she wanted to bring something fresh to the table, she would have to steer clear of nouvelle cuisine.

Paula soon met restaurant consultant George Lang, who quickly got Paula her first gigs. An early American restaurant consultant, Lang had been hired by the prestigious Manila Hotel in the Philippines to do something innovative: to serve authentic Filipino dishes in a five-star hotel setting. Lang prided himself on his eye for fresh talent. For the hotel, he had hired a dynamic team of young German chefs, but they needed help immersing themselves in authentic Filipino recipes. Lang had read *Couscous* and had seen that Paula had a unique ability to imbed herself in a foreign culture and understand its flavors, no matter how exotic.

With a team of German chefs in the Philippines

"George Lang said, 'Anybody who could write a book on Morocco like that could go to another country and learn the food really fast—I need you to go to the Philippines,'" Paula recalled. "So Bill takes care of my kids and I go off."

Working alongside Lang's chefs that summer, Paula proved that the methodology she had perfected with her party boxes and *Couscous* was portable—even into the kitchen of a five-star restaurant in Southeast Asia. She visited Manila home cooks and food markets and learned how to work with such ingredients as coconut milk and hearts of palm to elevate classics like *lumpia*—the Filipino spring roll—all with characteristic moxie.

About his time in Manila, in his memoirs Lang wrote, "One day, during one of the annual monsoon floods, I found her in the test kitchen standing up to her knees in water. She had just gone on cooking through the deluge."

Back in New York, Lang opened more doors for Paula. At his landmark restaurant Café des Artistes, he asked her to write down his chef's recipes for a potential cookbook. He also hired Paula to record the French fermentation methods at a Lower East Side bakery, where she kept baker's hours (midnight to dawn) in order to take meticulous notes. In the late 1970s, when Bloomingdale's invited French culinary legends such as Michel Guérard and Gaston Lenôtre to give classes, Lang recruited Paula to translate. In the process, she befriended many of the chefs.

⁂

Paula's teaching career also took off in late 1976, when she received a call from Anne Otterson, another *Couscous* fan. Otterson, who helped run the cooking school at The Perfect Pan, a cookware store in Mission Hills, California, invited Paula to teach her first of several Moroccan classes in January 1977. The Perfect Pan was one of dozens of new venues opening across the country that catered to the general growing interest in cooking. The classes got started, Paula remembered, "because women would get together to teach one another Julia Child recipes. All over America people were teaching Julia. But I guess that got old, so they moved on to other books."

Among the biggest stars on the circuit were Jacques Pépin and Marcella Hazan, both of whom made regular appearances at The Perfect Pan. Otterson was so impressed with Paula's debut Morocco classes that she raved about them to Pépin, who soon shared his list of cooking schools with Paula. With their help, Paula booked her first national teaching tour.

"That's what friends are for," Pépin said of his generosity. "I knew Anne well. I did the same for Marcella. I always admired Paula."

Starting in 1977 and continuing for the next decade, Paula taught classes in twenty to forty cities a year—often in four or five annual tours of roughly a half dozen cities each.

It's easy to understand why she generated such demand. Her classes typically followed the same format: over three hours, she pulled off what she and Jaidi (and a few assistants) did in five—prepared an entire Moroccan meal, including salads, a tagine, and a couscous or *bastilla*—all the while sharing mesmerizing stories of Moroccan adventures, cooking pointers, and bawdy jokes. Her appearances quickly became news around the country, in cities big and small. From New York to Milwaukee and Phoenix, food editors struggled to find the right words to describe these electric performances. Part preacher, part scholar, part magician, part circus clown, she defied categorization.

"When Paula Wolfert blew into town last week, the spices almost flew off the shelves, the green peppers nearly burst under the broiler, the fresh coriander shook like it had the chills, and the chickens almost got out of the pot and cackled," panted Michigan's *Oakland Press*. In *The Atlantic*, food writer Corby Kummer called her a

Both national magazines, such as *Bon Appétit*, left, and local newspapers, such as Michigan's *Oakland Press*, right, struggled to capture the energy and excitement of Paula's cooking classes.

"virtuoso teacher" whose "gestures and expressions are too good to miss." He added, "The cook has to be a cross between a stand-up comic and a professor. Wolfert, a self-described show-off as well as a food scholar . . . can galvanize an audience."

Not every class on these tours went flawlessly; Paula had a few memorable misadventures. Self-conscious all of her life about her stubbornly short, brittle fingernails, in Houston she took the suggestion of her host and had false nails applied before her class. Paula regretted that decision one city later, in Arizona, when the nails popped off in the middle of a couscous steaming demonstration.

But by 1977, she had a much bigger problem. Moroccan food wasn't like Italian, where the appetite for the cuisine in America appeared to be as bottomless as the repertoire itself. "Marcella could go two or three times a year to each place," Paula said about her teaching colleague, Italian food expert Marcella Hazan. "With Moroccan, once you learned your couscous, your tagine, people didn't want much more." To maintain her pace, Paula would need fresh material.

❧

Her teaching tours and restaurant consulting gave her the confidence to begin making inroads as a food journalist into the intimidating world of New York food media. Although still gossipy, it had grown considerably and now included bright new writers she had never heard of, such as *Vogue* contributor Barbara Kafka, *New York Daily News* food editor Arthur Schwartz, and *Town & Country* food editor and columnist James Villas. They worked in the wake of Gael Greene, who had transformed food writing with her brash, brassy *New York* magazine restaurant reviews—herself inspired by late-1960s New Journalists like Tom Wolfe and Gay Talese. ("In a town where snob, snoot and snub flower in perpetual renaissance, Lafayette is the 'most,'" Greene wrote in a 1970 review titled "Lafayette, We Are Leaving," excoriating a pretentious French restaurant in her typical irreverence.) "We were always causing trouble," Villas recalled.

Their outrageousness belied their accomplishments, however. Villas had a PhD in romance languages and comparative literature. Kafka had previously enrolled in a doctoral program to become a poet. Paula was well aware she had no degrees. She would have to bring her A game.

"In the late seventies, the food writers were the kings and queens," Paula said. "The chefs have since pushed us aside—and rightly so— we didn't do anything compared to what chefs do. But it was a time, like in the poetry world, where you had to fight for position, especially in New York, since the stakes were so small."

Couscous and *Mediterranean Cooking* both gave her entrée. Starting with a genteel, even timid essay on basil for a 1977 issue of *New Times*, by the end of that year Paula had written features for *New York* magazine and *Bon Appétit*. Her first big splash appeared in *New York* in December 1977, when she and Bill published an exposé called "A Delicious Little Recipe Scandal," in which they revealed that cookbook author Lady Pamela Harlech had plagiarized over 160 recipes from *Gourmet*.

Paula's writing—and endearing backstory—won her notice. Schwartz told me, "Her book had a great story attached to it: This Jewish girl from Brooklyn runs away to Tangier as a teenager with this asshole who then leaves her with two children and she's got to support herself? Who hobnobs with such great people in Morocco? She got great press."

Her palate also won her admirers. "I made pasta for her once using Trapani salt from Sicily," Schwartz recalled. "She asked, 'What kind of salt do you use?' I thought, 'My God, how can she detect the salt just from the pasta water?'"

"I don't think I have met anyone with Paula's palate, before or since," agreed Ruth Reichl, who befriended Paula in the mid-1980s when Reichl was a food writer for the *Los Angeles Times*. "She could just identify anything. It blew me away." For her palate—and her gift of gab—James Villas gave her the nickname La Bouche. Paula soon joined a a tight circle—some on the outside called it a clique—with Schwartz, Villas, Kafka, and other writers. Their home base was a chic Upper West Side restaurant called Le Plaisir. Like all of her favorite spots, Paula found adventure there.

And yet Paula remained so uncomfortable with competition that she attributed her success to superstition. One night in late 1977, George Lang invited her to a dinner to announce his new restaurant, Hungaria. At dessert, he served a strudel holding a lucky Hungarian gold coin, announcing that whoever found the coin would be guest of honor on Hungaria's opening night. Paula pulled out the coin. For for the next half-decade, she credited it with all of her good luck.

❖

Paula's new friend Barbara Kafka inadvertently helped her overcome her fear of knives and got her fresh material for her cooking classes when she invited her to become a contributor to *Cooking*. Later renamed *The Pleasures of Cooking*, the new monthly magazine was launched by the Cuisinart company and edited by Kafka. Paula joined the ranks of contributors like Pépin and Madhur Jaffrey. As Paula recalled, they each got early models of the Cuisinart to develop recipes.

One might assume that a traditionalist like Paula would eschew such a modern convenience. But the Cuisinart changed everything. When it was introduced in 1973 as the home version of a new French restaurant appliance called the Robot Coupe, it could have been tailored for Paula's vision problems. Its safety guards protected someone who lacked depth perception and was prone to cut him- or herself.

Outfitted with a machine with reliably sharp blades and a dough attachment, Paula finally felt fully equipped to tackle restaurant-grade recipes. With assignments from *Cooking*, she mastered French classics she had avoided because they involved too much handwork, like brioche, puff pastry, and phyllo dough. Through months of hard work, she developed unparalleled recipes for all of them tailored for the Cuisinart. For years to come, Cuisinart founder Carl Sontheimer sent new models of his machine to Paula from time to time.

Another great innovation, the word processor, helped Paula with a different challenge caused by her vision problems: organizing her thoughts on paper. Paula spent $4,000 (about $14,500 in today's dollars) to purchase a Lexoriter from Otterson's husband, who helmed the Lexor Corporation, an early computer company. Paula loved how it let her cut and paste paragraphs *and* put her on the on the technological cutting edge. "The only other people I heard of who had the Lexoriter were Julia Child and George Lucas. I was glad to be with them," she said.

In 1978, she convinced a publisher to give her a contract for a cookbook called *Wrapped in Pastry* and started teaching brioche and strudel classes around the country. But still she had a problem.

"I wasn't all that excited about that book because there were no stories behind the recipes," she said. "*Wrapped in Pastry* was not a world, just a bunch of procedures. Once I got the first six or seven recipes down, I didn't give a shit."

❧

But her luck, pluck, Le Plaisir contacts, and lousy book idea all got Paula back to France, where she finally discovered the Southwest.

First, her pastry interests (and charms) won her a free trip to Paris. After she translated for pastry genius Gaston Lenôtre during his visit to Bloomingdale's, he invited her to study puff pastry and brioche at his acclaimed cooking school outside the city.

In those days, airlines and hotels were generous with free tickets and housing for food writers with assignments. For example, TWA was eager to promote its new direct 747 flights from New York to Paris. She secured her TWA ticket (and a free room at the Paris Hilton) when she successfully pitched a story on Lenôtre's school to Le Plaisir regulars Michael and Ariane Batterberry. That year, in 1978, the couple founded *The International Review of Food and Wine*, now known simply as *Food & Wine*. They were eager to hire smart new voices. "While you're in France," she remembered Michael Batterberry asking her, "why don't you go down to Southwest France to do a story on cassoulet?"

Between teaching appearances, Paula began to research the pork, poultry, and bean stew. In the pages of *The Food of France* by Waverly Root, among other sources, she learned about the longstanding rivalries over who made the best version among southwestern French villages with fairytale names like Castelnaudary, Carcassonne, and Toulouse. Back at Le Plaisir, she bumped into another regular named Roger Yaseen, head of the Chaîne des Rôtisseurs, a prestigious international dining society, who often traveled to dine in France. She shared the news of her cassoulet assignment and asked if he knew anything about the dish. As luck would have it, that evening he was dining with Ariane Daguin, the teenage daughter of André Daguin, a star chef of Southwest France.

"That night was my first introduction to the foodie world of New York City," Ariane Daguin told me. "Paula mentioned she was working on an article about cassoulet. She was talking about the cassoulets of Castelnaudary, and I said, 'No no, there's much more to it than that. Let me send you to my family in Gascony.'"

"I hadn't even been planning to go to Gascony before they suggested it, because Waverly Root never mentioned it as a place for cassoulet," Paula said. "So I wrote to André Daguin. And he said, 'I don't make one cassoulet. I make three.'"

❖

In 1978, André Daguin was forty-three, three years older than Paula, and brimming with ambition. He had two Michelin stars for Hôtel de France, his restaurant and inn located in the Gascon town of Auch. He had inherited the hotel from his father, and his grandfather had cooked there in the 1880s.

Like many of his contemporaries, Daguin modernized French classics according to the precepts of nouvelle cuisine. But crucially, his innovations were grounded in place and history. He updated his region's iconic dishes, such as cassoulet, limiting himself to local ingredients: duck, Armagnac, prunes. He was the first chef to serve duck breasts like steak, seared medium-rare, and he invented prune and Armagnac ice cream, a whimsical play on a traditional Gascon after-dinner snack (recipe, page 149). Sharing Paula's love of technology smartly applied, he was also the first chef to use liquid nitrogen to

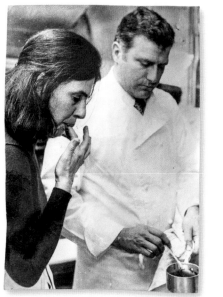

freeze ice cream, preparing his signature dessert in dramatic fashion in the restaurant dining room.

And he had a chip on his shoulder. In 1956 at his Paris cooking school, Daguin's teacher told him goose fat was worthless. "He was from the north and didn't know any better," Daguin later told Paula. "So when I began to cook, all of my ideas came in reaction against this stupid idea of ignoring the great food of my region."

He headed up a circle of like-minded, forward-thinking south-western French chefs, including the young Jean-Louis Palladin, who called themselves *la ronde des mousquetaires*, after Alexandre Dumas's *The Three Musketeers*, which is set in Gascony. He saw Paula as someone who could bring international attention to their efforts, and he invited her and Bill to stay a few nights at his hotel.

✤

That spring, Paula and Bill flew to Paris on a TWA 747 armed with two assignments from *Food & Wine* (cassoulet and Lenôtre) and two from *Cooking* (one on the chef musketeers, one on duck confit). They planned to share the cassoulet byline to justify Bill's free plane ticket and to help Paula get all the stories written on time. In Paris they connected with a French restaurant publicist named Yanou Collard, who led them to more chefs of the Southwest. Then Paula enrolled at Lenôtre's cooking school. Because she couldn't drive, every day at dawn she hitched a ride on the school's delivery truck from the Paris Hilton to the school in Versailles.

COUNTER-CLOCKWISE FROM UPPER RIGHT: Paula at Gaston Lenôtre's cooking school; tasting a sauce and discussing technique with André Daguin at his Auch hotel; and at a New York restaurant in the 1980s with Jean-Louis Palladin, seated, wearing glasses.

For their second week, Bill rented a car and they drove to the Southwest to investigate cassoulet. They spent their first several nights at Daguin's restaurant in Auch, where she and Daguin cooked together.

At first Paula felt intimidated by Daguin. But they quickly developed a profound mutual respect. Daguin invited a local reporter to observe their first day in the kitchen; in an article in the local paper, the reporter described "this astonishing American" with her deep knowledge of French cooking, who peppered the chef with questions, her notebook "blackened with recipes."

From Auch, Paula and Bill drove on to meet a half dozen more chefs in the region, including Daguin's closest compatriots, the other "musketeers," such as Lucien Vanel in the nearby city of Toulouse and Jean-Louis Palladin in the quirkily named village of Condom. Paula loved how Palladin's restaurant was built inside the vaulted ceiling of a converted monastery and was struck by his generosity as well as creativity: every weekday the young chef set a table for village pensioners, whom he served a discounted lunch. Paula's thank-you gift to each of the chefs was a metal tin of maple syrup, a gesture they seemed to appreciate.

She felt electric at all the innovations they shared with her, from Palladin's lightened sauces to Vanel's salmon rillettes. She reveled in her meetings with a handful of generous home cooks, like Pierrette Lejanou, a potato broker's wife and friend of Vanel's, whose cassoulet recipe Paula found to be one of the best in Toulouse (recipe, page 136).

Finally, Bill and Paula returned to Auch for a final lunch at Daguin's restaurant. Under the astonished stares of their fellow diners, Daguin served them all three of his cassoulets: a classic with Tarbais beans, another with lentils, the third with fresh fava beans, "because that's what the original cassoulet would have been made with before Columbus brought back Tarbais beans from America— favas are indigenous to Europe," Paula explained.

In the book, she described it as "a concoction of preserved duck and fresh fava beans, crisp on the outside, soft and buttery-tender within. The contrast of flavors and textures, the beans so full of spring and the Mediterranean, beans that absorbed the taste of the other ingredients and yet, almost paradoxically, maintained a fresh taste of their own—I could not quite believe what I was eating. It seemed a miracle."

Paula knew what her next book would be.

"I could have kicked myself," she said. "I had lived in France for eight years, and I had never been to Gascony, Toulouse, Béarn. No one had! I made the decision right then and there, this is what I'm going to do. *This* is an adventure!"

In *Food & Wine*, the Batterberrys gave the cassoulet story five pages.

"It was huge. It established me immediately as having the Southwest," Paula said. "Everyone else had butter, and I had goose fat!"

More commissions quickly followed—from *Bon Appétit*, *Travel + Leisure*, and *Cuisine*. Partly thanks to all the ink, Paula's *Couscous* editor Fran McCullough, who had moved to Dial Press, was able to snatch up Paula's proposal for *The Cooking of South-West France* for twenty-five thousand dollars. Paula began making regular trips to France to report on the region.

Through 1979, Paula became something of a culinary rock star. She began spending almost all of her time on the road, either touring southwestern France for the book or the United States for her ever-more-popular cooking classes on Morocco and Southwest France. During stints at home in New York, she became a centerpiece at Le Plaisir, enthralling food-writer friends with her wild tales.

All of the attention became a drug. Food became a twenty-four-hour, seven-day-a-week obsession. Whenever Bill suggested they do something that didn't involve food, like see a movie or a play, she increasingly waved him off.

She and Bill started to get on each other's nerves. Landing at the airport from her tours, she stopped going home to Bill (her children were in boarding school) and instead headed straight to Le Plaisir to share her latest discoveries with her adoring gang. When Bill told her he had started looking for a new apartment, he remembered, "she just didn't seem to hear me."

"Pretty soon," Paula said, "Bill walked out on me."

When Paula first told me this, she immediately changed topics, which suggested the pain of the breakup. When we revisited it, she acknowledged that she wasn't just caught off guard when Bill left, but devastated that a second (Harvard) man had given up on her. Did this make her unlovable? At least Bill didn't leave her for someone else, as her husband Michael had in 1969. She and Bill also were not married, nor was he her sole means of support, so the rest of her life did not fall apart as a result of his departure. In fact, many of her new food friends were not sad to see him go; Bill had a prickly side that had put many of them off.

She rented out her second bedroom to a food magazine editor. She and Bill remained friendly, and he continued to advise her on her articles and book. But she became determined to win him back.

In Bill's absence, she found a new companion in fellow food writer James Villas, with whom she fell "madly in love," though he was Protestant, a southerner, and gay. If only Paula had been born a man.

"We were one chromosome away from happiness," they both loved to joke.

Throughout 1979 and 1980, she also distracted herself with even more work: in addition to teaching tours in the US and regular return trips to Southwest France, she took on more articles, consulting jobs, and even cooked a few pop-up Moroccan dinners at the pioneering Brooklyn restaurant Huberts.

Amid this turmoil, Southwest France became home. Her descriptions of her return visits reminded me of how she now talks about the meditation she practices for her dementia: each new adventure recentered her mind. The Daguins put her up in a spare bedroom. Paula's eyesight prevented her from driving, so when she couldn't reach a chef by train or bus, Daguin would either drive her the whole distance or to a midpoint, where another chef would pick her up and ferry her the rest of the way.

Many of these chefs had never met an American before, let alone a trained female cook. To establish her bona fides, Paula and Daguin hatched a plan for Paula to cook a Moroccan feast for fifty of the region's best chefs and members of the press at Daguin's Hôtel de France. In November 1980, inside forty-eight hours, with a crew of young chefs to help her, she prepared *bastilla*, tagine with chicken and olives, lamb *mechoui*, Berber vegetable couscous, almond pastry ring, oranges with cinnamon, and Moroccan mint tea.

"It worked," André Daguin told me. "They saw she knew how to do everything in the kitchen."

The only people who didn't share recipes with her were other women. Remarkably, the Southwest was the only region where Paula continually struck out in her efforts to bond with women home cooks. She encountered a proud tradition among them of closely guarding recipes, not just from American food journalists but also from one another. In a headnote to cabbage soup with *miques* (bread dumplings), Paula described meeting a woman in the Périgord region so cagey about her recipes that, despite having invited Paula to her house to teach her how to make *miques*, the woman (whom Paula called Madame X) deliberately sabotaged the recipe to hide her tricks. After her *miques* failed to rise, her own family complained at their size and flavor, but "she pretended not to hear one word and gobbled up her portion," Paula wrote. "Still, the experience was fascinating," Paula added charitably, "an insight into the cult of 'secrets' and into the life-style of a peasant family." She went on to describe how she joined the family in grilling fresh chestnuts in the kitchen fireplace while they waited in vain for the *miques* to rise.

But elsewhere in the book, her frustration screamed off the page. "The tendency towards secretiveness is still prevalent . . . among some of the older, bony-faced 'mothers' in the tight black hats who, staring about a marketplace, can tell the difference in taste between two chickens squawking at their feet."

She told me, "I couldn't get the recipes from the women, so I went to their sons."

❖

The culinary innovations of the sons—the chefs of the Southwest such as André Daguin and Jean-Louis Palladin—proved so attractive in her classes that, by the end of 1980, she contemplated shifting the focus of her book to highlight *only* these chef techniques. Appealing to the fashion of the times, she considered renaming the book *Beyond Nouvelle Cuisine*. She tested the waters for her new idea that year and the next by writing several articles and teaching a series of cooking classes that showcased the work of these modernizers, their techniques such as *stratification* (detailed on page 146), and unusual combinations such as tomatoes with mustard and salmon. Needless to say, it might have turned out a very different book.

Although they were still separated, when Bill heard about Paula's latest plan, he wrote her an impassioned letter imploring her to drop it. He saw she had chosen the topic to chase a trend, not to please herself. He reminded her of a broader vision for her future. "Write a book you believe in," he wrote. "A book you want to write. A classical kind of book like *Couscous* or what Diana Kennedy writes—a book about a region—its cuisine, its lore, with a strong sense of place and personality based on extensive research in the field and good solid recipe writing and testing at home. The books that last are all like that—*Couscous, Cuisines of Mexico*, Hazan's stuff, Eliz. David. The other kinds of books are phony and dishonest."

❖

Paula recommitted to her original idea, to immerse herself in both the modern and the ancient cooking of the region. By early 1981 she had more than enough to fill that book. But she kept going back to the Southwest. In her travels she found some material so cutting edge, she wouldn't publish it until 2005, in her second edition. She pushed south to Basque country, at a festival in the village of Espelette, where she became among the first American food writers to taste *piment d'Espelette*, an experience that sparked a lifelong love of previously overlooked red peppers. At Restaurant Clavel in Bordeaux, chef

Francis Garcia introduced Paula to *sous vide*. The technique of cooking foods in vacuum-sealed pouches at highly regulated temperatures was widely used in France for industrial food production, but had only begun to make inroads into high-end restaurants; her description of it in the book's appendix is one of the first discussions of the method in English. In the tiny town of Poudenas, she became fast friends with a rare professional female chef, Marie-Claude Garcia (no relation to Francis), the first person Paula ever saw put salt on a chocolate cake. Garcia impressed Paula with her resourceful economy: she had started in the food business while a young woman, by selling rillettes, crocks of slow-cooked duck she made with meat she scraped off carcasses purchased from duck farmers at a discount at the village market. After Paula interviewed her, because the small town of Poudenas had no hotel, Garcia arranged for Paula to spend the night at a nearby château. By coincidence, the night of Paula's visit, the owner, a count, hosted a lavish dinner in celebration of a predawn stag hunt set to take place the next day. In one of the best stories in the book, Paula described the evening's Armagnac- and foie gras–fueled feast.

In October 1981, with the help of the Bordeaux chamber of commerce and Otterson of The Perfect Pan, Paula led a sold-out culinary tour of Southwest France for a small group of American women home cooks. Her itinerary showed her command of the region—of its wines as well as foods, at every level of dining, from Michelin-starred restaurants to forest huts. The trip entailed lunch at Jean-Louis Palladin's restaurant La Table des Cordeliers followed by dinner at Michel Guérard's spa, then predawn mushroom foraging led by a French pharmacist, capped with a breakfast of mushroom omelets. The rest of the week was filled in with cooking workshops and tours of the vineyards of Saint-Émilion and Sauternes.

But just as Paula was establishing herself as the go-to expert for Southwest France, to both her pleasure and her chagrin, American interest in Moroccan food surged, spurred by her own touring and by the Morocco-influenced collections of fashion designer Yves Saint Laurent (who lived in Marrakech and had purchased the Jardin Majorelle in 1980 to save it from demolition). The surge elevated her from insider's food hero to a minor national food star. It even brought her back into favor with her ex-mentor, James Beard, who wrote about renewing their friendship over couscous in a magazine story in 1979. But by 1981, she felt she had to campaign against her identity as *just* a Morocco expert.

"I've done my Morocco," she told the *Chicago Tribune* in August of that year, in a story titled "Tired of Couscous, Wolfert Crusades for Lighter French Fare." She may have experienced genuine *bastilla* burnout; she told the reporter, "I'm so sick of those smells I can't even eat the stuff."

She may have also experienced Morocco fatigue because that spring she had been forced to relive painful Tangier memories. *Rowing Toward Eden*, a mostly autobiographical book by former Tangier friend Ted Morgan, had appeared and included a chapter about the breakup of the marriage of his friends. He used pseudonyms but he described her and Michael circa 1969 from what Paula took to be Michael's point of view, mocking her hypochondria and superstitions, playing up her Paris indiscretion, and in general depicting her in such a callow, unflattering light that it was impossible to see what Michael had ever loved about her. "It was all about how I ruined Michael's life because I was too bourgeois and kept him from being the free spirit that he really was," she remembered with heavy sarcasm.

Reunited with James Beard in 1979, wearing the djellaba from the back cover of *Couscous*.

"That book really hurt her," Bill recalled.

Paula was clearly angry at the memory, but when I said it must have been an ordeal to read, she shrugged. "Some of our friends took Michael's side. I just kept going."

❖

Amidst all her travels, at home Paula plunged into testing the recipes for *South-West France*. Although the food revolution in America was well under way, she faced challenges similar to those posed by *Couscous*. She was more understanding now, however. This time she knew intimately from her cooking classes just how much of a struggle it would be for most Americans to re-create southwestern French flavors at home. She wrote all of the duck recipes for American Pekin ducks, though they were neither as flavorful nor as fatty as the classic Moulard of Southwest France. She became so obsessed with helping cooks use up all of the duck parts that she included a recipe for stuffed duck neck. Because her kitchen was so tiny, she set up a card table in her living room and leaned in close with her nearsighted right eye to do all of the stitching. "Make a patchwork of duck skins and sew them together to make one large piece," she wrote in her recipe for stuffed duck neck with *sauce Périgueux*.

To confirm that her facsimiles tasted genuine, she roped in chef André Daguin's daughter Ariane as a tester, for some of the time while she was a student at Barnard. In her exactitude, Paula taught her a new way to cook and eat. To judge how much salt a cook should sprinkle onto duck breasts before searing them, Paula asked Ariane to season some herself and slid a piece of paper between Ariane's fingers and the meat to measure how much fell. "It was sometimes grueling," Ariane recalled. "Those dinners obliged me to go deep down, to learn how to analyze a dish technically. When she asked how it tasted, it wasn't enough for me to say 'good.' I had to learn to decide—not enough of this, too much of that, what was missing."

When it came time to write the book, Paula had little confidence without Bill. But McCullough found a desk for her at Dial, and Paula wrote down the hall, bringing McCullough daily drafts. This time, they sifted some of her deep research into a long and charming appendix packed with tips, from how to cook *sous vide* to how to bring up the flavor in then-tasteless American tomatoes (sprinkle them not just with salt but also with sugar and vinegar).

But as the book took shape, Paula had fresh reason to panic. In her cooking classes, she saw Americans were falling under the sway of a new low-fat health craze, a concern for her upcoming ode to duck confit, foie gras, and goose fat.

"I didn't give up on fat, but I was aware of a problem," she said. She found a USDA pamphlet that she cited in the book's introduction, showing the favorable percentages of cholesterol in duck fat (9 percent) and lard (10 percent) compared to butter (22 percent). She also eloquently defended animal fat as a flavor, in a passage that feels prescient today: "I often use these animal fats for taste, the way I use a cinnamon stick in a red-wine compote of fruits."

❖

In March 1981, after a year in which she hadn't spoken to Bill, she heard that his mother had died. To wish him better luck in the coming days, she mailed him the Hungarian gold coin.

"He was so moved by that," she remembered. "We started slowly to get back together."

Over the coming months, the two rekindled their romance with help from story assignments from *Cuisine* magazine, then edited by Pat Brown, who had become Paula's roommate after Bill moved out. For *Cuisine*, Bill and Paula researched and cowrote several stories about far-flung romantic locales, from Alsace to Yugoslavia to Greece.

In August 1982, Bill won an Edgar Allan Poe Award for his mystery novel *Peregrine*. He told Liz Smith of the *New York Post* that it was all because of the Hungarian gold coin.

The following summer, in August 1983, Paula and Bill wed in a small ceremony on a bluff overlooking the ocean in Martha's Vineyard, just the two of them, with a local justice of the peace as their officiant. Afterward, they celebrated with some anise-scented butter cookies

Paula baked, a recipe she learned on a trip she and Bill had taken to the Greek island of Paxos (recipe, page 175).

Bill and Paula on their wedding day; at right, the Hungarian gold coin.

❧

The reception Paula received for *South-West France* could not have contrasted more with that of her first two books. At her book party that fall, two hundred people attended, among them André Daguin, Julia Child, chef Pierre Franey, and Paula's Le Plaisir gang. Paula stood at the center of the New York food world. A party guest quoted in the *New York Times* observed, "If a bomb went off here, America wouldn't eat for a month."

André Daguin told the reporters that Paula "has got to the roots of our kitchens better than most Frenchmen." Critical acclaim for the book was universal. In *Vogue*, Kakfa called it the "in" book of the year.

Paula was thrilled by all of the attention, by the recognition all her hard work received. But by the time the book appeared that winter, she had already moved on. The trips she and Bill had taken for *Cuisine* that summer to Corfu and other parts of Greece had already planted the seeds for her next book.

Her Gascon compatriots were sad to see her go. "When she wrote books about the other regions of the Mediterranean, it was a little bit of a letdown, you know?" Ariane said. "Because she was our ambassador. But eh, were we supposed to stop history? To have her known for Southwest France and nothing else would have been totally unreasonable."

Lunch in Southwest France

❖ ✳ ❖

This suggested menu spans the wide range of recipes in Paula's third book, *The Cooking of South-West France*, from humble staples (duck confit) to avant-garde chef innovations (scallops with a tangerine sauce), from the complex (cassoulet) to the simple (a puree of celery root and apple). All capture an approach to cooking that Paula so admired about the region: "a love of logic in recipes in which a dish is built, step by step, inexorably toward a finish that is the inevitable best result of all the ingredients employed."

FIRST COURSE

Mixed Greens Salad with Duck Fat–Garlic Croutons

MAIN COURSE

Cassoulet in the Style of Toulouse

or

Easy Oven Duck Confit

with

Celery Root and Apple Puree

or

Scallops in Tangerine Sauce

DESSERT

Prunes in Armagnac

and/or

Prune and Armagnac Ice Cream

Mixed Greens Salad with Duck Fat–Garlic Croutons

This deceptively spare salad is packed with subtle, brilliant touches. You can make it with prepackaged mixed greens, but you will be miss the fun—and flavor—of assembling your own blend. "Try to preserve a balance of flavors when choosing greens for this salad," Paula wrote.

Like the best of Paula's dishes, you can assemble the components an hour or two ahead and throw the salad together at the last minute. The recipe can also easily be doubled or tripled for a crowd. For a vegetarian version, sauté the croutons in olive oil.

---

1 (5-inch | 12.5-cm) section baguette, cut lengthwise into quarters and left out overnight to dry

2 garlic cloves, halved

2 tablespoons walnut oil

2 tablespoons extra-virgin olive oil

1 tablespoon sherry vinegar or verjus

Flaky sea salt and freshly ground black pepper

2 tablespoons rendered duck or other poultry fat or olive oil

3 cups (about 135 g) lightly packed torn mixed young greens, such as chicory, escarole, sorrel, arugula, and radicchio

1 to 2 tablespoons snipped mixed fresh herbs, such as flat-leaf parsley, chives, chervil, and thyme

Rub the crusts of the baguette with the cut sides of the garlic cloves until the crusts are shiny. Reserve the garlic cloves.

In a small bowl, whisk together the walnut and olive oils. Drizzle 1 tablespoon of the oil mixture evenly over the cut sides of the baguette lengths. Let stand for at least 30 minutes or up to 1 hour.

Peel and mince the garlic by hand and set aside (you should have about 1½ teaspoons). In a large salad bowl, whisk together the remaining oil mixture and the vinegar to make a dressing. Season with salt and pepper and set aside.

Tear or slice the baguette lengths into 1-inch (2.5-cm) croutons. You should have about 1¼ cups (300 ml). In a small frying pan, heat the duck fat over medium-high heat. Add the croutons and sauté, turning them a few times, until golden, about 4 minutes.

In a large bowl, combine the greens, hot croutons, and garlic. Drizzle with the dressing, toss to coat evenly, and transfer to salad plates. Sprinkle with the herbs and serve.

Serves 4

If you forgot to leave the baguette out to dry overnight, put it into a 350°F (180°C) oven for about 10 minutes, until dry.

Cassoulet in the Style of Toulouse

No one has recorded a better version of this ultimate southwestern French dish, nor is it likely anyone ever will. Paula learned it in the dining room of Pierrette Lejanou, a local Toulouse woman known to make the best. This is a three-day project, made more pleasurable if you can collaborate with a friend. The biggest challenges lie in the shopping: in addition to Tarbais beans and duck confit, the dish contains six kinds of pork. It's an ideal excuse to visit that new nose-to-tail butcher shop that just opened. The staff will be excited to hear you are tackling this and should have most items.

The cooking is relatively straightforward. On day one, you lightly cure the pork to enrich its taste. On day two, you make a dense ragout of onions, carrots, beans, and five of the six kinds of pork. The final day, you bake the ragout with the duck confit in a large pot (preferably a traditional clay *cassole*, see Notes), with the sausages nestled on top. I guarantee you will never forget the results.

---

2 pounds (900 g) dried Tarbais, cannellini, or other runner-type beans

1½ pounds (675 g) fresh ham hock with skin

1 pound (450 g) boneless pork shoulder, trimmed of excess fat and cut into 1-inch (2.5-cm) chunks

12 ounces (350 g) fresh pork skin with ¼-inch (6-mm) layer of hard fat attached

Flaky sea salt and freshly ground black pepper

⅓ cup (75 g) rendered duck fat

2 yellow onions (about 1 pound | 450 g total), chopped

3 small carrots (about 12 ounces | 350 g total), cut into rounds ¼ inch (6 mm) thick

8-ounce (225-g) piece ventrèche (French-style pancetta) or pancetta

1 head garlic, loose skins removed, plus 4 small garlic cloves, peeled

1 large Roma tomato, peeled, seeded, and chopped, or 1 tablespoon tomato paste or Tomato Magic (page 309)

Herb bouquet of 4 fresh flat-leaf parsley sprigs, 3 small celery ribs, 2 fresh thyme sprigs, and 1 Turkish bay leaf, tied together with kitchen string

2 quarts (2 l) lightly salted chicken stock

6 confit duck legs, homemade (page 143) or store-bought

4 ounces (115 g) pork fatback

1 pound (450 g) Toulouse or other mild fresh garlicky pork sausages (such as sweet Italian sausage)

2 tablespoons fresh bread crumbs

2 tablespoons walnut oil (optional)

Serves 10 to 12

The cassoulet takes 3 days to cook. Allow at least 1 additional day (if not 1 week) to shop for the ingredients.

DAY ONE

Rinse the beans and pick them over to remove any grit. In a deep bowl or pot, combine the beans with water to cover by at least 2 inches (5 cm). Let soak in the refrigerator overnight.

recipe continues →

In a shallow dish, sprinkle the ham hock, pork shoulder, and pork skin with ¾ teaspoon salt and 10 grinds of pepper. Cover and refrigerate overnight.

DAY TWO

In a saucepan, combine the pork skin with water to cover by 1 inch (2.5 cm) and bring to a simmer over medium heat. Cook until plump and supple, about 15 minutes. Drain and let cool. Roll up the pork skin, skin side out, and tie securely with kitchen string.

Meanwhile, pat the ham hock and pork shoulder cubes dry with paper towels. In an 8- or 9-quart (8- or 9-l) oven-proof stainless steel or enameled cast-iron casserole, heat the duck fat over medium-high heat. Add the pork shoulder and cook, turning occasionally, until lightly brown on all sides, about 7 minutes. Add the onions and carrots and sauté, stirring, until the onions are soft and golden, about 5 minutes.

Nestle the ham hock and ventrèche in the casserole and cook, turning occasionally, until browned a little around the edges, about 5 minutes. Add the garlic head and tomato and cook, stirring, for 1 minute. Add the pork skin and herb bouquet, pour in the stock, and bring to a boil, skimming off any scum that rises to the surface. Turn the heat down to low, cover, and simmer gently for 1½ hours.

Meanwhile, once the pork ragout has completed its first hour of cooking, start the beans. Drain them, then put into a large saucepan. Add fresh tepid water to cover by 1 to 2 inches (2.5 to 5 cm), place on the stove top, and slowly bring to a boil, skimming off any scum that rises to the surface. Adjust the heat to maintain a simmer for 3 minutes. Drain the beans immediately and add them to the simmering pork.

Re-cover and continue simmering the pork and bean mixture until the beans are tender, at least 30 minutes or up to 2 hours, depending on the age and type of bean. (The beans should be fully cooked. They will not further soften when baked on day three.) Remove from the heat, let cool, cover, and refrigerate overnight.

DAY THREE

Preheat the oven to 325°F (160°C). Remove the pork and bean ragout from the refrigerator and skim off any fat that has solidified on the surface, reserving 2 tablespoons. Set the ragout over low heat and rewarm to room temperature.

recipe continues →

Meanwhile, warm the duck confit to soften the fat: If using store-bought duck legs sealed in plastic pouches, submerge the pouches in a large bowl of hot water for 10 minutes or so. If using homemade confit, set the legs on a foil-lined sheet pan and rewarm in the oven. Pull the duck meat off the bones in large chunks. Discard the skin, bones, and any large, dark veins. Save any fat for another use (such as more confit). Set the meat aside.

When the ragout has come to room temperature, pick out the garlic head, separate the cloves, and squeeze each clove to extract the pulp from its skin; return the pulp to the ragout. Remove and discard the herb bouquet. Pick out the ham hock and ventrèche, discarding bones, large fatty parts, and skin. Cut the remaining meat into 1-inch (2.5 cm) cubes and set aside. Pick out and untie the pork skin and cut into 2-inch (5-cm) pieces. Place the skin pieces, fat side down to prevent sticking, in the bottom of a 5½- to 6-quart (5½- to 6-l) casserole, preferably earthenware and at least 4 inches (10 cm) deep.

In a food processor, combine the fatback and the 4 garlic cloves and process until pureed. Scrape the puree into the ragout and stir until blended. Bring the ragout to a simmer over low heat and cook for 30 minutes. Remove from the heat. Fold in the cubed pork shoulder and ventrèche.

Using a large slotted spoon or skimmer, add half of the ragout to the prepared casserole in an even layer, letting any excess liquid fall back into the pot. Scatter the duck confit on top of the ragout. Using the same spoon or skimmer, cover the confit layer with the remaining ragout. Taste the ragout cooking liquid and adjust the seasoning if necessary (there will probably be no need for salt). Ladle just enough of the ragout liquid over the ragout to cover it. Be sure to leave at least 1 inch (2.5 cm) of "growing space" between the ragout and the casserole rim. Dollop the surface with the 2 tablespoons fat reserved from the chilled ragout.

Transfer the casserole to the oven and bake for 1½ hours.

Meanwhile, prick the sausages in several places. In a large frying pan over medium-high heat, cook the sausages, turning them a few times as needed, until browned all over, about 10 minutes. Transfer to a plate. Cut larger sausages into 3- to 4-inch (7.5- to 10-cm) pieces.

recipe continues →

Remove the casserole from the oven and lower the oven temperature to 275°F (135°C). Gently break up the skin that has formed on the surface of the beans, being careful not to disturb the layers of confit and pork skin beneath. Spacing them evenly, nestle the sausages partway down among the beans. Dust the surface of the cassoulet with the bread crumbs.

Return the cassoulet to the oven and bake for 1 hour longer. If you like a dark brown crust, raise the heat to 400°F (200°C) after the first 30 minutes. After 1 hour, if the surface is still not browned to your liking, turn on the broiler (make sure the vessel you are using is broiler-safe). As needed, adjust the oven rack so that the rim of the cassoulet will be 7 to 8 inches (17.5 to 20 cm) from the heating element. Broil until richly browned, 2 to 5 minutes.

Remove the cassoulet from the oven and let rest for 20 minutes. (If you are using an earthenware vessel, place it on a cloth-lined surface to prevent cracking.) Just before serving, drizzle with the walnut oil, if using. Ladle onto plates and serve at once.

NOTES Fresh pork skin and ham hock (not smoked or cured) are essential to enrich the beans; they can be hard to find but are worth the effort.

When Paula published this recipe in 1983, Tarbais beans weren't available in the United States, but they are now and they are worth seeking out. Other white beans do not absorb as much flavor and cannot be cooked as long without collapsing. Heirloom bean retailer Rancho Gordo New World Specialty Food carries them, and recommends Ayocote Bianco beans as a substitute, as they are the Mexican beans from which the Tarbais were bred.

Paula devised this recipe to fit inside a clay cassoulet pot she purchased in France. Called a *cassole*, it is narrow at the bottom and broad at the rim, a shape that maximizes exposure of the ragout to the oven heat to ensure a better crust. If you do not have a 5½- to 6-quart (5½- to 6-l) earthenware vessel (or ovenproof mixing bowl), you can divide the cassoulet into two smaller vessels before the final baking, or simply halve the recipe. If you choose the latter option, halve everything except the sausage amount, as you'll want enough so that everyone gets at least half a link. If you divide the full recipe between two smaller vessels, keep all of the quantities the same except for doubling the bread crumbs. You'll want enough so that both vessels get a light sprinkling.

Easy Oven Duck Confit

There is a lot of mystique around this classic dish of Southwest France, starting with its fancy name. It could not be more basic, however: duck legs lightly cured overnight in salt and aromatics, poached in their own fat until meltingly soft, then crisped in a hot oven right before serving. Paula was not the first food writer to share a recipe, but she helped popularize the dish among food insiders in the 1970s and 1980s. Her recipe is the reason duck confit became a signature dish at Chez Panisse.

It is worth tracking down the first edition of *The Cooking of South-West France* for Paula's original six-page exegesis on the traditional method, which can be kept for up to 4 months, developing a wonderfully complex flavor. Over her career, she published several methods for achieving similar results, including one for duck confit *sous vide*. This shortcut oven method can't be put up for more than a few days, but it saves time and money, as it needs no additional duck fat, only six duck legs of whatever kind of duck you can find.

---

5 pounds (2.2 kg) fresh or thawed frozen duck legs, such as Moulard, Muscovy, or Pekin

3 tablespoons plus 1 teaspoon kosher salt (45 g total), preferably Diamond Crystal brand

1½ tablespoons coarsely chopped shallot

1½ tablespoons coarsely chopped garlic

1½ tablespoons chopped fresh flat-leaf parsley

2 teaspoons black peppercorns, lightly crushed

1 bay leaf, crumbled

1 fresh thyme sprig, chopped, or pinch of dried thyme

The night before, in a large bowl, toss the duck legs with the salt, shallot, garlic, parsley, peppercorns, bay leaf, and thyme. Cover with plastic wrap and refrigerate for at least 18 hours or up to 24 hours.

Serves 6 to 8

🕐 The duck legs marinate overnight.

The next day, preheat the oven to 225°F (110°C). Rinse off the salt and seasonings on the marinated duck under cool running water. Drain briefly; do not let the duck legs dry completely. Using the tines of a fork or a skewer, prick the fatty skin all over.

Place the duck legs, skin side up, in a single layer in a large, very heavy pot, such as a stoneware crock or enameled cast-iron casserole. Cut a round of parchment paper just to fit inside the pot and place atop the legs. Cover the pot with a tight-fitting lid and transfer to the oven. Cook without opening the oven door until the

recipe continues →

duck meat feels very tender, has begun to separate from the bone, and the joint between the leg and thigh is very loose, about 4 hours.

Turn off the oven heat and leave the confit in the oven for 1 to 2 hours longer to cool in the rendered fat. At this point, the duck can be refrigerated for up to 5 days. To refrigerate, stack the legs in a deep, narrow container, ladle the fat over to cover, and let cool to room temperature. Cover tightly and refrigerate. Scrape off all fat before using.

To serve, preheat the oven to 400°F (200°C). Arrange the legs, skin side up, on a rack set on a sheet pan. Bake until the skin is browned and crisp, about 10 minutes.

NOTE Gascon chefs taught Paula this ideal ratio for confit of 2 teaspoons kosher salt to 1 pound (450 g) meat, which she published in *South-West France*.

Celery Root and Apple Puree

Paula created this silky, subtly sweet puree, adapting it from a footnote in the *Michel Guérard's Cuisine Gourmande*. She visited the star chef on her first trip to Southwest France in 1978. In his ingenious riff on a classic French celery root puree, he used apples instead of potatoes. In her book, Paula called for Red Delicious, but the recipe works with pretty much any apple. She cautions, however, that "some apples are sweeter and some wetter. Just watch and taste as you go." If your puree seems too wet, you can simmer it for a few extra minutes to thicken it. For another sophisticated touch, she suggests a garnish of a few celery leaves fried in oil until crisp. Serve with duck confit or spoonable duck (pages 143 and 254, respectively), simple roast chicken, or pan-seared pork chops (page 169).

---

1 pound (450 g) celery root, peeled and cut into 1½-inch (3.75-cm) chunks

4 cups (1 l) whole milk

12 ounces (350 g) apples, such as Red Delicious, peeled, quartered, and cored

2 to 3 tablespoons (30 to 45 ml) heavy cream, if needed

Flaky sea salt and freshly ground black pepper

In a large saucepan, combine the celery root and milk over medium heat, bring to a simmer, and simmer for 10 minutes. Add the apples and simmer until the celery root is tender, about 10 minutes longer. Drain and discard the milk.

In a food processor or blender, puree the celery root and apple quarters in batches until smooth. Add the cream if needed to loosen the mixture. Season with salt and pepper, then serve.

Serves 4 to 6 as a side dish

🕐 The dish can be refrigerated for up to 2 days. Rewarm gently before serving.

NOTE For a dairy-free version, use water in place of the milk and full-fat coconut milk in place of the cream.

Scallops in Tangerine Sauce

A popular favorite in Paula's cooking classes, this dinner party dish showcases the wildly inventive mind of Jean-Louis Palladin, an avant-garde chef of the 1970s through the 1990s. Paula was among the first journalists to introduce him to the United States, before he moved to Washington, DC, to open Jean-Louis at the Watergate, his landmark restaurant.

Inspired by a scallops dish his mother made, Palladin created an intense sauce using stratification, a nouvelle cuisine technique taught to him by its originator, chef André Guillot. Rather than thickening his sauce with a roux (a mixture of flour and butter), Palladin "built" his sauce through a series of stratifications (reductions). First he reduced three liquids separately, then he "coagulated," or bound, them by reducing them together. He started by reducing an acid (in this case, tangerine juice), followed by a protein (fish stock), and finally a fat (heavy cream). As Paula taught in her classes, "The faster the evaporation, the better the coagulation!" The final reduction should take no more than 15 minutes.

---

16 large fresh sea scallops (1½ pounds | 675 g), preferably the same size and weight

3 tablespoons (45 ml) fruity extra-virgin olive oil

1 tablespoon coarsely chopped fresh flat-leaf parsley

1 tablespoon chopped celery leaves

½ teaspoon fresh thyme leaves, or 2 pinches of crumbled dried thyme

Flaky sea salt and freshly ground black pepper

1¼ cups (300 ml) lightly salted fish stock

1½ cups (360 ml) fresh tangerine or clementine juice

¾ cup (180 ml) lightly salted chicken stock

½ cup (120 ml) heavy cream

Juice of ½ lemon (optional)

1 tablespoon water, if needed

1 tablespoon unsalted butter, if needed

Serves 4

🕐 The scallops marinate for 2 to 3 hours. The sauce can be prepared up to 1 hour ahead.

Rinse the scallops and pat dry. In a large, shallow dish, toss them with the olive oil, parsley, celery leaves, and thyme. Season lightly with salt and pepper. Cover and marinate in the refrigerator for 2 to 3 hours.

Meanwhile, in a small saucepan, boil the fish stock until reduced to ¼ cup (60 ml). In another small saucepan, boil the tangerine juice until reduced to ⅓ cup (80 ml). In a third small saucepan, boil the chicken stock until reduced to 2 tablespoons.

Add the reduced fish stock and tangerine juice to the reduced chicken stock and bring to a boil over high heat. Add the cream and boil vigorously, without stirring, until large bubbles appear on the surface and the sauce begins to bind, 5 to 7 minutes. From time to time, test by stirring with a wooden spoon to see if the sauce has thickened. You should be able to glimpse the bottom of the saucepan for an instant (see photo below, at left). Remove immediately from the heat.

If the sauce is too sweet, adjust with a few drops of lemon juice and a few grinds of pepper. If the sauce turns oily, you have reduced it too much; in this case, add the water and it will immediately smooth out. If the sauce tastes too intense or feels too thin, swirl in the butter. (At this point, the sauce can be held in the top of a double boiler over barely simmering water for up to 45 minutes.)

About 15 minutes before serving, position an oven rack 4 inches (10 cm) from the heating element and preheat the broiler. Rewarm the sauce, if necessary. Remove the scallops from the refrigerator and arrange them on the rack of a broiler pan or on a rack set on a sheet pan. Broil the scallops, turning once, until lightly browned on both sides and just cooked through, about 2 minutes on each side.

To serve, spoon about 2 tablespoons of the warmed sauce onto each warmed individual plate. Tilt each plate to coat the bottom evenly. Set 4 scallops on each plate and serve at once.

Prunes in Armagnac

This sophisticated after-dinner treat is well worth the two-week wait. Prunes and Armagnac are longtime pantry staples of the Southwest. Paula wrote, "In the old days, Armagnac was distilled on practically every Gascon farm, in traveling stills hauled about by oxen."

After a couple of weeks, the spirit loses its fiery edges and the prunes are usable—but left for a few months, the Armagnac turns dark and syrupy and the prunes swell to an almost crisp plum-like texture. They're the essential ingredient for the Prune and Armagnac Ice Cream on the next page, and they are heaven eaten alone. Paula wrote, "one should drink off the thick, dark, aromatic syrup as slowly as possible, the longer to savor it."

---

3 cups (720 ml) boiling water

3 chamomile tea bags

2 pounds (900 g) unpitted prunes

1 cup (200 g) sugar

½ cup (120 ml) cold water

3 cups (720 ml) Armagnac, or more to cover

Makes about 45 prunes

🕐 The prunes marinate in chamomile tea overnight, then in Armagnac blended with a sugar syrup for at least 2 weeks or up to 1 year.

In a large heatproof bowl, pour the water over the tea bags and let steep for 5 minutes. Discard the tea bags. Add the prunes to the brewed tea. Cover loosely and let stand overnight.

The following day, drain the prunes and discard the tea. Place the prunes in a clean 1½-quart (1.5-l) widemouthed glass jar. In a small saucepan, combine the sugar and cold water and bring to a boil over high heat, stirring to dissolve the sugar. Boil undisturbed for 2 minutes. Remove from heat and let cool. Pour over the prunes. Add the Armagnac as needed to cover, stir gently, and cap the jar.

Let stand for at least 2 weeks before eating. The prunes will keep for up to 1 year in a cool, dark place or in the refrigerator. Add more Armagnac as needed to keep them covered and use clean wooden tongs or a wooden spoon to remove the prunes as needed.

NOTES Unpitted prunes are necessary here, as pitted prunes will change their shape, but you do not need a high-quality Armagnac.

In Paula's original recipe, she drained off the tea and rolled the prunes in paper towels to dry them, a step I found unnecessary. By skipping the drying, the Armagnac takes on a pleasantly more pronounced chamomile note, which I prefer. Feel free to follow her recipe to the letter and judge for yourself.

Prune and Armagnac Ice Cream

Boozy and not too sweet, this is rum raisin ice cream for grown-ups. As Paula writes, "It is perhaps the most elegant ice cream I know." Paula's friend chef André Daguin first thought to use prunes and Armagnac for making ice cream, which he presented in his dining room in dramatic presentation, freezing it to order with liquid nitrogen—probably the first chef to use the gas in a kitchen application. Paula translated his recipe for home cooks, adding her own touches, like a little heavy cream poured in at the very end. "This way, the butterfat in the cream will 'glide' into the chilled ice cream, endowing it with a satiny texture," she wrote.

---

2 cups (480 ml) whole milk

4-inch (10-cm) piece vanilla bean, split down one side, or ¾ teaspoon pure vanilla extract

5 egg yolks

½ cup (100 g) sugar

Pinch of flaky sea salt

15 Prunes in Armagnac (page 148), pitted, and 2 tablespoons of the syrup for the ice cream, plus extra prunes and syrup for garnish (optional)

¼ cup (60 ml) heavy cream

Prepare an ice-water bath. Set a sieve over a large bowl and set the bowl in the ice-water bath. In a heavy saucepan, combine the milk and vanilla bean (if using vanilla extract, you will add it later) and heat over medium-high heat just until small bubbles appear along the sides of the pan. Immediately remove the pan from heat.

Meanwhile, in a bowl, whisk together the egg yolks and sugar until the mixture is thick and pale and falls in a slowly dissolving ribbon onto the surface when the whisk is lifted. Whisk in the salt. While whisking constantly, pour the hot milk in a slow, steady stream into the egg yolk mixture, continuing to whisk until smooth. Pour the egg-milk mixture back into the saucepan and warm over low heat, stirring constantly with a wooden spoon, until the custard thickens enough to coat the back of the spoon and registers 170°F (77°C) on an instant-read thermometer. Immediately remove the pan from the heat.

Strain the custard through the sieve into the bowl, then stir the custard constantly until cool. If using vanilla extract, stir it in

Makes 1 quart (1 l); serves 4 to 6

🕙 The ice cream is ready to serve right away or can be frozen for up to 1 week.

recipe continues →

now. Pour the cold custard into an ice cream maker and freeze according to the manufacturer's instructions.

Meanwhile, coarsely chop the prunes with a sharp knife or pulse them in a food processor. When the ice cream is half-frozen, add the prunes and Armagnac syrup. When the ice cream is nearly frozen, pour in the cream.

When the ice cream is ready, transfer it to individual bowls and serve right away, or transfer it to an airtight container and place in the freezer for up to 1 week. Garnish each serving with a whole prune, if using, and drizzle with 1 teaspoon or so of the syrup. The ice cream is best served within 24 hours but can be frozen for up to 1 week.

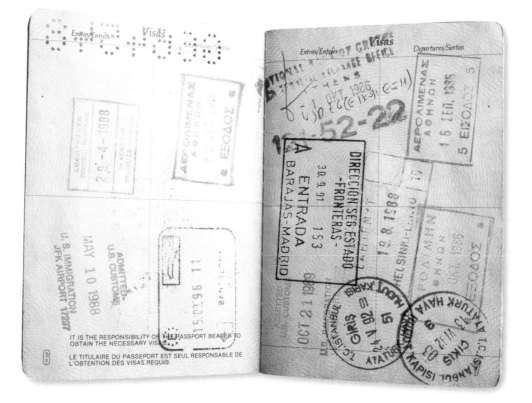

ΑΕΡΟΛΙΜΕΝΑΣ
ΑΘΗΝΩΝ
ΕΞΟΔΟΣ

2 Q - 4 - 1988

ADMITTED
U.S. CUSTOMS

MAY 10 1988
U.S. IMMIGRATION
JFK AIRPORT 1/2397

15.03.96 11

IT IS THE RESPONSIBILITY OF THE PASSPORT BEARER TO
OBTAIN THE NECESSARY VISAS.

LE TITULAIRE DU PASSEPORT EST SEUL RESPONSABLE DE
L'OBTENTION DES VISAS REQUIS.

6

NATIONAL
EXCHANGE OFFICE
ATHENS
-1 OKT 1986

ΑΕΡΟΛΙΜΕΝΑΣ
ΑΘΗΝΩΝ
16 ΣΕΠ. 1986
5 ΕΙΣΟΔΟΣ 5

DIRECCION SEG ESTADO
-FRONTERAS-
30.9.91   153
A ENTRADA
BARAJAS-MADRID

ΑΕΡΟΛΙΜΗΝ
ΑΘΗΝΩΝ
1986
ΧΟΡΟΣΙΣ

T.C. İSTANBUL
GİRİŞ
ATATÜRK HAVA

ATATÜRK HAVA
T.C. İSTANBUL
ÇIKIŞ 03
KAPISI

Searching for a New Country

NEW YORK AND THE
MEDITERRANEAN
❖ 1983 to 1988

"The ultimate test . . . is whether a dish is worth making a second time. Does this food taste true? Will I yearn for it some evening when I'm hungry? Will I remember it in six months' time? In a year? Five years from now? I don't think it's enough that a recipe be unique, interesting, odd-ball, previously unpublished, or simply 'new.' A dish worth repeating has to taste really good. That may, I confess, sound obvious, but in our current culinary scene, it is too often forgotten."

— Paula Wolfert in *Paula Wolfert's World of Food*

ALMOST THIRTY YEARS after the 1988 publication of her fourth book, *Paula Wolfert's World of Food*, Paula still felt superstitious about it. She cited it as a reason not to put her name in this book's title. "If you use my name, like *Paula Wolfert's World of Food*, your book will also go out of print!"

Although the book was Paula's biggest publishing failure, *World of Food* is among her most prescient, beguiling, and personal works. It won her a smaller but important new generation of chef fans, like Daniel Patterson, one of the country's most influential avant-garde chefs, who discovered the book in his early twenties.

"I love Paula's books because her recipes all have stories behind them," he told me. "She was always ahead of trends. In *World of Food*, she wrote about low-temperature salmon cooking (recipe, page 253) long before it ever became mainstream."

OPPOSITE: Paula's passport, imprinted with the intensive Mediterranean travel she undertook in the 1980s

Its recipes still feel modern, from foie gras sautéed with green grapes and a Greek-style slow-roasted *porchetta* to a home-cook version of chef Michel Bras's iconic *gargouillou* (recipe, page 172). Twenty years after its release, the *Washington Post* wrote that it was worth its weight in white truffles for all its brilliant ideas.

Yet for all its magic, *World of Food* lacks the focus or resonance of *South-West France* or *Couscous*. Reading it, I feel I'm chasing Paula as she flits around the sea like a Mediterranean sandpiper. Food writer John Thorne, one of her very few critics, noted that it contained the language of the tourist, not the convert. It's almost as though to write it, she used only her left eye, which can see distances, never her right eye to get up close.

"*World of Food* is like your handbag, where you've tucked away all this stuff," she told me. "Finally you sort it out, but you don't want to throw any of it away, even though they hold memories that don't work together. It's so scattered because I was looking for a new country."

❖

Paula in 1983 with her daughter, Leila

By the mid-1980s, Paula enjoyed considerable personal and financial freedom. She no longer relied exclusively on food writing to pay her bills. Bill had achieved enough commercial success as a crime novelist that he could support them both, but neither of them wanted him to. Financial independence was a point of pride for each of them. They have always split household expenses.

After the critical acclaim for *South-West France*, Paula could write any book she wanted. Her former editor, Fran McCullough, said that among publishers, after *South-West France*, "she somehow got into this magical circle where she and her work became really valuable without reference to sales figures." Exhibit A, for *World of Food*, Harper & Row gave her an advance of more than one hundred thousand dollars.

As often happens after a surprise success, Paula's first instinct was conservative, to replicate her previous hit. She thought she needed another overlooked region, another Southwest France.

But the American food movement had grown, and Paula now had a new generation of competitors to contend with, English-language food writers who, like her, claimed outposts around the Mediterranean to report on the local foodways. They included Giuliano Bugialli in Italy, Colman Andrews in Catalonia, and Patricia Wells in France.

Reluctant to encroach on anyone else's turf, Paula had trouble finding another big, empty place to claim as her own.

Working in Morocco and southwest France had taught her an essential lesson: to get the best recipes, she needed to connect with people, to learn their language first, and not only the language of the country but also of the regions—not every word, but the important ones: please, thank you, egg in both the singular and the plural, and what are we having for lunch?

After southwest France, she also formalized a practice she continued the rest of her career, of packing small gifts to hand out to anyone who gave her a recipe. Since the cans of maple syrup she had brought to Daguin and other chefs in the region proved too heavy, she switched to small kitchen tools, whether a garlic press, tomato peeler, or an electric immersion mixer. "You have to give before you take," she said.

First she considered Sicily. She became a regular at Azzurro, a Sicilian restaurant near her New York apartment. Through the chef and owner, Maria Sindoni, and a Sicilian poetry society in New Jersey, Paula built a list of Sicilian cooks to visit and taught herself some Sicilian dialect. In 1985, she and Bill took an extended trip to the island. She wrote four features, two with Bill, more than enough for a cookbook introduction and chapter headings detailing the island's history and *terroir*.

"Eggplants, tomatoes and olive oils varied with the soil," she wrote in *Bon Appétit*, "while differences in red mullets and sardines were due to the diversities of botanical life in the Tyrrhenian and Ionian seas." She gathered recipes for pumpkin *escabeche*, a marmalade of spring greens similar to her Moroccan herb jam, and, from Sindoni at Azzurro, a *caponatina* that still ranks among her favorite eggplant dishes (recipe, page 283). But when she bumped into Italian food writer Giuliano Bugialli, she sensed she might be stepping on his toes and ditched the idea of a Sicily book.

"I wasn't walking on anybody else's territory," she told me.

She moved on to Catalonia, a Mediterranean Spanish coastal region centered around Barcelona whose cuisine would not experience widespread acceptance in the United States until the rise of Catalan chef Ferran Adrià in the 1990s. In New York in the 1980s, Paula befriended and supported a number of pioneering Spanish-speaking chefs and restaurateurs, including Montse Guillén, cofounder of El Internacional, New York's first authentic tapas bar. Guillén also consulted for The Ballroom, the restaurant credited with first serving tapas in New York. (In kitchen of The Ballroom, Paula met an aspiring Latin American food historian named Maricel Presilla, who made the restaurant's amazing flan and today credits

Paula with discovering her.) Her interest sparked, Paula began studying basic Catalan and learned some classic dishes of the region from Guillén and her mother in the chef's SoHo loft.

In the summer of 1986, Paula traveled through Catalonia and acquired over twenty recipes, including three versions of Catalan seafood *a la planxa* (cooked on a cast-iron griddle), a technique that would become trendy in the United States a decade later. She even got a recipe for squid served in a sauce of its own ink from chef Juan Mari Arzak (a mentor of Guillén). On the Costa Brava, she learned a remarkable recipe for shrimp *suquet* (recipe, page 165), a kind of Catalan stir-fry. But in Barcelona she had lunch with food writer Colman Andrews, who shared a draft of his forthcoming masterwork, *Catalan Cuisine: Europe's Last Great Culinary Secret*, due to be released in 1988. Paula decided against doing her own Catalonia book.

Her friends tried to persuade her to throw out her elbows. "I told her, 'it doesn't matter what Colman and them are doing, paint your own Indians, sing your own song,'" Villas recalled. "In the long run, Paula did her own thing. But she can be very jealous when you stomp on her territory. I think she felt the other writers would react the same way."

A Vasco da Gama of cookbook writers, Paula wanted virgin territory. She saw competition as a zero-sum game: Either she'd "lose" because she published an inferior or less-recognized book (in which case, I think the thought of playing second fiddle to some other English-language Mediterranean food writer might have reminded her of the pain of life as the less-favored daughter after the arrival of her younger sister). Or she'd "win" because she published the best book. But, of course, that risked angering rivals she didn't want in the first place.

So she settled on a compromise. Inspired by her second book, *Mediterranean Cooking*, instead of celebrating one region, she would anthologize her best finds from all of them.

❖

Then her anthology took on a more pressing purpose. Through the mid-1980s, she began to position it as a counterweight to two trends she feared threatened American foodways: California cooking and celebrity chefs. She witnessed both firsthand through her cooking classes and through the biggest endorsement deal of her career. Courvoisier Cognac annually paid her tens of thousands of dollars for several years to promote its product in America. They booked her on radio stations in Los Angeles, New Orleans, and other major cities to promote Cognac to their biggest American market, urban African Americans.

"I'd talk about how to cook with Courvoisier, how you can sip it in Chinese restaurants in Chinatown, how some people mix it with Coca-Cola, whatever they asked me to talk about," she said. She felt comfortable promoting the spirit because she genuinely wanted more Americans to know about it, however they chose to consume it. Plus she loved the money, and the access.

Through Courvoisier, Paula met celebrity chefs and tasted California cooking in situ. In Los Angeles, she got to know

Author Paula Wolfert challenges amateur chefs to create original recipes that feature cognac and enter the Courvoisier Culinary Classic.

Promoting Courvoisier in the 1980s

Wolfgang Puck at his new restaurant, Spago, and tasted some of his first wood-fired pizzas. In New York, she met Jonathan Waxman, who in 1984 imported California cooking from his native Berkeley to a Manhattan restaurant, Jams, where Paula went often.

California cooking revolutionized American restaurants, fusing classic French and Italian technique with seasonal American ingredients (and sometimes Asian condiments) in dishes like wood-fired goat cheese pizza and mesquite-grilled fish or meat. The geographic focus offered a model for other regional revivalists like Jasper White in New England, Mark Miller in the Southwest, Norman Van Aken in Florida, and Paul Prudhomme in New Orleans. Paula liked the chefs personally and admired their creativity. But the food?

"I get so sick of that style of food," she told Colman Andrews in the *Los Angeles Times* in 1986. "They grill a piece of tuna and squeeze a little lime on it and call it cooking!" She added, "There's definitely a renaissance going on in this country today, just like there once was in Florence. The only difference is, back then everybody was talking about painting, painting, painting, and now it's food, food, food. The only trouble is, we don't have any Michelangelos."

Paula wasn't the first (or last) to complain about California cooking: her comments were echoed decades later when New York chef David Chang complained in 2009, "every restaurant in San Francisco is just serving figs on a plate." But it wasn't only California cuisine she found problematic. Finally food was trendy in America, but in a way that was opposite of what she'd hoped: a kitsch American version of nouvelle cuisine, stripped of history or context. "I'm not interested in shock value or trendy foods," she told a Milwaukee reporter in

October 1986. "I'm very interested in nuances. Every person in this room makes a brownie. One person makes it better. I'm interested in that extra dimension in cooking."

Clearly, Paula exaggerated her frustrations to play to the press and promote her new book. But she was also genuinely turned off. She offered her latest discoveries in the loose hope that American chefs might choose to emulate them, as examples of innovations grounded in flavor and tradition.

Despite these unsettling rumblings in the culinary world, Paula didn't deprive herself of trips to France—though she had new competition there, too, from food writer Patricia Wells. On one memorable jaunt in 1987, Paula, James Villas, and Ruth Reichl, among other writers, accompanied Wells on a tour of France via the Concorde. (The 1980s were truly a glory age of cookbook publishing.) On the supersonic jet, "Paula and I sat and smoked our heads off and drank and did nothing but look at guides of where to eat in Paris," Villas recalled. In her own book, Paula included a rare Parisian recipe, a riff on a trendy bistro dish that remains timelessly delicious: pork chops with a cornichon butter (recipe, 169).

Paula with James Villas and Ruth Reichl in France

The same trip, she and Villas visited a Paris restaurant known for its *pot au feu*, a classic stew. It turned out the owner so loved dachshunds, he kept several on hand as lap companions for patrons. Paula "got hysterical," Villas recalled—she had been terrified of dogs since she was a child. Villas calmed her down, so much so that, amazingly, Paula let one dog sit in her lap. "The next thing I knew, Paula was feeding her dog a little bit of her *pot au feu*," Villas recalled, laughing anew at the memory.

Paula also kept up with her friends from Southwest France now living in America. Jean-Louis Palladin flew Paula from New York to Washington, DC, for dinner at Jean-Louis, his celebrated restaurant in the Watergate Hotel, and gave her a recipe for ratatouille set in aspic for her book. In 1984, André Daguin's daughter, Ariane, launched the first company to sell domestic foie gras in the United States, which she named D'Artagnan. Paula helped her promote the products, publishing a foie gras feature in *Food & Wine*. The ingredient had been left out of *South-West France* because it had not yet been available in the United States, so *World of Food* became Paula's first book to include foie gras recipes.

On another trip to France, this one with Bill in 1986, Paula made one of the biggest finds of her career. A French friend told them about a gifted chef working in the "poor, almost savagely rural" Aubrac Mountains, as Paula later described them, in the south-central French town of Laguiole. After they completed the multiday journey, the young, bespectacled chef told her his restaurant was still closed for the off-season, but she was welcome to visit with him while he readied it for opening. The chef was Michel Bras, who remains one of the greatest legends in French culinary history. Paula wrote two stories on him, one for the *New York Times Magazine* and one for *Bon Appétit*, and became the first journalist to introduce him to a US audience. Bras showed her twenty-five of his dishes, each one astonishing her more than the last.

Asked about their time together, Bras said, "I remember her very well, she was very sensitive to my work." He recalled one instance when her curiosity got the better of her—leaning over a pot to study a dish, she dropped her glasses into the broth, much to the entire kitchen's amusement. They stayed in touch for years. To help him make his salmon with cracklings, she sent him a bacon press. For *World of Food*, she created a clever, tasty, home-cook-friendly version of his iconic *gargouillou*, a deconstructed vegetable ragout (recipe, page 172).

In her introduction to *World of Food*, Paula wrote a moving manifesto about these kinds of foods of nuance and history, foods that had what she called the Big Taste: "What do I mean by Big Taste? I mean food that is deeply satisfying, and that appeals to all the senses. I like dishes that leave their flavor with me, whose tastes and aromas I will never forget."

And yet, though fueled by such a worthy cause and vision, her book reveals a surprising tentativeness, a reluctance to boast about her finds, that's out of step with the bubbling enthusiasm in *Couscous* and *South-West France*. I owned the book for ten years before I put together that the recipe for Spring Vegetables in the Style of Laguiole was her version of Bras's *gargouillou*. The seemingly scattered volume hides countless gems. It's as though she needed a Madame Jaidi, a mother figure, to help root her in place, to get her to focus.

It would take until her next book for her to find an entire region of Madame Jaidis—Mediterranean women cooks who would help her write a book so groundbreaking that only today can we fully savor its impact.

Paula Wolfert's World of Food: Date-Night Dinner

❖ ❀ ❖

This menu highlights the creative and geographic range of Paula's most personal book. It showcases sentimental favorites like the butter cookies that she served at her wedding, and lesser-known treasures like her homage to the signature vegetable dish of legendary French chef Michel Bras. The main courses work best for an intimate date night at home for two. The mushroom caps and cookies are perfect make-ahead treats to serve a few—or a crowd. Along with (or in lieu of) the cookies, Paula also suggests a simple dessert of vanilla ice cream drizzled with warmed chestnut honey.

FIRST COURSE
Mushroom Caps Stuffed with Olives and Porcini

MAIN COURSE
Shrimp Suquet with Almond Picada
and
Catalan "Fried" Rice
or
Pan-Seared Pork Chops with Cornichon Butter

SIDE DISH
Vegetables in the Style of Laguiole

DESSERT
Greek Butter-Almond Cookies with Ouzo

Mushroom Caps Stuffed with Olives and Porcini

These umami-packed mushrooms are both wonderfully modern and a throwback to the era of cocktail parties (excellent with martinis). "Greek green-cracked olives are large, dark, and sharp, with a hint of bitterness and a slightly smoky flavor that mingles well with dried wild mushrooms," Paula wrote in the *World of Food*.

True to Paula, the recipe is both specific and forgiving, requiring two kinds of mushrooms and both butter and olive oil, yet the whole thing can be assembled up to a day ahead of time and reheated just before serving. It makes a great first course or side dish.

---

1 tablespoon extra-virgin olive oil

¾ ounce (20 g) dried porcini mushrooms

1 cup (240 ml) hot water

Flaky sea salt and freshly ground black pepper

16 to 20 firm fresh white mushrooms, caps about 1½ inches (3.75 cm) wide (about 12 ounces | 350 g total)

4 tablespoons (60 g) unsalted butter, at room temperature

¼ cup (10 g) chopped fresh flat-leaf parsley

¼ teaspoon dried oregano, crumbled

Juice of ½ lemon

10 to 15 pitted cracked green olives (about 90 g total), rinsed (see note on page 91) and finely chopped

---

Serves 4 to 6

The mushrooms can be assembled and refrigerated overnight before the final baking.

Preheat the oven to 325°F (160°C). Grease a 9-by-13-inch (23-by-33-cm) baking dish with the oil.

In a small bowl, combine the dried mushrooms and hot water. Add a pinch of salt and let stand for 20 minutes.

Meanwhile, wipe the white mushrooms clean. Trim off the stem ends, separate the stems from the caps, and finely chop the stems. You should have about 1 cup (70 g). Set aside (save any extra for another use).

Place the mushroom caps, gill side up, in the prepared baking dish. In a small bowl, mash 2 tablespoons of the butter with a pinch each of salt and pepper. Divide the butter evenly among the caps. Bake the caps for 10 minutes, until heated through and a little moisture is released. Remove from the oven and raise the oven temperature to 400°F (200°C).

recipe continues →

While the caps are baking, rub the dried mushrooms between your fingers in the soaking water to remove any grit, then lift out the mushrooms, squeeze them dry over the bowl, and finely chop them. Slowly pour the mushroom soaking liquid into a frying pan, stopping when you reach the grit at the bottom of the bowl. Add the chopped dried mushrooms and fresh mushroom stems to the frying pan and bring slowly to a simmer over medium-low heat. Turn down the heat to low and simmer gently, stirring occasionally, until all the liquid has evaporated and the mushroom stems are tender, about 15 minutes.

Transfer the mushroom mixture to a bowl and let cool to room temperature. Add the remaining 2 tablespoons butter, the parsley, oregano, lemon juice, and olives and work together with a fork until evenly mixed. Season with salt and pepper, then stuff each mushroom cap with about 1 tablespoon of the mixture. (At this point, the stuffed mushroom caps can be covered and refrigerated overnight before continuing.)

Bake the caps until tender when pierced with a toothpick and sizzling, 10 to 15 minutes. Serve hot or lukewarm.

Shrimp Suquet with Almond Picada

In the 1980s, Paula became so enamored of Catalan cooking that she considered doing an entire book on the Spanish region. This magical little dish, a kind of Catalan stir-fry from the Costa Brava, first opened her eyes to the cuisine's unusual combinations: shrimp simmered in a quick broth made from their shells, plus tomatoes, Cognac, and cinnamon (!), and a *picada* of almonds pounded with garlic and parsley. *Suquets* are fish stews popular along the Catalan coast, and their ingredients are typically easy to find. The Catalan "Fried" Rice is a fun accompaniment, but in a pinch, use plain white rice.

---

12 extra-large or jumbo shrimp in the shell

2½ cups (600 ml) water

Catalan "Fried" Rice, for serving (page 168)

3 large Roma tomatoes (about 12 ounces | 350 g total), halved lengthwise and seeded

5 almonds, toasted

¼ teaspoon finely chopped garlic

1 teaspoon finely chopped fresh flat-leaf parsley, plus more for garnish

Pinch of hot red pepper flakes

1 tablespoon olive oil

Flaky sea salt and freshly ground black pepper

2 tablespoons finely chopped yellow onion

2 tablespoons Cognac

Pinch of ground cinnamon

Pinch of sugar (optional)

Peel and devein the shrimp and set the shrimp aside. In a medium saucepan, combine the shells and water and bring to boil over high heat. Turn down the heat to medium-low and simmer for 12 minutes. Strain the stock through a fine-mesh sieve into a measuring pitcher and discard the shells. You should have about 1⅔ cups (390 ml) stock. Measure out ¼ cup (60 ml) plus 2 tablespoons for this recipe and use 1 cup (240 ml) to start the rice.

While the rice cooks, continue with the *suquet*. Use the large holes of a box grater, and with the cut side against the grater, grate the tomato halves and discard the skins.

To make the picada, in a mortar with a pestle, pound the almonds until they release their oil and form a paste. Add the garlic and parsley and continue to pound until a smooth paste forms. Alternatively, to make the picada in a mini food processor, process the almonds with 2 tablespoons of the shrimp stock, then add the garlic and parsley and process until a smooth paste forms.

Serves 2

🕐 Start the rice after making the shrimp stock so things come together at the same time.

recipe continues →

In a large nonstick frying pan or wok, heat the red pepper flakes and olive oil over medium-high heat for 1 minute. Add the shrimp and a pinch of salt and sauté, turning the shrimp often, until they are just white throughout, about 2 minutes. Transfer the shrimp to a plate.

Add the onion and tomatoes to the pan, turn down the heat to medium-low, and cook, stirring, for 5 minutes. Add the Cognac, cinnamon, and the ¼ cup (60 ml) shrimp stock and simmer for 1 minute. Season with salt and pepper and with the sugar if needed to balance the acidity.

Scrape the picada into the sauce and cook, stirring, for 30 seconds. Return the shrimp to the pan and mix gently. Remove from the heat and let stand for 5 minutes before serving. Quickly reheat and serve hot with the rice. Sprinkle on some parsley for flourish.

NOTE The dish can be doubled or even tripled, but it retains a certain delicacy when cooked for two.

Catalan "Fried" Rice

Unlike Chinese fried rice, this simple steamed version relies on a light toasting of the raw grains in olive oil as a way to boost the flavor of plain white rice. Although part of the beauty of this dish is Paula's resourceful use of the shrimp shells from the *suquet*, you don't need shrimp stock to enjoy it. Lightly salted chicken or vegetable stock also work. The white pepper and nutmeg subtly highlight the toasty character of the rice.

1½ tablespoons olive oil

½ cup (90 g) jasmine or other long-grain white rice

1 cup (240 ml) shrimp shell stock from shrimp suquet (page 165) or lightly salted chicken or vegetable stock

Flaky sea salt and freshly ground white pepper

Freshly grated nutmeg

Serves 2

In a small frying pan, heat the oil over medium-high heat. Add the rice and cook, stirring constantly, until the grains are lightly toasted, about 9 minutes. Add the stock and a generous pinch each of the salt, pepper, and nutmeg. Stir once, then cook uncovered over medium-high heat, rotating and shaking the pan a few times to ensure the rice cooks evenly, until the liquid is absorbed and the rice is tender, about 20 minutes. Serve hot.

Pan-Seared Pork Chops with Cornichon Butter

Although Paula lived in Paris for eight years, this lovely date-night bistro-style main course with an unforgettably good pan sauce is one of the few Parisian recipes she ever published. For a complete Francophile dinner, serve with Potato Gratin Dauphinois (page 272).

MARINADE

1 garlic clove, thinly sliced

1 teaspoon minced fresh flat-leaf parsley

1 teaspoon minced fresh tarragon

1 shallot, thinly sliced

1 tablespoon olive oil

PORK AND BUTTER SAUCE

2 bone-in loin or rib pork chops, each about 1½ inches (3.75 cm) thick (see note)

1½ tablespoons unsalted butter, at room temperature

4 or 5 cornichons, rinsed and finely chopped (1½ tablespoons)

2 teaspoons olive oil

Flaky sea salt and freshly ground black pepper

2 tablespoons sherry vinegar

2 tablespoons water

1 teaspoon minced fresh flat-leaf parsley

1 teaspoon minced fresh tarragon

Serves 2

To make the marinade, in a shallow dish, combine all the ingredients and mix well. Add the pork chops and rub with the marinade to coat both sides evenly. Cover with plastic wrap and let stand at room temperature for 2 hours or refrigerate overnight and bring the pork back to room temperature before proceeding.

For the butter sauce, in a small bowl, using a fork, mash the butter with the cornichons. Set the butter aside in a cool place.

Pat the pork chops dry with paper towels. In a heavy 10- or 12-inch (25- or 30-cm) frying pan, heat the olive oil over medium-high heat, swirling to coat the bottom. When the oil is hot, add the chops and cook, turning once, until browned on both sides but not yet cooked through, about 6 minutes total. Transfer the chops to a plate and sprinkle with salt and pepper.

Pour off the fat in the pan and discard. Return the pan to medium-high heat. Add the vinegar and water to the pan and boil, scraping up any browned bits from the bottom of the pan, until reduced by half (2 tablespoons total). Add the cornichon butter and swirl to make an emulsion.

recipe continues →

Return the pork chops to the pan, turn down the heat to low, and cook, basting with the pan sauce, until an instant-read thermometer inserted at the thickest part away from bone registers 140°F (60°C) for medium, about 9 minutes.

Transfer to a platter and let rest for 5 minutes. Sprinkle with the parsley and tarragon and serve.

NOTE Paula wrote this recipe for 4 thin pork chops (each about ½ inch | 1.25 cm thick) and served 2 chops to each diner. But thin bone-in chops are difficult to find today, so the more widely available thick chops are used here. If you can find the thinner chops, follow the recipe as written but shorten the final cooking time to about 4 minutes.

Vegetables in the Style of Laguiole

This is Paula's brilliantly approachable take on one of the most iconic restaurant dishes ever invented, the *gargouillou* of chef Michel Bras of Laguiole, France. Paula introduced Bras to the United States in an article she wrote about him in 1987. Like all her favorite chefs, he elevates the humble peasant foods of his region. *Gargouillou* is traditionally a Laguiole vegetable soup flavored with ham. Bras deconstructs it, blanching the vegetables separately, tossing them with crisped pancetta, and garnishing them with foraged flowers and weeds. That version has since spawned dozens of homages around the world. But when Paula published this recipe in *World of Food* in 1988, its name was little known, so she called it Spring Vegetables in the Style of Laguiole.

In Paula's home-cook adaptation, the vegetables are sequentially blanched in the same pot, starting with the ones that need the most water. The process yields a pleasingly intense vegetable stock for the sauce. Don't let the long list of vegetables intimidate you. In fact, Paula wrote, "There is no precise way to execute the following recipe; the fun is playing around with it."

---

2 quarts (2 l) water, preferably filtered

Flaky sea salt and freshly ground pepper

GROUP A: GREEN VEGETABLES

4 slender inner celery ribs

4 ounces (115 g) Swiss chard leaves, torn into 2-inch (5-cm) pieces

2 ounces (60 g) haricots verts or slender green beans, trimmed

2 ounces (60 g) red cabbage leaves

GROUP B: ALLIUMS

4 thin green onions or 2 young leeks (3 to 4 ounces | 90 to 115 g total), halved lengthwise

4 shallots, halved (2 to 3 ounces | 60 to 90 g total)

GROUP C: ROOT VEGETABLES

2 small carrots (2 ounces | 60 g total), peeled and cut on the diagonal into slices ¼ inch (6 mm) thick

2 baby turnips (2 ounces | 60 g total), quartered

3 radishes (2 ounces | 60 g total), quartered

----

4 ounces (115 g) pancetta, cut into slices ⅛ inch (3 mm) thick

2 tablespoons unsalted butter

1 tablespoon mixed fresh herbs, such as tarragon, chives, flat-leaf parsley, and chervil, snipped if desired

Serves 4

In a deep 4-quart (4-l) saucepan over high heat, bring the water and 2 teaspoons salt to a rolling boil. Working through each group in alphabetical and listed order (first the celery, then the chard, the haricots verts, and so on of Group A, then Group B, and then Group C), blanch each vegetable until tender. Each vegetable

recipe continues →

should take 2 to 3 minutes, depending on its size. Use the same water for all of the vegetables groups. As the water evaporates, the heat can be lowered to medium-high or medium, as long as the water remains at a healthy simmer. As each vegetable is ready, use a slotted spoon or spider to transfer to a colander and then rinse under cool running water and let drain. Transfer to a sheet pan lined with paper towel or a dishtowel to rest. Repeat with the remaining vegetables.

When all of the vegetables are cooked, remove the saucepan from the heat and reserve ½ cup (120 ml) cooking liquid for the sauce. Reserve the remainder for soup or stock.

Set a 12-inch (30-cm) frying pan over medium heat. Add the pancetta slices and cook, turning once, just until crisp, about 10 minutes total. Pour off the fat in the pan and reserve for another use. Add the reserved ½ cup (120 ml) cooking liquid to the pancetta in the pan, raise the heat to medium-high heat, and bring to a boil, scraping up any browned bits from the pan bottom. Boil until reduced to ¼ cup (60 ml).

Add the butter and swirl to form an emulsion. Immediately add the vegetables and cook, tossing, until heated through and glazed with the sauce, about 2 minutes. Taste and adjust the seasoning with salt and pepper, then remove the pancetta if you like.

Artfully arrange the vegetables on a platter, drizzle with the sauce, and sprinkle with the herbs. Serve hot.

NOTE If you can't find these exact vegetables, Paula offered many alternatives: Group A, spinach, green cabbage leaves, Brussels sprout leaves, asparagus, snow peas, zucchini; Group B, green garlic, ramps; Group C, celery root, beets. Sturdier vegetables such as the zucchini, celery root, or beets should be cut to ¼-inch-thick matchsticks that can be cooked to tenderness within 2 to 3 minutes.

For a vegetarian version, omit the pancetta (in its stead, add about 1 teaspoon white or yellow miso paste with the butter at the final step).

Greek Butter-Almond Cookies with Ouzo

These aromatic, slightly sweet butter cookies echo Mexican wedding cookies or Russian tea cakes, with an anise scent from the Greek liqueur ouzo. You can swap in a similar spirit like pastis or absinthe, but the anise notes may not be as strong. Paula first discovered these cookies for sale at a small corner store on the Greek island of Paxos in 1983. She loved them so much that she baked them for her wedding later that year.

Impossibly light, these cookies all but shatter into powder when you take a bite. A few tricks help achieve that lightness: three siftings of low-gluten flours, extended beating of the clarified butter, and extra baking powder.

1⅓ cups (180 g) all-purpose flour with a low gluten content, such as Gold Medal bleached

½ cup (65 g) cake flour

1¼ teaspoons baking powder

1 cup plus 2 tablespoons (235 g) clarified butter, chilled

¼ cup plus 3 tablespoons (55 g) confectioners' sugar, plus more for dusting (optional)

1 egg yolk

1 tablespoon ouzo

½ teaspoon pure vanilla extract

¼ teaspoon pure almond extract

¾ cup (80 g) almond meal

Working over a bowl or a sheet of waxed paper, sift together the all-purpose flour, cake flour, and baking powder. Resift the mixture twice; set aside.

In a stand mixer fitted with the paddle attachment, or in a bowl using a handheld mixer, beat the butter at medium speed until very light and fluffy, at least 5 minutes. (The more you beat, the lighter the cookie.) Gradually beat in the confectioners' sugar, then continue to beat for 2 minutes. Add the egg yolk and beat for 2 minutes longer. Add the ouzo and vanilla and almond extracts and beat for 1 minute.

Using a rubber spatula, carefully fold the flour mixture into the butter mixture, always working in the same direction, just until combined. Gently fold in the almond meal just until incorporated. The dough will be quite soft. Cover the bowl with plastic wrap and

Makes about 3 dozen

🕑 The cookies only improve with time, so feel free to make them several days ahead.

recipe continues →

refrigerate until the dough is cold enough to shape into small balls, about 45 minutes.

Preheat the oven to 350°F (180°C). Shape the dough into rounds, each about 1 inch (2.5 cm) in diameter and ½ inch (1.25 cm) tall. As you work, place them ½ inch (1.25 cm) apart on an ungreased sheet pan (preferably light colored, as darker pans can brown the cookies).

Bake until just firm to the touch, 12 to 15 minutes. The cookies will be pale, not brown. Transfer the pan to a wire rack. Immediately sift confectioners' sugar, if using, generously over the cookies. Let the cookies cool for 5 minutes, then remove them from the pan and roll them in additional sifted confectioners' sugar until well coated and set them on a rack. If you are not coating them with sugar, let cool on the pan for 5 minutes, then transfer them directly to the rack. Let the cookies cool completely. Store the cookies in an airtight tin at room temperature for at least 2 days before serving to allow them to mellow. They will keep for up to 10 days.

NOTE For a lower-sugar version (and stronger ouzo flavor), omit the dusting of confectioners' sugar. For guidance on clarifying butter, see the second paragraph on page 311.

On the
Pepper Trail

CONNECTICUT AND THE
EASTERN MEDITERRANEAN
❖ 1988 to 1994

> "This is *nouvelle* Paula. . . . It requires, first of all, a very
> hands-on type of cooking I find extremely pleasing, and
> it brings together a variety of diverse ingredients—the
> tastes sour and sweet, the textures crunchy and soft—
> into a finely tuned and delicious equilibrium."
>
> —Paula Wolfert on *The Cooking of the Eastern Mediterranean*
> in a profile by Molly O'Neill in the *New York Times Magazine*, 1994

A STRONG CASE CAN BE MADE that Paula's fifth book, *The Cooking of
the Eastern Mediterranean*, changed American food culture in more
ways than any of her other works. Yet *Eastern Mediterranean* has
never received nearly the recognition that her best-known titles,
Couscous and *Southwest France*, have garnered.

Many of the Middle Eastern culinary practices commonplace in
the United States today owe their prominence in no small part to
Eastern Mediterranean. This is true not only of the popularity of
mezes (small plates) but also of the elevation of vegetables to a main
dish (and the relegation of meat to a condiment) and the regular use
of such pantry staples as sumac, pomegranate molasses, and Aleppo,
Marash, and Urfa peppers.

But when the book appeared in 1994, such notions were so radical that even Paula's most ardent fans knew the book was *too* far
ahead. In the *Chicago Tribune*, William Rice, her former editor at
Food & Wine, wrote, "On the inside covers and facing pages of Paula

OPPOSITE:
In the early
1990s, with
Greek food
writer Aglaia
Kremezi

Wolfert's arresting new book . . . is a map that alerts the prospective reader/cook to just how far outside the American culinary mainstream Wolfert has stepped."

In restaurant terms, if *Couscous* was a late bloomer and *South-West France* was an instant hit, *Eastern Mediterranean* was that hole-in-the-wall that only industry insiders know about—but they're all regulars. The book influenced three food pioneers in particular: Alice Waters, Ana Sortun, and Ari Weinzweig, each of whom shepherded a different one of the book's ideas into American culinary consciousness.

In Berkeley, Chez Panisse founder Alice Waters had been giving vegetables equal ground with meat in her advocacy for farmers' markets and school gardens when *Eastern Mediterranean* helped her articulate a key notion. "To make vegetables the main dish, that was just utterly impressive," Waters said. Paula didn't just describe the eastern Mediterranean practice in the book's introduction: she adopted it as an organizing principle for the entire book, whose structure is arguably even more unorthodox than *Mediterranean Cooking*. (While *Eastern Mediterranean* includes conventional chapters on fish, poultry, and meat, of its first nine chapters, a whopping six are dedicated to vegetables. One is titled "Vegetables"; the other five have such quirkily specific titles as "Small Cooked Vegetable Dishes" and "Small Uncooked Salads.") These recipes informed Waters's burgeoning political activism. She founded her first Edible Schoolyard, or school garden and kitchen, at a public school in Berkeley in 1994, the same year *Eastern Mediterranean* appeared. Today, there are Edible Schoolyards across the country, and their vegetable-centric menus draw in part from Paula's book.

Ana Sortun, who heads up Oleana restaurant in Cambridge, Massachusetts, is considered among the first chefs in the United States to serve upscale, modern takes on Turkish mezes. As this chapter details, she discovered the country's cuisine through Paula.

Ari Weinzweig, founder of specialty foods emporium Zingerman's in Ann Arbor, Michigan, became the first major importer of Turkish Marash and Urfa peppers to the United States thanks to Paula, who described the vibrant Middle Eastern red pepper flakes in the book. A 2002 story in *Los Angeles* magazine also credited Paula with first introducing Aleppo pepper to American chefs. And at the specialty foods store Sahadi's in New York, Charlie Sahadi told me, "we've imported Aleppo pepper since at least the 1960s, maybe since we opened in the 1940s. But very few people not from the Middle East asked us for it before Paula wrote her book."

Today, Aleppo pepper on avocado toast has become a foodie cliché (though war in Syria has moved much of the pepper production to

Turkey), vegetable-centric diets are on the rise, and Middle Eastern flavors appear on high-end restaurant menus across the country. Many restaurants now describe themselves as "eastern Mediterranean." Yet Paula's foundational role in these trends is little known. She was so far ahead of her time, her achievements have become obscured, even forgotten.

Today, chefs and more recent cookbook authors (particularly Yotam Ottolenghi) are most often credited with the surge of interest in eastern Mediterranean cooking in America—and deservedly so. In a 2015 article in *Saveur* magazine, Michael Solomonov of the ground-breaking Philadelphia Israeli restaurant Zahav wrote, "It's great to see the food of the Middle East finally get its due here in the States. . . . Let's give some props to some early adopters: Before it was even cool, Mourad Lahlou in San Francisco was making couscous by hand, and Ana Sortun of Oleana in Cambridge, Massachusetts, had been expertly using Turkish flavors for years."

When I spoke with Solomonov, he cited Paula as an influence, just as his peers have. Mourad Lahlou acknowledges her in the Morocco chapter (page 78). Read on to learn how Paula helped lead Ana Sortun—and the rest of America—to Turkey and beyond.

❖

When Paula started *Eastern Mediterranean* in 1988, she was fifty years old and didn't need to break fresh ground. Although *World of Food* had gone out of print, it did nothing to tarnish her icon status in the food world. On the contrary, she had been recast as an expert not just for Morocco and Southwest France but for the entire Mediterranean. She could have revisited any of her earlier regions to publish spinoffs, as successful cookbook authors often do. Instead, in her pursuit of new flavors, she undertook the most adventurous work of her career, traveling to regions that weren't just remote but downright risky, such as Dagestan and Syria.

Paula was looking for fresh territory, which was when she often cast the widest net. By the late 1980s, her place in the food world had shifted. Her recipes from distant locales drew less interest as Americans began to explore good foods closer to home, like artisanal bread, craft-brewed beer, and better coffee from so-called first wave roasters like Starbucks. Increasingly, new chef stars like Thomas Keller, Charlie Trotter, and Bobby Flay overshadowed food writers. Cookware stores could no longer afford to fly in teachers, and Paula taught fewer cooking classes. Her attentions shifted to newly established conferences on food, where she now lectured. But she wanted to keep learning, to keep pushing the envelope.

She also remained ever vigilant about not competing with other English-language cookbook authors, tiptoeing around regional authorities she admired, such as Claudia Roden, to collaborate with emerging Mediterranean food journalists who published in their own languages and saw Paula as a mentor rather than a competitor. With their help, Paula gerrymandered a map of the eastern Mediterranean subregions that captivated her—ones that, to her mind, remained underreported: Slavic Macedonia, northern Greece, southeastern Turkey, Syria, and the barely Mediterranean Soviet Georgia. In the book she described her snaking route as "following the pepper trail."

As with much of Paula's life, her pepper trail quest started from unlikely circumstances. She didn't wake up one morning and decide to write about the eastern Mediterranean, despite her past visits to the region. Instead, she chose it on a 1988 junket to the decidedly non-Mediterranean Soviet Union. The last year before the Berlin Wall fell, Paula, almost on a lark, joined three dozen food stars on a three-week tour of the USSR.

❧

Organized by the Soviet Union, the USSR tour included some old East Coast writer pals such as Arthur Schwartz, plus West Coasters whom she got to know on the trip, such as Alice Waters. The group traveled to Kiev, Moscow, Leningrad, and the Baltic republics, where they sampled unremarkable, sometimes awful food (a layer of unidentifiable fat often floated atop the borscht served at Moscow restaurants) and drank a great deal of vodka.

Then they got to Georgia. "I took one bite of this eggplant dish and I went wild! We were finally in a place where people really knew how to cook. I spent the rest of the trip figuring out how I was going to get back to Georgia to learn the rest," Paula said of the recipe on page 206. Georgia stood at the intersection of Indian, Persian, and Armenian culinary traditions. Paula loved its pungent flavors, its unusual combinations of fresh herbs and rarer spices like sumac and red pepper pastes. The country reminded her of Morocco, especially in its warm hospitality. "In Georgia, guests are treated like a gift from God," she said.

But *Food & Wine* balked at a story, explaining that no one knew or cared about Georgian food. She persuaded them by fibbing that their rival *Gourmet* was interested in a few recipes. She hired a New York University student to teach her basic Georgian (not an easy feat, given that its Kartvelian script and structure bear no relation to the Cyrillic alphabet of Russia—or to the Arabic, French, Spanish, Catalan, Sicilian, or Serbian languages that Paula had already studied), and perused Georgian cookbooks written in Georgian. Finally, in the winter of 1988, she found a small, new American-Soviet culinary exchange program called Peace Table. It was run by a Washington State baker named Jerilyn Brusseau, who arranged a three-week stay for her and Paula in the Tbilisi home of a woman named Tsino Natsvlishvili, whose friend Tamara translated. By luck, the women turned out to be excellent cooks themselves, with Paula-level dedication to tradition.

A snapshot Paula took of the elderly women bread bakers of Khunzakh.

"Our first day," Brusseau recalled, "Tsino and Tamara were clustered in this little kitchen, wringing walnuts with their bare hands to make walnut oil."

Paula's Georgia adventures show just how far she was now willing to travel for good recipes. Paula and Brusseau crisscrossed the country, exploring villages along the Armenian border in the south and along the Black Sea coast to the west. Paula even talked their way into Chechnya and to the edge of the Caspian Sea in the east, persuading an official from bordering Dagestan to fly them to the capital city of Makhachkala. But at the Tbilisi airport, their flight to Makhachkala left early, stranding them, so the official hired a taxi to take them that night. They spent eleven hours in the back seat of the tiny car, climbing steep roads with turns so tight that the driver often had to stop and back up. They passed through the Chechen capital of Grozny by moonlight. They pulled into their hotel in Makhachkala at two o'clock in the morning, then rose before dawn to drive up into the mountains another eight thousand feet above sea level to the village of Khunzakh, where they watched an ancient bread-baking ritual at sunrise. Paula wrote, "seven elderly local women, in black dresses and black shawls, appeared . . . from the icy air and began to kiss us. They had come, they explained, to teach us to make corn bread. I can still feel the parchment-like texture of their deeply weathered cheeks."

Yet all this buildup and romance could not soften Paula's standards. The food was not good, so she omitted their recipes from the book. However, before departing Makhachkala, their hosts gave her a delicious recipe for pork skewers marinated in dill (recipe, page 209).

Back in the States, Paula did her utmost to spark interest in Georgian food, but the only interest came in the form of an interview with the *Times-Picayune* in New Orleans. She couldn't write a whole book on Georgian food—not least after she learned that her publisher, HarperCollins, had signed Russian studies expert Darra Goldstein to do a seminal Georgia book, which released in 1993. But her time there sparked her curiosity about the seasonings of Georgia and its neighboring countries in the eastern Mediterranean. She saw an opportunity to honor Georgian food in a book about the condiments of the Middle East. "No one had written about the region the way I wanted to, by exploring its ingredients, its pantry," she told me. She came up with a way to justify her inclusion of Georgia by applying the transitive quality of equality: Georgia is considered the birthplace of wine, wine is essential to the Mediterranean, ergo, Georgia could be considered part of the eastern Mediterranean. She sold the idea as the first of a two-book deal to HarperCollins.

From Georgia, Paula wanted to venture to truer centers of eastern Mediterranean cooking, such as Iran, Lebanon, and Armenia (Armenia is no more Mediterranean than Georgia, but she knew from her travels that "Armenians lived all over the Mediterranean," she said, and had influenced its cooking in myriad ways). But conflicts in all three regions prevented her from getting in. She decided to leave Persian cooking out of the book but doggedly called Armenian churches around the United States to build a collection of community cookbooks that she could later reference.

As she shared her new book idea with food insider friends in New York, she was told repeatedly that she needed to get to Syria and Turkey because they had some of the best food in the eastern Mediterranean.

Few Americans, let alone any American food writers she knew, had been to Soviet-allied Syria. She contacted the State Department and charmed a Syrian desk officer there into connecting her to an attaché at the Syrian embassy in Washington, DC. The attaché turned out to know a surprising amount about the culinary ambitions of his country's ruling elite. He wrote a letter on Paula's behalf to Syria's minister of defense, Lieutenant General Mustafa Tlass, whose wife had recently published an Aleppo cookbook. Maybe they would invite her to Syria to study the cuisine?

Soon, a gold-embossed letter on heavy cream stock from Tlass arrived in the mail. The Syrian government offered to fly Paula and Bill from Jordan to Damascus, to cover their hotel stay, and to provide a car and driver.

Paula's invitation to Syria from Defense Minister Mustafa Tlass

On the flight in, Bill read up on Tlass and learned that he was a notorious anti-Semite—author of *The Matzah of Zion*, a book that promoted the patently false myth of the Jewish blood libel, the ancient fiction that Jews in Damascus slaughtered non-Jewish children to bake their blood into matzoh. And, in his role as a henchman for President Hafez al-Assad, he presided over the horrific Hama massacre of 1982.

This time Bill was the nervous one. When Paula woke up from a nap, he suggested they not go. She talked him into going forward, promising that she would not reveal they were Jewish—a tall order for someone so voluble.

In their hotel room, their driver, a young uniformed soldier named Ayman Ramadan, placed his finger to his lips, turned on the faucet, and pointed to the ceiling. "You're probably being bugged," he told them. (For that, he was not only included in the book's acknowledgments, but more important, Paula and Bill wrote letters in support of his visa application to the United States just a few months later.)

They stayed three weeks. The general gave them one of his staff cars, with a general's star affixed to it, which gave them exceptional access, even driving through the car-free medina of Damascus. They toured sites that have since been destroyed by war, from the modern cities of Homs and Aleppo to the glorious arches of the ancient city of Palmyra. Paula fell in love with Aleppo pepper at a restaurant so centered around the spice that all of its foods were red.

A snapshot by Bill Bayer of their visit to Palmyra

They had to suffer through only two meetings with the general. The first was at a party for several hundred at his villa. When the general shook hands with Paula in farewell, she succeeded in keeping a straight face as she felt him lightly wiggle his index finger against the inside of her palm, a gesture she knew to be a crass come-on. Once they left and were safely in their car back to their hotel, she shared what had happened and laughed when their driver noted wryly, "His excellency fancies himself quite a ladies' man."

Toward the end of their trip, the general invited them to a more intimate lunch. On a tour of his library, he unlocked a steel door to his inner sanctum. It was crammed with gold-plated daggers and guns, Persian carpets, and creepy acrylic-on-velvet seminude paintings of Hollywood actresses like Brooke Shields. Of the few books, the general drew their attention to a set titled *The Jewish Encyclopedia*, then pointed to his forehead. "Know your enemy," he chuckled. Paula kept her mouth shut. They were able to leave the country without incident.

❧

Ever since visiting the Ionian islands and southern Greece in the 1960s, Paula had wanted to explore the northern part of the country—and she knew that few English-speaking food writers had covered it. In New York, a Greek importer offered to introduce her to Aglaia Kremezi, an Athens journalist. E-mail for the masses wouldn't arrive for years, so Paula faxed Kremezi, who quickly faxed back.

Fluent in English, Kremezi was a successful magazine editor and photographer at work on her first cookbook when she came upon *World of Food*. Kremezi had been reading American cooking magazines and knew Paula's reputation. She was particularly impressed by the high quality of Paula's Greek wedding cookies (recipe, page 175). As a journalist, she greatly appreciated the book's reportorial approach.

"It was one of the most engaging and intelligent collection of recipes I had seen," she said. "I thought the voice behind that book belonged to somebody I would like to meet."

It turned out that neither of them had explored much of northern Greece. Through fax communications, the women plotted a three-week trip to explore Macedonia, Epirus, and Thrace. Kremezi worked her many contacts and volunteered to drive. Paula bought a Pimsleur method kit to teach herself basic Greek. "At least enough that I could read the map!" she said. They each purchased separate copies of encyclopedic regional Greek cookbooks (written in Greek) and created their own lists of recipes they hoped to find.

Paula had never before collaborated this closely with a fellow food writer. Kremezi would become among the first of few food writers to witness Paula's methods so closely. They met for the first time in May 1991 at the airport in Thessaloniki, and within hours felt like lifelong friends. In the book, Paula described the road trip as their "nonviolent version of *Thelma & Louise*." It's a fitting comparison: Kremezi the younger, more reserved Geena Davis, Paula the older, more ribald Susan Sarandon. "We shared the same hotel room every night. How could she not become one of my best friends?" Paula asked.

At first Kremezi was struck by Paula's anxieties about even minor travel inconveniences, like finding a legal parking spot in Thessaloniki. (Paula didn't realize that parking "illegally" was commonplace in

Greece.) "Her anxieties seemed strange for someone so traveled," Kremezi said. "But then she relaxed. And we clicked."

In the field, Kremezi realized that Paula's fears underlined the seriousness of her work. "She took everything very, very seriously," she said. "Really—she wasn't taking things lightly at all. Ever." Kremezi also admired Paula's horse sense—and relentlessness—about finding the best cooks. In many villages, using Kremezi's contacts, they gathered women together and quizzed them about their cooking repertoires to find out who might have the best recipe for the dishes on their lists. Because these were just conversations in a room, they could not taste these dishes, nor watch the women cook, so they had to gauge whom to trust based on instinct and observation. "In Greece," Kremezi said, "when you ask somebody what they cook, everybody will tell you the most obvious things, like roasted lamb with potatoes. Paula has this intuition in choosing which cooks to ask, what to ask, and how to get things. And she doesn't take no for an answer. She'd point to one woman and tell me, 'Ask her! No, she hasn't spoken, ask this one!' And they would turn out to be the ones who knew."

Paula used intuition and charm to coax recipes from guarded women such as these Macedonians.

"I follow their eyes," Paula said. "I must have learned it in Morocco. If you ask who makes the best version, all the other women will look to one or two women. They know!"

For her part, Paula was so taken with Kremezi, she felt comfortable enough to work with her in a way that she had never done with any American food writer. Their collaborations did not end with finding good recipes; on the contrary, back home in their respective kitchens, still comparing notes by fax, they began the hard work of finessing— each giving their own versions a different spin. They began a decades-long practice of publishing divergent takes on similar recipes in their respective books. For example, in *Eastern Mediterranean*, Paula published an unusual northern Greek pie of wild greens, its crust made from a mere sprinkling of cornmeal (recipe, page 228). Kremezi later published a similar pie under its Greek name, *hortopsomo*.

When Kremezi expressed concern to Paula about competitors stealing their recipes, Paula told her not to worry about it. As much as Paula avoided competition herself, she knew the value of generosity in winning over rivals.

"Paula said, 'if you help people, it will come back to you,'" Kremezi recalled. "Now a lot of people write to me, and I go out of my way to help everybody. And it really has paid back."

Paula also advised Kremezi on which recipes to include in her debut cookbook. "Paula gave me some of the best advice I ever got, which I think every food writer should have: she said only choose recipes that you *love* to cook and *love* to eat, that you want to make again and again. It helped me from then on with all of my books."

❧

From her research, Paula knew that some of the best eastern Mediterranean cooking would be found in Turkey. In her travels she had experienced the culinary influence of the Ottoman Empire. In the book she wrote, "If one thinks of the eastern Mediterranean as an arc, Turkey is the keystone, a country that not only synthesized the cooking styles of the many nations it conquered but also reinterpreted and then exported these ideas to the farthest reaches of the greater Mediterranean."

In the early 1990s, Paula sat on a panel at a food conference in San Francisco with Turkish Sufi cooking expert Nevin Halici and seized the moment, confessing she had never been to Turkey but was dying to go. Halici not only invited her to stay for a week with her in her town of Konya but also gave her a list of the twenty-five best chefs in the country. In a departure from her language-first approach, Paula wrote all the chefs in English to ask if she could visit and learn their food. In closing, she added a last-ditch suggestion (in English): "I know you don't speak English, but can you hand this letter to someone who does, who might be willing to help me?"

Three chefs managed to write back. In Gaziantep, Burhan Çağdaş, said to be the best baklava chef in the country, took the letter to Ayfer Tuzcu Ünsal, a popular local English-speaking reporter.

"So I read this letter," Ünsal said. "I didn't know who Paula Wolfert was, I was not in the food world that much at the time, it was not that popular, you know? But she had left a fax number, and we had a fax. So I faxed her a few short lines, something like, 'You are looking for me!'"

In another lifetime, Ünsal and Paula could have been sisters. Born fourteen years apart, both women had rich alto voices, infectious laughter, and strong opinions. Ünsal, the younger, is almost more energetic and stubborn than Paula. When they met, Ünsal was working as a social worker and political journalist active in Armenian–Turkish relations. Her father founded the biggest newspaper in Gaziantep, where she was on staff. He had three goals for his daughter: to learn to cook, to marry well, and to speak English. She achieved all three and then some. To polish her English, as a high school student in 1970, Ünsal spent a year as an exchange student with an American family in Topeka, Kansas. Back home, already an accomplished Turkish cook, she special ordered buns and taught herself how to grind meat to prepare American hamburgers. After college, she studied English to work for the United Nations. She had always wanted to make Gaziantep an internationally renowned city, not least for its food: too few people recognized it as Turkey's gastronomic capital. She saw Paula's fax as an opportunity. But she had no idea that what came next would change the course of both their lives.

"The following morning, she got crazy!" Ünsal recalled. "She sent me a fax back that went on for at least eight pages!" In these early days of thermal fax printers, Paula's eight pages spooled out in a single roll onto the floor. The scroll-like missive explained who she was, followed by detailed descriptions of the specific ingredients and foods she was after.

Ünsal invited Paula to stay with her and her family for two weeks. Within no time, Ünsal became the second international journalist after Kremezi whom Paula helped recruit into food writing. For the next fourteen years, Paula returned to Turkey at least once a year to explore its foods with Ünsal.

Ayfer Ünsal, right, and Filiz Hösükoğlu, bottom left, at dinner with Paula in Turkey in the early 1990s.

For all of her time there, Paula never learned Turkish. "By the time I really started to go to Turkey, I could no longer learn languages," she told me. "Your mind does go down a bit when you get older." Paula was then in her sixties; it's possible Alzheimer's had begun to set in.

Ünsal found another Gaziantep woman to serve as Paula's translator, Filiz Hösükoğlu, whom Paula also won over to food.

"I have a degree in mechanical engineering and never thought about the importance of the culinary cul-

ture on our lives till I met Paula," Hösükoğlu wrote me in an e-mail. Above all, she was struck by the humanity of Paula's methods.

"Paula has a beautiful way of approaching people," Hösükoğlu said. "Although there is great competition in this world, she never made us feel it. Her common denominator is food, and we are all searchers." Hösükoğlu also admired how Paula tailored her questions to her interviewees: "It was fascinating how she grasped their social status and experience, even though she does not speak Turkish." Inspired by her time with Paula, Hösükoğlu began a second career offering her services as a culinary-culture consultant to writers and filmmakers traveling to the area.

In Turkey, Paula's key ideas for *Eastern Mediterranean* coalesced. With her dynamic duo of Ünsal and Hösükoğlu, Paula explored virtually every nook and cranny of the country but especially the southeast. Ünsal took Paula to such romantic settings as the banks of the Euphrates, the northern edge of the Fertile Crescent "where it all began!" Paula exclaimed (meaning agriculture, as well as civilization). In their travels to cities with exotic names like Nizip, Paula met dozens of women home cooks who, like Madame Jaidi, embraced her like family and shared their most cherished recipes.

To bolster her eclectic choice of regions for her book, Paula noted the many similarities found in the cooking of southeastern Turkey, northern Greece, and Syria. They shared boundaries and had occasionally swapped population segments, after all. She loved the emphasis on vegetables and the relegation of meat to a condiment. With Ünsal's help, she made a pilgrimage to the mountaintop café of the maker of the finest *manti* (Turkish dumplings) in the country. Ünsal also introduced her to two key Turkish red peppers: the bright, citrusy Marash and the earthy Urfa. For years, Ünsal arranged through an importer friend for Paula to receive annual three-pound shipments of canisters of Marash pepper flakes. Paula embraced the role of spice ambassador, handing out the canisters to leaders of the American food scene, and talking up their Aleppo and Urfa cousins.

Thanks to Ünsal, Paula also developed a profound obsession with kibbe, kebabs covered with a bulgur-and-meat shell, of which Paula published a list of fifty recipes in *Eastern Mediterranean*. (She couldn't fit all the recipes into the book and invited readers to mail her if they wanted the unpublished ones. Only one person took her up on it.)

In 1995, a year after the publication of *Eastern Mediterranean*, Cambridge chef Ana Sortun discovered the mezes and flavors of Turkey with the help Paula and Ünsal. Through a mutual friend, Ünsal invited Sortun to retrace Paula's steps in Turkey. Back home, Sortun used *Eastern Mediterranean* as a textbook on Turkish flavors to develop the menu for Oleana, her first restaurant, which she opened in 2001. While she also consults Middle Eastern cookbooks by Paula's peers, such as Claudia Roden, *Eastern Mediterranean*, Sortun says wryly, "opened the can of worms."

Sortun became one of many chefs and food writers in the 1990s who got to know Paula in person through Oldways Preservation & Exchange Trust, a food advocacy organization whose initial work focused on the Mediterranean. Founded in 1990 and based in Boston, Oldways worked in parallel to do much of what Paula did with her cookbooks, though on a grander scale, organizing conferences around the Mediterranean largely funded by olive-growing Mediterranean countries and the United Nations–chartered International Olive Oil Council (today the International Olive Council). Attended by chefs, food writers, nutritionists, anthropologists, and food importers from all over the globe, the events promoted the healthful and hedonic benefits of tradition-based Mediterranean foods. Between 1991 and 1993, the organization partnered with Harvard and the World Health Organization to design the Mediterranean Diet Pyramid, which emphasized fruits and vegetables over meat and olive oil over butter and cream—and would help Paula promote her book. Paula objected only that the pyramid lacked a section for herbs and spices—that it lacked flavor—but she liked the philosophy of Oldways and greatly benefitted from the organization's activities. (Once again she was ahead of her time; after consulting with scientists, Oldways added herbs and spices to the pyramid in 2008.)

As the reigning queen of the Mediterranean, Paula was one of the first authorities Oldways approached to participate in its conferences as a speaker and a resource to help them tap local authorities, such as Ayfer Ünsal in Istanbul.

"There are so many amazing food writers and cookbook authors, Paula was special because she talked in stories, which made these Mediterranean traditions come alive," said Oldways president Sara Baer-Sinnott. "She was also incredibly generous with her expertise in a way that not everybody is or was. She wants you to experience her discoveries like she does. She gets so excited she can barely stand it," she said fondly. "I know food retailers said it helped them come back [from conferences] and sell food in the United States in a more meaningful way. Paula helped them explain whatever the food was because she talked in stories."

Behind the scenes, Paula often drove everyone crazy with her nerves. The presentations before so many esteemed colleagues were very high stakes for her. Despite years of practice teaching, she often panicked in the hours leading up to them. But by many accounts, her presentations were revelatory. "Her going on those [Oldways] trips was a sort of edible education for many people I know," said Alice Waters.

The conferences proved vital to Paula not only for her on work on *Eastern Mediterranean* but also for every book that followed. The gatherings gave her new reach, allowing her to share finds with culinary leaders who could act on them immediately. It was on a bus to visit a food producer that she raved to Ari Weinzweig about Aleppo pepper from Syria and Marash and Urfa peppers from Turkey.

"Because I loved her work so much, and trusted her taste, I didn't hesitate to act on it when she told me something was that good," Weinzweig said. Paula introduced him to Ünsal. With their help, his company, Zingerman's, quickly became the first major US importer of Urfa and Marash peppers into the United States.

Thanks to Oldways, Paula got to compare her research style against that of rival American food writers in the field. It tickled her to see how some of her closest competitors needed to take such thorough notes. In those days, though she had lost the ability to learn new languages, her food memory remained so efficient that she could scribble two lines, go home, and re-create the entire dish. Observing her at a 1993 conference, *Vogue* food writer Jeffrey Steingarten wrote, "Paula seems to breathe in recipes the way I breathe in air."

❖

Paula always had wanderlust, but through Oldways, she hit peak travel. In addition to eastern Mediterranean recipe hunting, she may have had a new reason for getting away: to escape the suburbs. In 1989, after Bill had sold several books to Hollywood, the couple moved to Newtown, Connecticut. Bill had originally wanted to move to San Francisco, but Paula resisted living so far from her children, who were both grown and living on the East Coast. She also worried she would have trouble finding close friends out West. He proposed Santa Barbara, but she couldn't bear to live in a small and unfamiliar town where she might have to play second fiddle to the biggest food star in the country, Santa Barbara resident Julia Child. They compromised with the move to Connecticut.

They both eventually regretted the move. "Bill calls them the lost years," she said. "We lived there for five years, and neither of us can remember practically anything we did there; it's like we wasted time."

Paula had resisted a suburban life since she was a teenager in the 1950s and her parents moved to Westchester. To a certain extent, she found Connecticut undeniably exotic. After Bill sold the movie rights to one of his novels for a small fortune, he splashed out on a twelve-room Georgian colonial farmhouse with a millpond large enough to accommodate its own small island. The house had a literary heritage of sorts, as it was once owned by Rea Irvin, the founding art director of *The New Yorker*. Paula and Bill employed a maid, a gardener, and two part-time drivers to chauffeur Paula the hour and fifteen minutes back to Manhattan whenever she wanted.

In certain ways, the Connecticut years proved to be surprisingly fruitful. Life in the country sharpened two skills that would inform her next book, *Mediterranean Grains and Greens*. In Newtown, for the first time since Tangier, she could garden—on acres, not just square feet. In the surrounding fields and forests she also studied how to forage—for wild grape leaves, purslane, nettles.

"I made a deal with a neighbor that I'd weed his garden if I could keep his purslane," she said. To the chagrin of her gardener, she also let nettles run wild on her three-acre lawn. Through a nearby Greek Orthodox church, she found a Middle Eastern market that carried all the ingredients she needed for testing. If she had questions on her recipes, she faxed Kremezi or Ünsal.

Striking a pose on the porch of her Connecticut home

But she also felt isolated and lonely. In the summers, Bill went to their vacation house on Martha's Vineyard to write. Paula insisted on staying behind to watch the property. She filled the time by hosting friends on overnight stays. She started an annual tradition, an exclusive summer feast for three dozen of her closest friends. "I would do twenty dishes. Ayfer would come, Molly O'Neill, Jimmy Villas, Suzanne Hamlin. We would cook for days. I was always doing something that I knew people had never had before. Show-off meals," she said.

But the house spooked her. "It was a bad-luck house," she said. This time her superstitions appear to have been tragically well-founded: in 1990, their maid asked her husband, their gardener, for a divorce, and the gardener stabbed her to death and then killed himself. "It took us a long time to get over that," Bill said.

In January 1994, a blizzard struck. While on the roof clearing snow, Bill stepped through the skylight above his office. In his fall to the floor below, he punctured his lung and broke three ribs. On the gurney into surgery, he firmly announced, "We're moving to San Francisco."

An Eastern Mediterranean
Meze Spread

❖ ❀ ❖

When Paula began reporting on the foods of the eastern Mediterranean in the late 1980s, she helped introduce the tradition of Middle Eastern mezes to American food circles. From her earliest magazine articles, she showed a surprisingly adaptable attitude, encouraging home cooks to supplement homemade dishes with easy store-bought meze such as hummus, baba ghanoush, and grape leaves. She loved to inspire her own guests to alter the flavors of the meze themselves, offering them "dramatic piles of fresh pita" and "a plate of freshly picked untorn leaves," such as fresh mint, cress, and arugula.

These recipes reflect the geographical reach of Paula's work exploring the eastern Mediteranean. Altogether, they form a dream meze spread. Some of the recipes double as main dishes, such as the mussels and pork skewers, while others are wonderful side dishes, such as the stuffed eggplant.

SYRIA

Muhammara

GREECE

Mussels Saganaki

TURKEY

Cracked Green Olive, Walnut, and Pomegranate Relish

ISRAEL

Deconstructed Hummus

GEORGIA

Eggplants with Creamy Walnut Spread and Pomegranate Seeds

DAGESTAN

Pomegranate-Glazed Pork Skewers

Muhammara

Paula is one of the first American food writers to publish a recipe for this tangy-sweet Syrian bell pepper and nut spread. Although she traveled to Syria for the book, she learned this recipe in Brooklyn, from the family owners of the Middle Eastern grocery store Sahadi's. Its name is Arabic for "brick colored," the color that results when sweet bell peppers are pureed with meaty walnuts and tart pomegranate molasses. In her original recipe, Paula called for wheat crackers. Today, on her gluten-free diet, she has found crisp rice crackers also work.

2½ pounds (1.1 kg) red bell peppers

1 to 2 small fresh hot red chiles, such as Fresno

1½ cups (180 g) walnuts, coarsely ground

½ cup (30 g) wheat or rice crackers, crumbled

2 tablespoons pomegranate concentrate (page 314) or molasses

1 tablespoon fresh lemon juice

¾ teaspoon flaky sea salt

½ teaspoon ground toasted cumin, plus more for garnish

½ teaspoon sugar (optional)

2 tablespoons extra-virgin olive oil, plus more for garnish

2 teaspoons pine nuts, toasted, or peeled and chopped unsalted pistachios, for garnish

Pinch of mild red pepper flakes, preferably Aleppo or Marash, for garnish

Pita chips or crudités, for serving

Serves 4 to 6 as a meze

🕐 The flavor of the spread improves if made 1 or 2 days before serving. The spread will keep for up to 1 week.

Light a medium fire in a charcoal grill. Set the bell peppers and the chiles on the grill and cook slowly, turning occasionally, until they are blackened and blistered all over, about 15 minutes. Alternatively, in batches, set the peppers and chiles on a gas burner with the flame turned to medium-high and rotate them as needed until blackened and blistered all over. Transfer the peppers and chiles to a large bowl and cover with a plate or plastic wrap. Let steam for 10 to 15 minutes. Using your fingers or a paring knife, peel the peppers and chiles, then stem and seed them. Spread the peppers and chiles, skinned side up, on paper towels and let drain for 10 minutes.

In a food processor, combine the walnuts, crackers, pomegranate concentrate, lemon juice, salt, cumin, and sugar (if using) and process until smooth. Add the bell peppers and process until creamy, scraping down the sides as necessary. With the machine

recipe continues →

on, add the olive oil in a thin stream. Add the chiles to taste and process until smooth. If the spread is too thick, thin with 1 to 2 tablespoons water.

Transfer the spread to a serving dish, sprinkle with the pistachios, red pepper flakes, and a good pinch of cumin, and drizzle with olive oil. Place the dish on a platter, arrange the pita chips alongside, and serve right away. Alternatively, transfer the spread to an airtight container and refrigerate for at least overnight to allow the flavors to meld. Return to room temperature before serving.

NOTES In Aleppo, this spread is traditionally prepared with raw peppers. Unable to consistently obtain the proper Syrian varieties, the Sahadi family uses roasted bell peppers, which impart a meatier, sweeter flavor that Paula prefers.

Mussels Saganaki

Packed with fragrant fresh herbs, briny feta, and zingy powdered mustard, this Greek coastal dish, a classic of Thessaloniki, quickly became a household favorite for Paula. The term *saganaki* is used for both the dish and the traditional shallow, two-handled pan in which it is cooked, though any medium frying pan will do.

---

3 pounds (1.4 kg) mussels

Flaky sea salt and freshly ground black pepper

½ cup (120 ml) water

¼ lemon

1 tablespoon extra-virgin olive oil

⅓ cup (12 g) chopped fresh flat-leaf parsley, plus 2 tablespoons for garnish

1 serrano chile, seeded and finely chopped (2½ teaspoons)

½ cup (90 g) peeled, seeded, and diced tomatoes (fresh or drained canned)

5 large fresh mint leaves, shredded

1 teaspoon powdered mustard

½ teaspoon crushed garlic

¼ teaspoon crumbled dried oregano, preferably Greek

Pinch of hot red pepper flakes

3 ounces (90 g) feta cheese, preferably Bulgarian

Country-style bread, for serving (optional)

Rinse and scrub the mussels and pull off their beards (the short brown "threads" hanging from between the closed shells). Discard any mussels that have broken shells or that don't clamp shut when tapped. If wild-caught (ask your fishmonger), soak the cleaned mussels in a bowl of lightly salted cool water to cover for at least 30 minutes to purge them of sand, then lift them out, leaving the sand and water behind. If using farmed mussels, skip this soaking step, as they will be sand-free and soaking them will dilute their flavor.

In a wide, deep frying pan or saucepan, combine the mussels and the water, cover, and bring to a boil over high heat. Cook, shaking the pan occasionally, just until the mussels open, about 3 minutes. Using tongs, transfer the opened mussels to a bowl to catch their juices. Continue to cook any unopened mussels for about 1 minute longer, uncovering the pot as necessary to remove them as soon as their shells open. Discard any mussels that refuse to open.

Line a fine-mesh sieve with cheesecloth, strain the cooking broth through the sieve, and reserve. When the mussels are cool enough

Serves 4 to 6 as a meze or 4 as a light main course

The mussels can be shelled up to 1 day ahead. The dish can also be prepared up to 2 hours in advance except for the addition of the feta and then finished just before serving.

recipe continues →

to handle, pull them from their shells and pull off any remaining beard threads. Spread the mussels in a wide, shallow dish. Sprinkle them with a few grinds of black pepper and with the juice from the lemon quarter. Strain any liquor that collected in the bowl through the sieve, adding it to the reserved broth. (At this point, the mussels can be covered and refrigerated overnight.)

In a 9-inch (23-cm) saganaki pan or frying pan, heat the olive oil over medium-low heat. Stir in the parsley and 2 teaspoons of the chile and cook, stirring, until the parsley is wilted and bright green, about 1 minute. Stir in the tomatoes, mint, mustard, garlic, oregano, red pepper flakes, and ¼ teaspoon black pepper.

Add the mussel cooking broth to the pan, raise the heat to high, and quickly bring to a boil. Lower the heat to medium and simmer vigorously, stirring often, until the sauce has thickened and reduced, about 5 minutes. If desired, add the remaining chile to taste, raise the heat to medium-high, bring the sauce back to a boil for a moment, and then remove from the heat. Let cool to warm, about 10 minutes. Add the mussels to the warm sauce, cover, and refrigerate for at least 30 minutes or up to 2 hours.

Twenty minutes before serving, soak the feta in cold water to cover for 15 minutes, then drain and cut into small cubes. Reheat the mussels and sauce in the same pan over medium-low heat; do not allow the sauce to boil. Stir in the feta and cook until warmed through, about 2 minutes. Season with salt, pepper, lemon juice, and powdered mustard if needed. Transfer to individual plates, sprinkle with the 2 tablespoons parsley, and serve at once.

NOTE The recipe can be halved or doubled.

Cracked Green Olive, Walnut, and Pomegranate Relish

This incredible recipe is from Ayfer Ünsal, an acclaimed Turkish food journalist and gifted cook from Gaziantep and one of Paula's closest friends. It combines ingredients you would never expect to go together in such perfect balance: cracked green olives, crunchy walnuts, tangy pomegranate seeds, and zingy lemon juice. It is a lovely accompaniment to grilled fish or meat (such as pork skewers, page 209), Oven-Steamed Salmon (page 253), or melon.

8 ounces (225 g) cracked green olives, pitted, rinsed (see note on page 91), and coarsely chopped

2 tablespoons extra-virgin olive oil

¾ cup (90 g) walnuts, finely chopped by hand

2 green onions, white and light green parts, minced

¼ cup (10 g) chopped fresh flat-leaf parsley

⅛ teaspoon mild red pepper flakes, preferably Aleppo or Marash, or more to taste

2 teaspoons pomegranate concentrate (page 314) or molasses

1 tablespoon fresh lemon juice

Flaky sea salt and freshly ground black pepper

½ cup (85 g) fresh or thawed frozen pomegranate seeds

Serves 4 to 6 as a meze or side dish

In a bowl, combine all the ingredients and stir to mix well. The relish can be served the same day it is made. However, if covered and refrigerated for 1 to 2 days, it will mature and develop peak flavor. Bring to room temperature before serving.

Deconstructed Hummus

This recipe is a rare instance where Paula (reasonably) compromised on authenticity. She published numerous hummus recipes, including one in the 1994 edition of *Mediterranean Cooking* that many consider the gold standard (Google "Paula Wolfert hummus"). She learned this deconstructed version from Israeli food scholar Dalia Carmel in the 1990s. Called *musbacha*, it consists of whole chickpeas smothered in a thick, creamy tahini-lemon sauce loaded with fresh parsley. The original version calls for miniature chickpeas, which are soaked overnight, simmered for 5 hours, and peeled. After establishing that the added flavor did not justify the extra work, Paula called for ordinary chickpeas. You can decide for yourself if she was right: the miniature chickpeas are sold at Indian groceries and labeled *kana chala*. This recipe goes one step further and gives the option of canned chickpeas. Whichever you choose, do peel them—chickpeas without their skins are a revelation.

---

1 cup (200 g) dried chickpeas, picked over and soaked overnight in water to cover, or 1 (14-ounce | 400-g) can chickpeas

Flaky sea salt and freshly ground black pepper

4 garlic cloves, peeled

¼ cup plus 1 tablespoon (75 g) tahini, stirred in the jar before measuring

¼ cup plus 1 tablespoon (75 ml) fresh lemon juice

About 3 tablespoons (45 ml) ice water

⅓ cup (15 g) chopped fresh flat-leaf parsley

1 small serrano or jalapeño chile, seeded and finely chopped (about 2 teaspoons)

1 teaspoon extra-virgin olive oil, plus more for garnish

Pita triangles, for serving

If using soaked dried chickpeas, drain the chickpeas, rinse, and place in a saucepan. Add water to cover by 1 inch (2.5 cm) and a few pinches of salt and bring to a boil over high heat. Lower the heat to medium and simmer, uncovered, until tender, 45 minutes to 1 hour. Drain the chickpeas and let cool until they can be handled. If using canned chickpeas, drain and rinse. Whether using cooked dried chickpeas or canned chickpeas, rub them to slip off the skins. Do your best. Not every chickpea needs to be peeled.

Using a mortar and pestle, the back of a heavy knife and a cutting board, or a mini food processor, crush together the garlic and 2 or 3 pinches of salt, forming a paste. In a food processor, combine the tahini, ¼ cup (60 ml) of the lemon juice, and ½ teaspoon of the

Serves 4 to 6 as a meze

🕙 The dried chickpeas (if using) are soaked overnight; the tahini sauce mellows for 1 hour before serving.

recipe continues →

garlic paste and process until smooth. With the motor running, drizzle in the ice water, 1 tablespoon at a time, and process until the mixture is the consistency of mayonnaise. Transfer the sauce to a bowl and gently fold in all but 1 tablespoon of the parsley. Set aside ¼ teaspoon of the garlic paste for adding to the chickpeas and use the remainder to season the sauce if needed. Let the sauce stand at room temperature for 1 hour to mellow and develop flavor.

Shortly before serving, in another bowl, toss the peeled chickpeas with the reserved ¼ teaspoon crushed garlic paste, the remaining 1 tablespoon lemon juice, half of the chile, and the olive oil. Season with salt and pepper, then taste and adjust with any remaining garlic paste or chile if needed.

Arrange the chickpeas on a shallow serving dish and spread the sauce on top. Garnish with the remaining 1 tablespoon parsley and a drizzle of olive oil. Serve with pita triangles.

Eggplants with Creamy Walnut Spread and Pomegranate Seeds

This stunning meze combines two of Paula's great loves: eggplants and stuffed vegetables. It's no wonder it ignited her love of Georgian cooking when she tasted it on a junket to the USSR in 1988. She admired the technique of steam-sautéing the eggplants, which "eliminates greasiness without sacrificing taste," as she wrote. She also enjoyed the contrast of flavors and textures in the silky eggplant, creamy pureed walnuts, lively herbs, and crunchy pomegranate seeds. Dried marigold petals are a Georgian staple but turmeric is a worthy stand-in.

---

12 baby eggplants or 6 slender Asian eggplants with stems (about 2 pounds | 900 g total), halved lengthwise

1¾ teaspoons flaky sea salt

2 cups (200 g) walnuts

1 garlic clove, finely chopped

½ teaspoon hot smoked paprika (pimentón de la Vera picante), or more to taste

¼ teaspoon ground marigold petals or ground turmeric

⅓ cup (80 ml) ice water

⅓ cup (15 g) chopped celery leaves

⅓ cup (15 g) chopped fresh cilantro

¼ cup (10 g) shredded fresh basil leaves

¼ cup (25 g) minced red onion

2 tablespoons mild vinegar, such as cider or rice

¼ cup (45 g) fresh or thawed frozen pomegranate seeds, plus more for garnish

2 tablespoons extra-virgin olive oil, plus more as needed

Fresh flat-leaf parsley leaves, for garnish (optional)

Svaneti salt (page 313), for garnish (optional)

Serves 4 to 6 as a meze or side dish

Line a sheet pan with paper towels. Sprinkle the cut sides of the eggplants with 1 teaspoon of the salt and arrange them, cut side down, on the prepared sheet pan. Weight the eggplants down with plates and let stand for 20 minutes. Rinse the eggplants under cool running water, then squeeze gently with paper towels to draw out excess moisture.

Meanwhile, in a food processor, combine the walnuts, garlic, paprika, marigold petals, and the remaining ¾ teaspoon salt and process until an oily paste forms, about 2 minutes. Add the ice water and process until the paste is light and smooth, about 30 seconds. Transfer to a bowl, add the celery, cilantro, basil, onion, and vinegar, and stir to mix. Fold in the pomegranate seeds. Taste and adjust the seasoning with salt and vinegar if needed. Cover and set aside.

recipe continues →

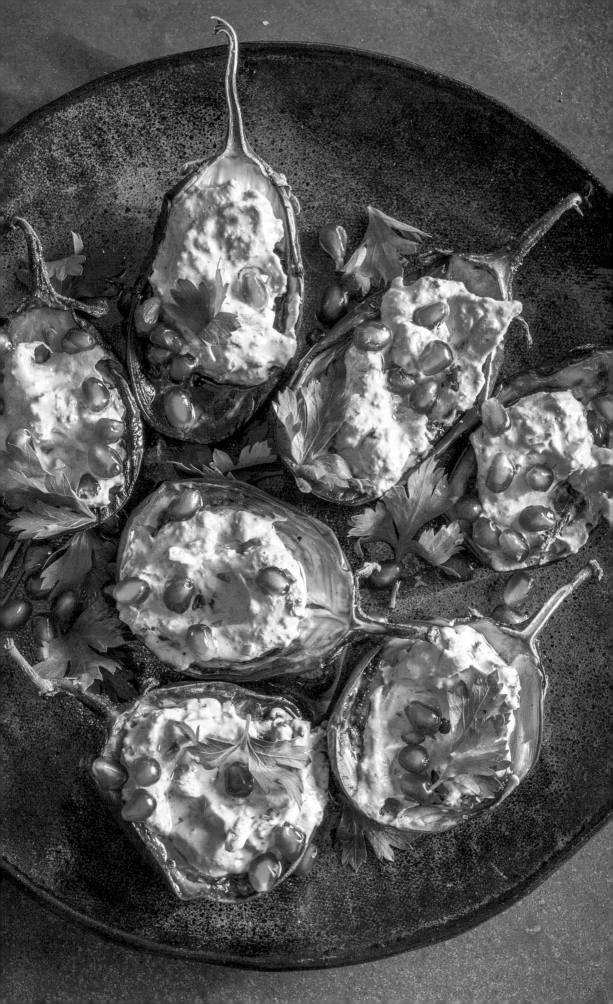

Line a sheet pan with paper towels. In a large nonstick frying pan with a tight-fitting lid, heat the olive oil over medium-low heat. Working in batches if necessary, add the eggplant halves, cut side down, cover, and cook until the cut sides are golden brown and the eggplant flesh is very tender when pierced with a knife, 15 to 20 minutes. Transfer the eggplant halves to the prepared sheet pan and let drain and cool to warm or room temperature. As needed, add 1½ teaspoons more oil to the pan before frying the second batch.

Using your fingers or a fork, split open the cut side of each eggplant half along the center, creating a cavity. Mound an equal amount of the walnut filling in each cavity. Garnish the eggplants with more pomegranate seeds and with the parsley leaves and Svaneti salt, if using. Serve warm or at room temperature.

Pomegranate-Glazed Pork Skewers

Paula learned how to make these herby, tangy skewers on an adventure in the Caucasus Mountains. The same marinade is also delicious with chicken thighs or extra-firm tofu. The onions are traditionally grated by hand, but the marinade comes together in seconds in a food processor. The onion-parsley salad is a classic kebab accompaniment Paula was taught by a master of kebabs, Burhan Çağdaş of Gaziantep, Turkey.

½ cup (75 g) coarsely chopped yellow onion (½ medium onion)

6 tablespoons (90 ml) water

4 tablespoons (60 ml) pomegranate concentrate (page 314) or molasses

2 tablespoons olive oil, plus more as needed

½ teaspoon flaky sea salt

½ teaspoon freshly ground pepper

1½ tablespoons chopped fresh dill

1½ pounds (675 g) boneless pork shoulder, cut into 1¼-inch (3-cm) cubes

Burhan's Onion-Parsley Salad (recipe follows), for serving

Grilled lemon halves, for garnish (optional)

In a food processor, combine the onion, ¼ cup (60 ml) of the water, and 1 tablespoon of the pomegranate concentrate with the olive oil, salt, and pepper and process until pureed. Transfer to a bowl and stir in the dill. Add the pork and stir to coat well. Cover and refrigerate overnight or up to 2 days.

About 1 hour before serving, thread the pork onto 4 metal skewers, each about 10 inches (25 cm) long (or thread the meat onto wood or bamboo skewers that have soaked in water for 1 to 2 hours); discard the marinade. Let the skewers stand at room temperature for 30 minutes.

Light a medium fire in a charcoal or gas grill, or position an oven rack about 5 inches (12.5 cm) from the heating element and preheat the broiler. Lightly oil the grill rack or oil the rack on a broiler pan.

In a small bowl, combine the remaining 3 tablespoons (45 ml) pomegranate concentrate and the remaining 2 tablespoons water.

Place the skewers on the grill rack directly over the fire, or on the broiler pan and slip under the broiler. Cook, turning the skewers

Serves to 6 as a meze, or 4 as a main dish

The pork marinates for at least overnight or up to 2 days.

recipe continues →

occasionally, until the pork is cooked and charred at the edges but still juicy within, about 15 minutes. Toward the end of cooking, brush on a bit of the diluted pomegranate concentrate to glaze.

Serve the skewers with the remaining diluted pomegranate concentrate for dipping and accompany with the onion-parsley salad and grilled lemon halves (if using).

Burhan's Onion-Parsley Salad

Very thinly slice a small red onion; you should have about ½ cup (55 g). In a colander or sieve, toss the slices with ½ teaspoon flaky sea salt and then let stand for 5 minutes to soften and reduce the harshness. Rinse and drain well. Transfer the onion to a bowl and toss with ½ cup (20 g) chopped fresh flat-leaf parsley and 1 teaspoon ground sumac. Serve within 30 minutes.

If heat at once

Adds 2 salsa

Sauté salsa after onion

Then the greens —
cold.
        broth —

Sometimes I mix up all
the greens —

Most tasty is the

—————————————

Hindibah

Kenan story

Used to think it
was sin to eat.
Children warned.

Araps Köjik
chopit cooks it for
Good for jajik

old garlic grows
steep rocks
always dangerous
to avoid them.
No became the
...taste so you

Yarpuz — for toothaches
        for headaches.
smell it crushed — opens nose

—————————————

When she was 6 or 7 years
take the cattle so she
to pass the time — she would
pick the greens.

plants enough for everyday

—————————————

Strong mint — mix in salad —
Yarpuz

—————————————

BR type of mallow with little leaves
Stems, broth, Steams
with red pepper

Forager

SAN FRANCISCO AND
THE MEDITERRANEAN
❖ 1994 to 1998

> "Aside from the greens offered in the typical American supermarkets there are more than eighty different edible greens that I believe will in time be cultivated and/or foraged for consumption. Just as we now often find wild mushrooms in stores, I foresee a time when purslane, nettles, mallow, lamb's quarters, and wild fennel will be on the produce counter along with mesclun, radicchio, frisée, arugula, braising mixes, and baby spinach leaves, which, though previously rare, are now thankfully commonplace."
>
> —Paula Wolfert in *Mediterranean Grains and Greens*

IN 2008, for a story in *Food & Wine* about an aristocratic Sicilian winemaker, I was given a recipe with a wild Mediterranean herb so obscure that the cook provided its Latin botanical name, *S. vulgaris*. The magazine ordinarily avoided ingredients no one could find. But suddenly, thanks to chef-foragers like Daniel Patterson and René Redzepi, wild greens were cool. I just needed to offer a store-bought substitute. For help, I e-mailed two Italy-based food writers and, for insurance, Paula. The first two were stumped. Paula responded within the hour.

"*Silene vulgaris*," she wrote. "It's called bladder campion in English. For a sub, you can use a combo of young spring greens like pea shoots, baby spinach and arugula. See Grains and Greens, p. 348."

OPPOSITE:
One of Paula's research notebooks from a trip to Turkey in the 1990s, with wild greens pressed into the pages

In the introduction to this book, I called Paula a messenger from a future we now inhabit. But that's not entirely true. *Mediterranean Grains and Greens*, her sixth book, published in 1998, describes a future that's not yet here: a world in which supermarkets stock wild greens such as hop shoots and stinging nettles along with kale and chard, and home cooks sort greens by flavor—sweet spinach, for example, versus peppery arugula—and then blend them the way the winemakers blend grapes.

"Blending salad and cooking greens may sound a bit like alchemy," she wrote, "but if done properly it can add great depth to leafy green dishes. I encourage you to experiment; mixing greens can be an endless pleasure."

In *Grains and Greens*, Paula pursued some of the most creative work of her career, especially in the field. In a wonderful merging of an old love with a new—her longtime romance with travel, and a revived passion for gardening (and weeds)—she "picked her way around the Mediterranean," as she put it, to uncover breathtaking variety in two humble plant categories. She took new liberties with her recipe titles, too, using whimsical turns of phrase like Best-Ever Bugulama, a Turkish pilaf (recipe, page 227) or Biblical Breakfast Burrito, essentially a Greek salad with feta rolled up into a durum flatbread slathered in *hrous*, a Tunisian pepper spread similar yet superior to harissa (hrous recipe, page 312).

In every introduction to her books she took a different stab at explaining her approach; in *Grains and Greens* she got closest to the truth. She disputed her reputation as an anthropologist, instead admitting that her work was more imaginative. "Even though I work hard to achieve authenticity in my recipes and never make dishes up out of my head, I don't consider myself a cultural anthropologist. Far from it," she wrote. Her approach—and the art of cooking—required too much "instinct" and "improvisation." In *Grains and Greens*, Paula performed a bold, book-length improvisation on two notes.

"This book was a turning point for me in many ways," she told me. "My earlier books are not as daring as I got in this book. But I knew enough now [that] I could really jump in and do things. This was like putting your hands in the earth."

But where the innovations of *Eastern Mediterranean* achieved widespread acceptance over time, amplified by a handful of food leaders, the improvisations of *Grains and Greens* still need a microphone.

It's possible Paula would never have written *Grains and Greens* had she not moved to San Francisco. In the Bay Area—the most Mediterranean of all US cities—she saw big changes afoot in the grains and greens Americans would soon eat, changes that would inspire her to write the book. Yet for all its Tangier-esque produce and eccentric characters, she didn't like the city at first. In December 1994, Paula left the East Coast, "kicking and screaming," as she told the *San Francisco Chronicle*. Bill used the proceeds from his best-selling crime novels to lease a stunning prewar apartment high on Russian Hill, with gorgeous views of San Francisco Bay to the north and east and a roomy kitchen.

Paula loved the views. She also felt a little better about living on the West Coast after her son, Nicholas, moved to Los Angeles in 1997 to work in the movie business. (Her daughter, Leila, then a wine wholesaler, still lived on the East Coast, in the Hudson Valley north of New York City, where Paula visited her regularly.)

She struggled to feel at home in San Francisco, however. She didn't like walking the hills (she always hated exercise). And she had no idea what to make of the food world, which felt almost *too* friendly compared to cutthroat New York. "Everyone was so *nice*," she recalled, still bewildered. She reunited with old friends Alice Waters and Judy Rodgers (whom she met when Rodgers was a teenaged apprentice in Southwest France) and became close with food writers like Peggy Knickerbocker. In 1995, *San Francisco* magazine wrote, "Paula Wolfert moving to San Francisco (as she did last year) is like Barry Bonds being traded to the Giants—a veritable coup for the home team."

With San Francisco friends, including Alice Waters and Peggy Knickerbocker (second and third from right, respectively)

But for once she felt uneasy about all of the attention. She wasn't sure who liked her because she was Paula Wolfert and who liked her for *her*. She told *Boston Globe* food editor Sheryl Julian, "When you live in New York, you come up in the trenches shoulder to shoulder. In San Francisco, it takes a long time to make a best friend."

She quickly chose a new book topic, one that required many more visits to her friends across the Mediterranean. But the topic had roots in San Francisco's exploding supply of organic produce. During the second half of the 1990s, the number of farmers' markets around the country shot up. The organic-driven supermarket chain Whole Foods expanded its reach; its first San Francisco outpost was just a few blocks from Paula's apartment. To save her from walking the steep hills, her new friend Knickerbocker gave her rides to Whole Foods during the week, and to the pioneering new Ferry Building farmers' market on Saturdays. Seeing all of this easy urban access to such good food, Paula predicted Americans could soon take on two next-level ingredients: wild greens and alternative grains.

Grains made a certain amount of sense. In 1994, William Rice wrote in the *Chicago Tribune*, "After years of going against the grain, so to speak, potato-loving Americans are being tempted to try grains with such names as couscous, bulgur, millet, barley, polenta, quinoa and amaranth as well as rices such as Italy's arborio, India's basmati, Spain's Valencia and the Orient's jasmine."

Greens, too, had gained cachet for their nutritional qualities— particularly bitter leafy ones. But wild ones?

"Weeds are the coming thing," Paula insisted to a Connecticut publication in 1994.

In a literal sense she was right: more organic produce meant fewer herbicides, which meant farmers had more weeds on their hands, many of them edible. But could they become trendy?

For evidence of a coming trend, in San Francisco she could point to Rodgers, who bought wild greens for Zuni Café and connected Paula to her source. Or to Chez Panisse, where her new friend, chef Catherine Brandel, was also an enthusiastic forager. Paula also remembered urging on the trend herself at the Ferry Building, where one Saturday she spoke through a bullhorn to implore farmers to bring mallow, purslane, nettles, and other weeds to the market for her (and everyone else) to buy. To add enticement, she spoke and wrote about their nutrition, as well. "The best part of the Mediterranean diet is the weeds," she told the *San Francisco Chronicle* in 1995. "That's why these people are so strong. Purslane and nettles and amaranth and goosefoot—these are the future greens, and they're delicious."

Fran McCullough, her former editor, came up with the book's title, though she was not its editor. "She knew where the cutting edge was," McCullough said. "Grains and greens were very popular at the time. She was doing it through gritted teeth, but she *really* wanted to have a big commercial hit. To me the idea seemed perfect, where everything was headed."

Paula does not remember wanting a hit. "There is something wrong with me," she said. "I never did the right things to make money. I could have created a product, a line of cookware, or gone on television. I just did the things that interested me." Whatever her motivations for picking the initial topics, the book soon lost any potential for mass appeal as it traveled down the rabbit hole of Paula's mind.

Grains had interested her since she discovered couscous. Wild foods also pop up like weeds along the path of her career. She bought her first wild mushrooms in the Tangier markets in 1959; she cooked her first purslane and mallow with Madame Jaidi in 1972 to prepare a wild greens jam (recipe, page 90). In the 1980s, she first studied foraging with the best: chef Michel Bras, among the earliest haute chefs to "pick" for his restaurant. She later honed her skills at her and Bill's vacation home in Martha's Vineyard and in Connecticut.

But she didn't think she wanted to dedicate a portion of a book to wild greens until she had her first Mediterranean foraging adventure in 1991. While researching *Eastern Mediterranean*, in a village outside Gaziantep, Ayfer Ünsal introduced her to Zeliha Gungoren, a gifted Armenian Turkish cook who announced they would pick lunch in a field by her house. To Paula, the field looked as barren as the moon (see picture). But Gungoren, who had looked after her family flock as a child, had learned to forage from fellow shepherds. Paula wrote in *Saveur*, "Soon my notebook is filled with pressed specimens—corn poppies, wild mustard, nettles, mallow, and more." Gungoren transformed their haul into a dozen dishes, including a robustly flavored *bugulama*, a warm grain salad (recipe, page 227). Paula could hardly believe that so many flavors could spring from such seemingly bare terrain. She became obsessed with learning all she could about edible weeds. "I went on a greens binge," she said.

Paula's 1991 snapshot of her first foraging adventure with Zeliha Gungoren, outside Gaziantep, Turkey.

From 1994 to 1998, Paula picked her way across Greece, Israel, Italy, Turkey, Tunisia, and Spain, tapping her old friends for new greens (and grains) intel. She timed many of her trips to coincide with Oldways conferences, making her arrangements to do her field work before, during, and after the events to take maximum advantage of the free airplane tickets.

In Greece, Paula first learned about the Mediterranean practice of blending greens for richer flavors. Aglaia Kremezi, her research partner, didn't have much experience with weeds, having grown up in Athens. (Paula says that Kremezi's knowledge has since surpassed her own.) When she learned of Paula's interests, Kremezi tracked down Mirsini Lambraki, a wild greens expert who took them foraging in Crete. There, Lambraki introduced them to the Mediterranean tradition of apron greens, something Paula later found in Turkey and Italy. Before heading out to pick, home cooks (mostly women) donned three-pocketed aprons so they could easily sort their finds by flavor: one pocket for sweet greens, one for peppery, one for bitter (or for roots and mushrooms). They often cooked their blends into stuffings or sauces. These blends gave Paula the idea that all greens, wild or cultivated, should be mixed by taste. She included suggestions in the book.

In Israel, Paula had her ultimate foraging experiences. On a press trip to Jerusalem, she met Moshe Basson, a chef known for modern takes on ancient Middle Eastern recipes. Having foraged since he was a boy, Basson took Paula into the hillsides around Jerusalem to pick wild purslane. She liked the greens so much, she engineered a return about a year later in the early spring, when wild greens peak.

Sara Hatan foraging with her flock, photographed in Israel by Paula

On her second trip, she heard her first warning about the potential unpopularity of the topic, even in the Mediterranean. On a farm in the Galilee, a Kurdish Iraqi woman named Sara Hatan took Paula picking at dusk, a journey during which they worked their way through a dazzling profusion of over thirty edible weeds, including a patch of sow thistle so thick that Paula named it "sow thistle alley."

"I was in a state of bucolic exhilaration," she wrote. Hatan told her, however, that even Israelis weren't interested in eating wild greens anymore—for poignant reasons. "Mallow and nettles had kept both Israelis and Arabs from starvation during the austere wartime period following Israeli independence," Paula wrote. Eating them reminded them of those bitter years.

Undaunted, Paula forged ahead. Recognizing that it was impractical for cooks to rely solely on foraged wild greens, in the book Paula introduced both lesser-known varietals and new ways to cook store-bought greens. She urged readers to plant Lacinato (Tuscan) kale, which was not yet available in stores. She predicted that the variety was "a vegetable success story waiting to happen, much like radicchio a few years back." (She was correct.) She found traditional but unorthodox cooking methods, such as salting and massaging chopped greens for *bugulama*, or presalting greens to concentrate their flavors before cooking them in an unusual northern Greek sprinkle pie (recipe, page 228).

Ever eager for new discoveries, Paula looked for little known but delicious grain dishes. Since everyone knew about paella from Valencia, she asked Spanish food expert Janet Mendel to help her research the more obscure *arroces* (rice dishes) from the nearby coastal region of Alicante.

In Italy, polenta turned into an obsession. While in the Marche, Paula became enamored with the use of polenta boards, the tradition of pouring just-cooked soft polenta out onto long planks, then topping it with a sauce. Although the porridge-like cornmeal dish traditionally requires long stirring, in San Francisco she stumbled on a no-stir, oven-baked polenta (recipe, page 237) that brings out the corn flavor of the cornmeal. In a classic example of her thoroughness, she even studied an American equivalent with an expert home cook from North Carolina, James Villas's mother.

"Mother said, 'Don't tell me about polenta, honey. In the South we just call that corn mush,'" Villas recalled. "Well, that intrigued Paula, and she immediately had to know everything about corn mush. That's the closest I ever knew Paula to come to American food."

In Tunisia, Paula finally learned to hand-roll couscous (recipe, page 109). Despite her reputation as the queen of couscous, she'd never learned this in Morocco because, she was told, it was only rolled (and sun-dried for storage) once a year, when the semolina was freshest. She also saw little point to including the method in *Couscous*, as it required two sizes of semolina grains, neither then available in the United States. By the mid-1990s, however, two of her favorite mail-order food retailers, Sahadi's and Kalustyan's, carried both sizes, so

Giving a couscous-rolling demonstration at the Culinary Institute of America at Greystone in Napa, California

she began teaching classes on hand-rolled couscous in San Francisco and New York.

In Morocco for an Oldways conference in 1994, Paula barely recognized heavily developed Tangier. She visited the old villa where she and Bill had lived, only to despair that her garden had been stripped of its many fruit trees. But at a dinner arranged for her at the home of the grandson of El Glaoui, the famed pasha of Marrakech, she enjoyed the best Moroccan meal of her life—including a pigeon tagine with hand-peeled grapes—which she described in a 1995 story for *Saveur*.

There is a frantic quality to Paula's late-1990s travels, as though she sensed these might be her last adventures. The book, too, displays a manic quality that suggests a race to squeeze in everything she could. It is possible she had begun to experience early Alzheimer's symptoms; friends say her anxieties peaked in these years. She turned sixty in 1991 and started to regard her mortality as a burdensome inconvenience.

"I need five more lifetimes to accomplish everything I want to do," she told *San Francisco* magazine.

To impose a little reader-friendly organization, Susan Friedland, her editor at HarperCollins, suggested they alphabetize the grains and greens. But Paula stood her ground. She wanted everything in the order she had assembled it, according to her interests.

Paula photographed in *People* magazine, blanketed by greens

"I lost that battle, but it was her name on the book," Friedland said. "The subject matter was very ahead of its time."

Had it been published today—now that purslane and nettles are available in high-end supermarkets, foraging has become fashionable, and many people have gone gluten-free, creating a new market for alternative grains—the book might have become an overnight sensation. But in 1998, the two topics still seemed so obscure that the book provoked genuine frustration, even among her most devoted fans.

In *Saveur*, for example, magazine cofounder Dorothy Kalins wrote, "I wonder, as I confront her deceptively simple new title . . . if focusing on just two kinds of ingredients isn't like trying to write a novel without the vowels? But no. Wolfert's book is more like culinary science fiction, where you encounter an entire cast of alien ingredients."

Other reviews poked fun at the book, at how it all but made a farce of Paula's obsessive ways. *People* magazine justifiably warned readers, "Although she

coaxes recipes for primal dishes like Cretan Snail and Fennel Stew out of a friend's deaf Greek aunt, Wolfert's tantalizing dishes for edible weeds require knowledge of foraging, and the book is not illustrated."

In a more favorable review in *Slate* by Nicholas Lemann titled "The Diva," the subtitle read, "Paula Wolfert is very high-maintenance, but she's worth it." Lemann wrote, "The sense-memories that linger after a week of cooking from *Mediterranean Grains and Greens* are of an intensity, a range, and an unusualness of flavor that you just don't get from more conventional cookbooks." At the same time, "the ratio of Wolfert advantages (daring, refusal to compromise, authenticity, unconventionality) to Wolfert disadvantages (her tendency to induce an overwhelming feeling of 'why bother?') is as high here as it has ever been."

Today the book is out of print. But it shouldn't be. It is a wonderful expression of Paula's passions, and its time feels nearly here. It may seem farfetched, but hop shoots are now available every spring in Oregon. The day does not seem far off when Whole Foods will stock them, if only in their freezers.

When *Mediterranean Grains and Greens* appeared in 1998, Paula seems to have worked more aggressively than usual to promote her ideas. For about a year and a half, she wrote articles, gave talks and hosted dinners, and introduced food editors and chefs to the flavors of wild and blended greens. She still cooks with them at home. But in her work, as always, her curiosity got the best of her. She soon moved on. She had a new territory to explore: Sonoma.

She and Bill had bought a weekend house there not long after moving to San Francisco. It had everything she'd loved about Tangier: a warm, almost Mediterranean climate with near-constant sun, amazingly fresh local produce, a small plot to grow her own vegetables (and weeds), and a cast of oddball characters. In the warmth of its embrace, she felt ready to try a personal first, something trailblazing in these quickening, Internet-driven times: slowing down.

Six Ways of Looking at Grains and Greens

Starting with a spare yet surprising salad of shredded fresh mint and grated egg and ending with a polenta so distilled to its cornmeal essence that you don't even stir it, these dishes showcase six of the most unorthodox but memorable ways to cook grains and greens that Paula uncovered as she picked her way around the Mediterranean in the 1990s.

TURKEY

Mint and Egg Salad

Bulgur with Blended Greens

GREECE

Sprinkle Pie

TUNISIA

Couscous with Greens

EGYPT

Megadarra

ITALY

No-Stir Polenta

Mint and Egg Salad

This is nothing like your grandmother's egg salad. Instead of a heavy mayonnaise dressing, eggs are tossed with vibrant slivered mint leaves and a light dressing of olive oil and lemon. What makes this salad unforgettable is Paula grates the eggs, so they are ethereally light. (As her longtime editor Fran McCullough notes, grating also makes traditional egg salad velvety smooth.) Paula offered this recipe as an accompaniment to *köfte*, Turkish grilled meat skewers. But it's so good, it's been doubled here to be enjoyed as a stand-alone or with a green salad as a light meal.

---

4 large eggs

1 to 2 cups (30 to 60 g) slivered mint leaves (depending on the intensity of the mint)

1 cup (90 g) thinly sliced green onions, white and green parts

2 teaspoons mild red pepper flakes, preferably Marash

2 tablespoons fruity extra-virgin olive oil

Juice of ½ lemon

Flaky sea salt

Serves 4 as a first course or side dish

In a saucepan, combine the eggs with water to cover by 2 inches (5 cm) and bring to a boil over high heat. Lower the heat to medium-high and cook for 6 minutes. Drain and place under cool running water to cool. Peel the eggs.

Using the large holes of a box grater, and working over a large bowl, grate the eggs. Add the mint, green onions, and red pepper flakes and mix well. In a small bowl, whisk together the olive oil and lemon juice to taste, then drizzle over the egg mixture and toss to coat lightly and evenly. Season with salt. Serve at room temperature or slightly chilled.

Bulgur with Blended Greens

Lemony, garlicky, peppery—this rich yet nutritious Turkish dish infuses the cracked wheat with the intense flavor of greens by massaging together the uncooked grain, greens, chopped onion, and seasonings before cooking. Paula perfected this *bugulama* (literally "steamed food") in collaboration with Turkish food writer Ayfer Ünsal and translator Filiz Hösükoğlu, working from a recipe by their friend Gülay Karsligil and called it "Best-Ever Bugulama." To heighten the flavors of the greens, less onion and garlic is used here than in Paula's original.

---

1 pound (450 g) flavorful leafy greens, such as Russian kale, Swiss chard, beet and/or turnip greens, or a combination (see notes), stemmed and finely slivered

1 cup (140 g) chopped yellow onion (1 medium onion)

1 cup (150 g) coarse-grind bulgur

¼ cup (60 ml) extra-virgin olive oil

2 or 3 garlic cloves, finely crushed with 1 teaspoon flaky sea salt

2 to 3 teaspoons red pepper paste, such as hrous (page 312) or harissa (optional)

½ teaspoon freshly ground black pepper

¼ teaspoon mild red pepper flakes, preferably Marash, or more to taste

Flaky sea salt

About ½ cup (120 ml) water

1 to 2 thinly sliced green onions, white and green parts, for garnish

Lemon wedges, for garnish

In a large, deep saucepan with a tight-fitting lid, combine the greens, onion, bulgur, olive oil, garlic paste, pepper paste (if using), black pepper, and red pepper flakes. Season generously with salt. Using your hands, massage well to moisten the bulgur with the greens. Add the water a few tablespoons at a time, massaging it in between additions, until the mixture is moist but not wet; you may need more or less than the ½ cup (120 ml).

Lay a paper towel over the greens, cover the pan with the lid, and place the pan over medium-low heat. Cook until the bulgur is just tender, about 30 minutes. Serve hot, at room temperature or cold, garnished with the green onions and lemon wedges.

Serves 4 as a first course or side dish

⏱ This pilaf is fast enough for a weeknight supper and reheats well for a work lunch the next day.

NOTE Paula typically makes this with Russian kale, but in Turkey she also had it made with young grape leaves and corn poppy leaves. She wrote, "A wild edible such as corn poppy, which you can grow from seed and harvest before it flowers, will impart a sweet buttery flavor with undertones of hazelnut. In southeastern Turkey, it's the green of choice for this dish." Experiment with fresh, local greens.

Sprinkle Pie

Although this Greek pie has all the savory richness of quiche, it's both egg-free and gluten-free. It gets its intensity from both a blend of greens and an unusual cooking technique. The greens are massaged with salt, then left to stand for about an hour, and finally squeezed to extract excess moisture, a technique that intensifies their flavor. They are then blended with feta cheese and encased in an equally remarkable and unorthodox "crust": a light sprinkling of cornmeal moistened in the liquid released by the greens. Typical of Paula's most radical recipes, it shouldn't work, and yet it does.

---

2 pounds (900 g) leeks (about 5), white and light green parts quartered lengthwise, then cut crosswise ½ inch (1.25 cm) thick

Flaky sea salt and freshly ground black pepper

1¾ pounds (800 g) spinach leaves

2 small handfuls each of at least two different greens (cultivated greens such as arugula, young Swiss chard, baby dandelion greens, lamb's quarters, or sorrel, or wild greens such as purslane, mallow, or nettles; about 2 ounces | 60 g total)

3 tablespoons (45 ml) extra-virgin olive oil, plus more for greasing

12 ounces (350 g) sheep's milk feta, preferably Bulgarian, crumbled

2 tablespoons snipped fresh dill (optional)

⅓ cup (55 g) fine stone-ground yellow cornmeal

Serves 6 to 8 as a first course or light lunch

The leeks and greens can be cooked and refrigerated overnight before assembling the pie.

Put the leeks in a large sieve and sprinkle with 1½ teaspoons salt. Using your hands, massage the salt into the leeks. Let stand for 1 hour, then rinse under cool running water. Working in small batches, squeeze the leeks tightly in paper towels to extract as much moisture as possible, capturing the released liquid in a small bowl. Set aside ¼ cup (60 ml) of the liquid for the pie; reserve the remainder for stock or soup if desired.

Meanwhile, shred the spinach and greens and any tender stems; discard any tough stems. Put in a sieve or bowl, sprinkle with 1 teaspoon salt, toss well, and let stand for 45 minutes. Rinse under cool running water. Working in small batches, squeeze the greens tightly in paper towels to extract as much moisture as possible, capturing the released liquid in a small bowl. Add ¼ cup (60 ml) of the liquid to the leek liquid; reserve the remainder for stock or soup if desired.

recipe continues →

In a 10-inch (25-cm) frying pan, heat 1½ tablespoons of the olive oil over medium heat. Add the leeks, cover partially, and cook until they are just heated through, about 2 minutes. Transfer to a large plate or sheet pan and let cool. Add the remaining 1½ tablespoons oil to the frying pan, and when it is hot, add the greens and cook, stirring, until the leaves turn bright green, about 2 minutes. Transfer to the plate or pan with the leeks and let cool. (At this point, the greens, leeks, and the reserved greens liquid can be covered and refrigerated separately overnight.)

Preheat the oven to 400°F (200°C). In a small saucepan, gently warm the reserved greens liquid over low heat. In a large bowl, combine the leeks, greens, feta, and dill (if using) and mix well. Season with salt and pepper.

Lightly grease a 9-inch (23-cm) round or 8-inch (20-cm) square baking dish, preferably nonstick, with olive oil. Add ¼ cup (40 g) of the cornmeal to the prepared dish and then rotate the dish to coat the bottom and sides evenly. Using your fingers or a fork, lightly sprinkle the cornmeal with just enough of the warm greens liquid to dampen it. Gently scrape the leek-cheese mixture into the cornmeal-lined dish and smooth the surface with a rubber spatula or moist palms. Sprinkle the remaining cornmeal in an even layer on top. Using dry hands, lightly press the cornmeal into the mixture. Sprinkle the cornmeal with just enough of the remaining greens liquid to dampen it lightly.

Bake the pie until the cornmeal forms a crisp, lightly browned crust, about 1 hour. Transfer the pie to a wire rack and sprinkle with a few drops of tap water. Let cool for at least 20 minutes before cutting into squares. Serve warm or at room temperature.

NOTE Greens that have been salted, rinsed, and squeezed dry, as they are in this recipe, are also lovely sautéed in olive oil with sliced garlic and mild red pepper flakes (preferably Aleppo or Marash), drizzled with balsamic vinegar, and then served over pasta or No-Stir Polenta (recipe, page 237).

Couscous with Greens

It may seem sacrilegious for Paula, a renowned Moroccan expert, to admit, but this Tunisian couscous is her all-time favorite version. And no wonder: fragrant, smoky, and tangy, it hits on all notes. Called *kuski ffawwar*, it is simpler than traditional Moroccan couscous, as the grains are steamed only once, and a powerful mix of steamed greens and spices are folded into the couscous as it cooks. She learned it on a trip to the Tunisian island of Djerba in 1993, and received guidance on polishing it from Abderrazak Haouari, one of her favorite chefs in Tunisia (or anywhere). Because it does not have the traditional Moroccan broth, it should be made with instant (not hand-rolled) couscous. It is also a bit on the dry side, so it is tastiest served with glasses of cold, tangy buttermilk (which tastes a little like thinned yogurt).

---

8 ounces (225 g) fresh dill leaves or fennel fronds, or a combination (8 to 10 packed cups)

8 ounces (225 g) fresh flat-leaf parsley leaves (8 to 10 packed cups)

1 handful (½ ounce | 15 g) of celery leaves (½ cup loosely packed)

1 handful (½ ounce | 15 g) of carrot tops (½ cup loosely packed)

4 ounces (115 g) green onions, white and light green parts, sliced crosswise ¼ inch (6 mm) thick

1 small leek, including light green parts (4 ounces | 115 g), sliced crosswise ¼ inch (6 mm) thick

½ cup (120 ml) extra-virgin olive oil

1 cup (140 g) chopped yellow onion (1 medium onion)

3 tablespoons (50 g) tomato paste or Tomato Magic (page 309)

8 large garlic cloves, peeled (2 cloves crushed, 6 cloves left whole)

2 teaspoons sweet smoked paprika (pimentón de la Vera dulce)

2 teaspoons flaky sea salt

2 teaspoons ground coriander or tabil (see note)

1 teaspoon ground caraway

1½ to 2 teaspoons mild red pepper flakes, preferably Aleppo or Marash

2 cups (480 ml) water

2½ cups (1 pound | 450 g) instant couscous

1 fresh hot green chile, such as serrano, seeded and minced

1 red bell pepper, cut lengthwise into sixths and seeded

Buttermilk, for serving

Roughly chop the dill, parsley, celery leaves, and carrot tops. Fit a large pot with a steamer basket, add water to the pot to just below the base of the basket, and bring the water to a boil over high heat. Add the dill, parsley, celery leaves, carrot tops, green onions, and leek. Cover and steam for 30 minutes. (If all the greens won't fit

Serves 6 to 8 as a main course

recipe continues →

under the lid, divide them in half, steam half until wilted, about
3 minutes, and then add the remaining half.) Remove from the
heat, uncover, and let cool. Squeeze out the excess moisture. Set
aside. Leave the water in the pot.

In a 10- or 12-inch (25- or 30-cm) frying pan, heat the olive oil over
medium heat. Add the onion and cook, stirring, until starting to
soften, about 3 minutes. Stir in the tomato paste and cook, stirring,
until the paste glistens, about 2 minutes. Stir in the crushed garlic,
paprika, salt, coriander, caraway, and red pepper flakes, mixing
well. Lower the heat to medium-low and cook, stirring, until the
mixture is quite fragrant and well blended, about 1 minute. Add
1 cup (240 ml) of the water, cover, and cook for 15 minutes.

Meanwhile, bring the water in the steamer pot back to a boil,
adding more water if needed to return it to its original level. Line
the steamer basket with muslin or cheesecloth.

Add the couscous to the frying pan and stir until thoroughly coated
with the spice mixture. Add the steamed greens mixture and fresh
chile and stir until well mixed. Scrape the contents of the frying
pan into the steamer basket. Using tongs, tuck in the bell pepper
pieces and the whole garlic cloves. Cover and steam until the
couscous is tender to the bite, about 30 minutes.

Retrieve the whole garlic cloves and red pepper slices and reserve.
Turn out the couscous onto a warmed large serving platter. Using
a long fork, break up any lumps. Sprinkle the remaining 1 cup
(240 ml) water over the couscous and fluff with the fork just until
incorporated. Taste and adjust the seasoning with salt and red
pepper flakes if needed. Tent with foil. Let stand in a warm place
for 10 minutes before serving.

Decorate the couscous with the red pepper slices in a star pattern
and place the whole peeled garlic cloves in the center on top. Serve
with glasses of buttermilk.

NOTE Tabil is a traditional Tunisian spice blend; to make
your own, combine 1 tablespoon ground coriander and
1 teaspoon ground caraway with ¼ teaspoon each ground
red pepper flakes (such as Marash or Aleppo), curry powder,
and garlic powder (optional).

Megadarra

The humble combination of lentils, rice, and fried onions shouldn't taste this good. This Middle Eastern dish has become so popular that many versions of it have lately appeared in magazines and cookbooks. This one is the best. It is Paula's take on a recipe from one of her heroes, Claudia Roden, who included it in *A Book of Middle Eastern Food*, published in 1968. Paula ups the flavor by seasoning the lentils and rice with a whopping 2 teaspoons freshly ground black pepper, plus fried onions and the onion cooking oil, which give the vegetarian dish all the richness and floral brightness of steak au poivre.

1 yellow onion (about 9 ounces | 270 g)

1½ cups (300 g) brown or green lentils, picked over, rinsed, and drained

4 cups (1 l) water

1 cup (180 g) long-grain white rice

2 teaspoons freshly ground black pepper

Flaky sea salt

½ cup (120 ml) extra-virgin olive oil

Svaneti salt (page 313, optional)

Turkish Yogurt Sauce, for serving (page 315)

Crushed dried mint leaves and mild red pepper flakes such as Marash, for garnish (optional)

Using a sharp knife, a mandoline, or the slicing blade of a food processor, slice the onion lengthwise ⅛ inch (3 mm) thick. Squeeze the onions dry in a kitchen towel. Line a sheet pan with a second clean kitchen towel. Spread the onions in a single layer on the second towel and let stand at room temperature for 1 hour.

Serves 6 to 8

Meanwhile, in a saucepan, combine the lentils and water and bring to a boil over high heat. Lower the heat to medium and simmer for 10 minutes; the lentils should still be slightly firm.

While the lentils are cooking, rinse the rice in several changes of water until the water runs almost clear; drain well.

When the lentils are ready, add the rice, pepper, a pinch of sea salt, and hot water to cover if needed. Raise the heat to high and return to a boil. Turn down the heat to low, cover, and simmer until the rice and lentils are tender, about 20 minutes. Remove from heat and let cool slightly.

Meanwhile, in a 10- to 12-inch (25- to 30-cm) frying pan, heat the oil over medium-high heat until an onion slice sizzles when

recipe continues →

dropped into the hot oil. Line a plate or sheet pan with at least three layers of paper towels. Add the onion slices to the hot oil and fry, stirring occasionally and lowering the heat as needed, until they are a rich golden brown but not burnt, about 15 minutes.

Using a slotted spoon or spider, transfer the onion slices to the paper towel–lined plate or pan to drain; reserve the cooking oil. Season the onion slices lightly with a pinch of salt. After about 5 minutes, gently transfer the onions to the second layer of paper towels and discard the top layer. Let stand until crisp, at least 30 minutes or up to 1 hour.

When the rice and lentils are ready, using a long fork or chopsticks (a spoon will smash the lentils and make the mixture pasty), lightly fluff the mixture, cover partially, and let stand. When the onions have finished drying, add half of the onion slices and all of their cooking oil and fold in gently. Let the stand, uncovered, for 10 minutes.

Fluff once more before serving. Serve warm or at room temperature, piled in a mound on a large platter or in small, deep bowls. Sprinkle with the remaining onions and if using, Svaneti salt, dried mint, and red pepper flakes. Pass the yogurt sauce at the table.

NOTE Drying the onion slices before frying ensures they will turn out crispy. But on a rainy or very humid day, they will never crisp up. Don't worry—even with less than shatteringly crisp onions, this dish tastes wonderful.

No-Stir Polenta

You'll never stir polenta again.

---

2 tablespoons unsalted butter or olive oil, plus more for greasing

2 cups (320 g) polenta, preferably organic and stone-ground

7 to 10 cups (1.6 to 2.5 l) water or a mixture of water and whole milk (see notes)

2 teaspoons flaky sea salt

Preheat the oven to 350°F (180°C). Grease a 4-quart (4-l) ovenproof saucepan, a 12-inch (30-cm) heavy ovenproof deep-sided frying pan or cazuela, or a 9-by-13-inch (23-by-33-cm) earthenware, ceramic, or glass baking dish. Add the polenta, water, salt, and butter and stir until blended. (As Paula wrote in the original recipe, "It will separate, but don't worry—it won't come together for more than half the cooking time.")

Serves 6 to 10

Bake uncovered for 1 hour and 20 minutes. Using a long fork, stir the polenta, season with more salt if needed, and bake for 10 minutes longer. The polenta should be tender, fluffy, and glossy. Remove from the oven and let rest for 5 minutes.

To serve, pour onto a wooden polenta board or pizza peel, into a buttered bowl, or simply bring to the table in its baking vessel.

NOTES To vary the consistency of the cooked polenta, simply adjust the amount of liquid. Paula offered a range for the liquid measurement so you may dial in your preference. To achieve firm, medium-soft, or soft polenta, respectively, use 7 cups (1.75 l), 8 cups (2 l), or 10 cups (2.5 l) of water or a combination of water and milk.

Paula prefers a wide pan because the greater surface area coaxes out more polenta flavor by toasting the grain as it cooks. Her favorite pan was a 12-inch (30-cm) "Peking" pan, a wok developed by Joyce Chen.

The recipe can be halved, though leftovers are arguably the best part. To halve the recipe, use a 10-inch (25-cm) baking dish or 2- to 3-quart (2- to 3-l) saucepan. Reduce the initial cooking time to 45 minutes.

Cover and refrigerate leftover polenta for up to 3 days. To make polenta cakes, cut into pieces, brush with butter or oil, then sauté or grill.

Confidence in the Kitchen

SONOMA ❧ 1998 to 2003

> "By the time I got to *Slow Mediterranean Kitchen*, I knew that I had found my voice. That's when I really found out how much I loved cooking."
>
> —Paula Wolfert in an interview with the author, December 2015

WHEN FRIENDS ASK ME to recommend a first Paula Wolfert cookbook, I ask them what kind of adventure they want to take. If they need weeknight ideas, I recommend *Eastern Mediterranean*. If they prefer to entertain, I recommend *The Slow Mediterranean Kitchen*. It's both her most complex and her simplest book. In it, she explores the idea of time as a flavor enhancer: the hours a good dish takes to cook on its own and to rest once it's done. The book is jammed with her favorite long-cooking classics, and many of the recipes are so hands-free and forgiving, they make throwing a dinner party a cinch.

Nothing about Paula's first sixty years was slow. But in 1998, she decided to pull back. It's possible she felt a need to retreat in the face of early, undiagnosed Alzheimer's symptoms, such as her difficulties processing new information, like learning a new language. But she was also nearing retirement age. And she wanted something new.

Her Mediterranean world was disappearing. Her beloved women home cooks no longer wanted to cook as much. In 1998, she told writer Patricia Mack, "Maybe I romanticize this mother-to-daughter thing. It's a beautiful vision of mine—women learning from one another and sharing the food," she said. "The truth is, it's pretty

OPPOSITE: Thumbtacked behind Paula's desk in Sonoma is her memory wall, a collage of favorite photos of friends, family, and places she has visited.

boring. In many places the lives of women are hard. Do you think it's fun to spend your entire summer preparing food for winter and in the winter sewing clothes for the summer? Today young people don't want to do that. The change isn't all bad."

Paula's fame was also fading. The American food scene had come so far and had embraced so many of her discoveries that it now took them for granted. A 2000 *New York Times Magazine* story on Aleppo pepper left a particular sting for failing to mention her, even though Paula had introduced the pepper in a 1990 article for the same publication. She called the author, Amanda Hesser, with whom she was friendly.

"I realized as I was telling her, 'Hey, Aleppo pepper, I was writing about that ten years ago!' that I shouldn't have opened my mouth. That was a mistake on my part," Paula told me. "They'd forgotten how much I'd done. I wasn't going to go out and fight for it; I couldn't do it anymore. I could no longer sleep on anyone's floor."

But she didn't run away in indignation. After twenty years immersed in the food world, she became truly curious about what life might be like away from it. Now the most exotic people in the world, the most "other," were her new Sonoma neighbors who had never heard of her. "Nothing against my friends in San Francisco, but I wanted to be out of touch," she said. "In Sonoma, nobody knew who the hell I was. For some reason, that *fascinated* me."

Bill and Paula had bought the Sonoma house for weekend getaways, but Paula increasingly wanted to stay there during the week. Since Bill still wanted to spend his weeks in San Francisco, she needed a means to commute there by herself. So she made her best, last effort to learn to drive. In San Francisco she called Ann's Driving School, aimed at women, founded by a former FedEx driver named Judy Lundblad who specialized in "panic-stricken New Yorkers," according to the *New York Times*. Although Lundblad had taught since 1994, she had never worked with anyone with Paula's vision problems. I asked her what it was about Paula's eyesight that had always prevented her from learning to drive.

"Oncoming traffic would be so scary for her because she couldn't judge it," Lundblad explained. Paula was also distractible, Lundblad said, laughing. "She'd be so excited talking to me about her cooking, she wouldn't be concentrating on the driving. I'd try to bring her back to task, but I was interested in her cooking, too. So it was complicated at times."

Sometimes Lundblad let Paula drive the dual-control car six miles from Russian Hill out Geary Street to stock up on pomegranate molasses and other necessities at an eastern European market in the

Outer Richmond (almost the entire length of San Francisco, which is only seven miles square). After two years of lessons, Paula mustered the courage to take a driving test. She failed—but decided it was for the best. During the week, when Bill returned to the city, Paula simply stayed behind. By that time she had made enough friends in Sonoma to give her rides.

She also didn't need to leave the house much. In Sonoma she began to savor the life she had already lived. In her new office, she tacked up six decades of her favorite photographs behind her desk, assembling them in a six-foot collage she called her Memory Wall: images of her grandparents on their New Jersey farm, Madame Jaidi, André Daguin and his fellow musketeers, Ayfer and Aglaia, even the German chefs she had consulted with in the Philippines for George Lang in 1976. She also lined her office and the hall with the fifteen-hundred-volume cookbook library she had accumulated over her career.

Bill had paid for the house, but Paula treated herself to a dream kitchen. In her past homes, she had always felt cramped while cooking. She'd always wanted a kitchen island so big, she said, "I couldn't reach the center."

An architect helped her unite the house's small galley kitchen and adjacent two rooms into an airy, sloped-ceilinged space so peaceful it could pass as a church altar. The six-sided kitchen island was "as big as a queen-size bed," she boasted. She set out all of her mortars, pestles, and scissors. She hid her knives and other less romantic necessities, like sheet pans and measuring cups, in deep drawers and cupboards. Open shelves that encircled the room displayed her favorite clay pots in another kind of memory wall, as each pot reminded her of different adventures. Her collection, which had ballooned into the hundreds, included Moroccan tagines, French *daubières* (potbellied vessels for simmering hearty meat-vegetable *daubes* or stews), Turkish *guveçs* (squat pots used for cooking the eponymous vegetable casserole), and more.

She kept the previous owners' refrigerator and bought an everyday range, ovens, and dishwasher, so she would be testing recipes on the same type of appliances the average home cook uses. But she splurged on a waist-high fireplace large enough to accommodate a Tuscan grill and a Florentine motorized rotisserie. In a story about the renovation for *Metropolitan Home*, food writer Janet Fletcher wrote, "remembering how a guest had to hold a flashlight for her while she cooked paella in Alice Waters's hearth, she installed recessed lights."

As Fletcher noted, a traditional kitchen designer would wince at the inefficient work triangle (Paula had to circle her massive island to get to the sink or stove from the refrigerator). But efficiency was the last thing from Paula's mind.

"I'm not a cook who stands at the stove and does a lot of last-minute sautéing," she told Fletcher. "Most of what I do is long, slow cooking."

She settled on slow food as her next book topic, but not as an indulgence. Always looking to offer something new, she thought she could position it as a counterpoint to Food Network and magazine stars like Rachael Ray and her thirty-minute meals, which debuted on television in 2001—and to the ever-more-dominant Internet, which made life as a whole move faster.

"Everyone was quick, quick, quick. I thought, where's the fun in that?" she asked.

She wrote in the book's introduction, "Yes, fast cooking can be exciting, but it is also stressful and exacting. A few seconds off, and you can ruin a dish. Slow cooking is relaxing and also more forgiving."

She got more encouragement from the burgeoning Slow Food movement. Started by Carlo Petrini in Italy in 1989, it got a big lift in the United States from Alice Waters, who had no trouble roping Paula in to promote its cause of handcrafted foods. Paula also felt buoyed that American home cooks could do more than ever. Certainly they had access to better ingredients.

"Today in the United States we have more exciting food to play with and enjoy than we've ever had," she told a reporter for *Friends*, a magazine for seniors. "The quality is getting better and better. Almost better than in Europe. It's not available in every nook and cranny, but if you're willing to do mail order, you can cook with fresh ingredients anywhere."

American home cooks also seemed willing to tackle harder stuff. For proof, Paula could point to the ambitious new magazine *Saveur*, to which she contributed project dishes like hand-rolled couscous, or to her new column in *Food & Wine* called "Master Cook," where she shared complex recipes such as daubes and homemade vinegar.

In the book, she expanded the definition of slow food, advocating that in addition to making a lovely meal, people ought to linger and chat afterward. She played with the idea of time as a flavoring. With all the extra space on that huge kitchen island to let pots sit out for a while, she discovered that her dishes often acquired more nuance when she let them rest, whether on her counter, on the back of the stove, or in the receding heat of the oven. She elegantly widened the definition of "cooking" to include allowing bread to become stale.

"To my mind, creating stale bread—by leaving it out on the counter to dry so as to acquire texture and absorbency—is the most relaxed form of slow cooking around the Mediterranean," she wrote. Presaging the current mania for toast, she included a small section of recipes for savory foods served on toasted stale bread, including one inspired by a recipe she found in a cookbook by Spanish chef Ferran Adrià that married avocados and sardines (recipe, page 250).

She called on her Mediterranean musketeers, Ayfer Ünsal in Turkey and Aglaia Kremezi in Greece, for help researching undiscovered slow recipes. But even as Paula innovated, much of *Slow Kitchen* was about looking back. She revisited recipes in her archives that were among her slowest and most unorthodox, ones she had downplayed in earlier books because of their strangeness, such as a Minorcan recipe for duck set over a bed of vegetables and steamed until the meat is so soft it can be eaten with a spoon. She re-introduced an overlooked cooked greens "salad" from *Couscous* as a provocative "herb jam" (recipe, page 90) and won a new cult following for it. She explored her cookbook collection, pulling out volumes she hadn't had the time to linger over before. A turn-of-the-century Périgord cookbook by a French woman known as La Mazille inspired her to craft another cult favorite that became known as Paula Wolfert's spoon lamb, a leg of lamb braised for seven hours in an orange muscat dessert wine with sixty cloves of garlic.

Her new kitchen refreshed her cooking confidence. It might seem unbelievable that someone so experienced would need more bravery at the stove, but with less travel, she didn't feel the same pressure to re-create the exact flavors she had experienced in the field. Of all her books, she could recall many of the recipes in *Slow Kitchen* with the most ease and detail. "This is *me*," she said, flipping through them. "These are the recipes where I started to build on my own voice, not everybody else's."

But lest we get the wrong idea that *Slow Kitchen* brought her instant Zen, there's one recipe, for a French pastry called *canelé de Bordeaux*, that shows she still had plenty of competitive fire.

"A magical bakery confection, a cake with a rich custardy interior enclosed by a thin caramelized shell," Paula wrote, "it's a brilliant construction developed long ago by an anonymous Bordeaux cook, whose innovation has been subjected to 300 years of refinements." For nearly twenty years, Paula was the only American with the authentic recipe, though she didn't realize it for most of that time. A Bordeaux baker had given it to her in the 1980s, shortly after *The Cooking of South-West France* appeared. But she had filed it away and forgotten about it because she felt the pastries had fallen into almost total obscurity. Plus, special copper molds greased with beeswax were required to make them (even Paula had her limits).

But by the 2000s, *canelés de Bordeaux* had become trendy, not only in Bordeaux but also in New York, Los Angeles, and Tokyo. Inauthentic versions like *canelés* with raspberries began to appear. To defend the original, eighty-eight Bordeaux bakers had formed a *confrérie*, or brotherhood, and then locked their recipe in a vault and pledged never to give it away. No one remembered that Paula had already been given a copy—not even Paula herself, until she read about the trend and realized it sounded familiar. She went to her files, compared her recipe against versions online, and was thrilled to see she had the real thing. For three months, she stopped all work on *Slow Kitchen* to master and perfect the recipe. On a trip to Bordeaux in 2001, she reached out to her source, told him she had the recipe, and requested his permission to put it into her book. He was so impressed with her thorough understanding of the pastry that he gave her his okay, on the condition she publish it only in English, not in French.

"The secret is to add the butter with the flour," she revealed to me. "In everyone else's recipes, the butter is added with the milk. It makes a difference in the texture, in how it holds itself together. If you see custard inside, it's their recipe. If it's more cakey, it's everyone else's."

Although she had already begun work on a revision of *South-West France*, due out in 2005, she rushed to get the *canelés* into *Slow Kitchen*, released in 2003, because, she said, "I wanted to be the first one to get it into print!"

It quickly became the professional standard in America. In San Francisco, her friend, Gascon chef Laurent Manrique put Paula's Canelés on the menu at his restaurant, Campton Place.

The *canelés* appear among the color photographs in *Slow Kitchen*, the first photographs in any of her books since *Couscous*, taken by *Saveur* cofounder Christopher Hirsheimer. To Paula's chagrin, the stylist who baked them accidentally created small air bubbles in their tops. But she has learned to live with it. By the standards of Paula's other books, *Slow Kitchen* hit the jackpot, selling more than twenty-five thousand copies when it came out in 2003.

Paula was delighted, but distracted. In late 2003, she was still recovering from a near-death experience caused by one of her beloved clay pots. However harrowing, as the next chapter explains, this medical crisis would not dissuade her from dedicating her next book to the pleasures and adventures of cooking in clay.

A portion of Paula's library (and awards)

A Slow and Easy Feast

This menu from *The Slow Mediterranean Kitchen* is one Paula has often served at her Sonoma home. True to her favorite entertaining recipes, these dishes offer big flavor for relatively little effort. In fact, the word *slow* here could refer to the relaxed attitude of the cook more than the time any of these recipes needs to cook. Only the duck and the Leblebi require real time in the oven, but it's all hands-free (and can be done a day ahead). As the dishes simmer, the cook can set the table and prepare the rest of the meal, so as to be at ease when guests arrive.

See individual recipes for side dish suggestions. For dessert, Paula favors a simple pairing of fresh fruit and squares of her favorite Valrhona dark chocolate. Feel free to serve any of the desserts in this book or a personal favorite.

FIRST COURSE
Avocado and Sardine Toasts (Canary Islands, Spain)

MAIN COURSE
Oven-Steamed Salmon (Laguiole, France)
or
Duck You Can Eat with a Spoon (Minorca, Spain)
or
Leblebi (Tunisia)

Confidence in the Kitchen   **249**

Avocado and Sardine Toasts

These toasts remain among Paula's entertaining favorites because they are so easy to throw together—and avocados and sardines are so good for brain (and heart) health. She adapted them from a recipe by iconic Catalan chef Ferran Adrià. How are they "slow"? It's all about staling the bread, a hands-free kind of "cooking" that brings Paula tremendous joy.

¼ cup (60 ml) extra-virgin olive oil

2 tablespoons chopped fresh flat-leaf parsley

1 scant tablespoon sherry vinegar

Flaky sea salt and freshly ground black pepper

Good pinch of mild red pepper flakes, preferably Aleppo or Marash (optional)

2 (4½-ounce | 135-g) cans whole sardines packed in olive oil, preferably Moroccan, drained

1 large firm, ripe Hass avocado

4 to 6 thin slices day-old country-style or gluten-free bread

4 green onions, white and green parts, cut into very thin strips and/or slices

Fresh chives, cut into batons or snipped, for garnish

Serves 4 to 6

🕐 The bread is left out overnight to stale; the sardines marinate for 1 to 2 hours.

In a shallow bowl, whisk together the olive oil, parsley, and vinegar. Season with salt and black pepper and with red pepper flakes, if using. Divide the sardines into fillets and discard any bones. Add the sardines to the vinaigrette and marinate at room temperature for 1 to 2 hours.

Using a mandoline, cut the whole avocado with its skin and pit lengthwise into paper-thin slices. Pull off the skin and pop out the pit from each slice as you go.

On a charcoal or gas grill over a hot fire, on an oiled stove-top grill pan preheated over medium-high heat, under a preheated broiler, or in a toaster, lightly grill or toast the bread.

Lightly brush the top side of each toast with the vinaigrette. Cut each toast into halves or thirds, if desired. Divide the avocado slices among the toasts, top with a portion of the sardines, and scatter green onions and chives on top. Serve at once.

NOTES For easier slicing, chill the avocado in the refrigerator for 1 hour.

If you do not have a mandoline, you can slice the avocado the conventional way (halve, pit, peel, and then thinly slice just the flesh, not the skin or pit). Although you lose the dramatic oval of the whole slices, none of the flavor is lost.

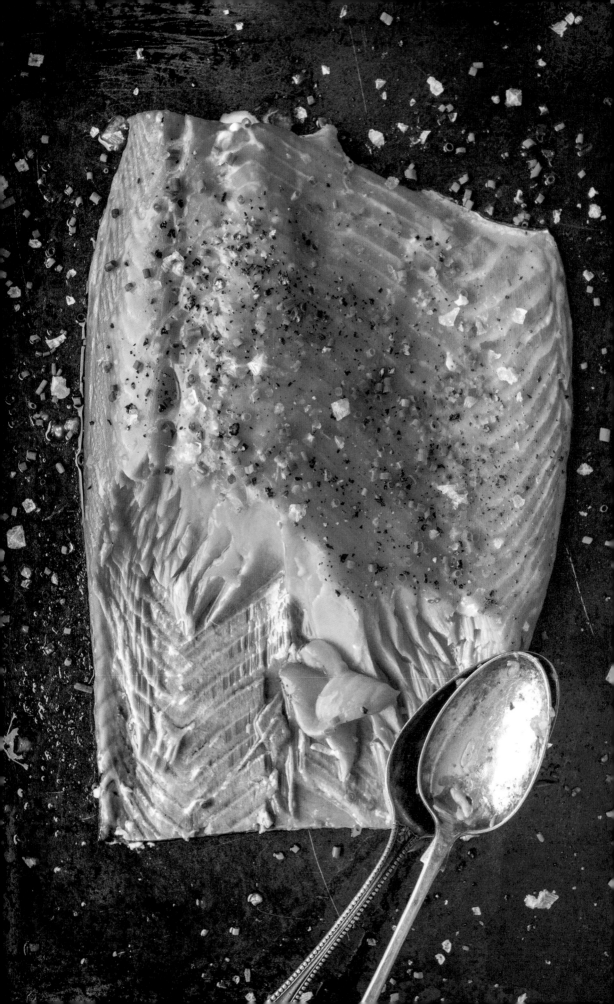

Oven-Steamed Salmon

This technique, which Paula learned from legendary French chef Michel Bras, is so simple and forgiving that it deserves a permanent place in everyone's repertoire. The salmon is cooked briefly in a very low-temperature oven filled with steam, emerging tender and incredibly moist. Pass a fork through the fish and you'll meet no resistance.

Paula liked it so much, she published two versions, one in *Paula Wolfert's World of Food* and one in *The Slow Mediterranean Kitchen*. The two versions have been merged here. The recipe is highly adaptable, working with almost any size salmon fillet, at any oven temperature between 225°F (110°C) and 275°F (135°C). A center-cut piece of wild-caught Alaskan king or sockeye salmon yields the best results. Be sure to use your thinnest metal pan; glassware or enameled cast iron takes too long to heat up for the salmon to cook through properly. Serve with any number of the salads or relishes in the book, such as the cracked green olive relish on page 202.

Olive oil, for greasing

Center-cut salmon fillets, preferably wild-caught Alaskan king or sockeye, 1 inch (2.5 cm) thick and of any size between 5 ounces (150 g) and 2½ pounds (1.1 kg)

Flaky sea salt and freshly ground black pepper

Snipped fresh chives, for garnish (optional)

Position an oven rack in the lower third of the oven and a second rack in the upper third. Preheat the oven to between 225°F (110°C) and 275°F (135°C). Grease a thin sheet pan with olive oil.

Serves 1 to 8, depending on the quantity cooked

Carefully place a frying pan of just-boiled water on the lower oven rack. Arrange the salmon on the prepared sheet pan, season generously with salt and pepper, and place on the upper oven rack. Bake until an instant-read thermometer inserted into the thickest part registers 110°F (43°C) for rare, 115°F (46°C) for medium-rare, or 125°F (52°C) for medium. This should take 10 to 12 minutes for 5-ounce (150-g) fillets or 20 to 25 minutes for a 2½-pound (1.1 kg) fillet. (The color of the salmon will not turn dull and the texture will be very juicy.)

Transfer the salmon to a platter or one or more individual plates and season with more salt and pepper, if desired. Sprinkle with chives, if using, and serve.

Duck You Can Eat with a Spoon

For this exquisite dinner party dish, "the most forgiving and delicious duck dish you'll ever find," according to *Food & Wine*, Paula slowly cooks a whole duck over a bed of vegetables scented with herbes de Provence. The meat takes on a confit-like, spoonable tenderness. Then she broils it to caramelize and crisp the skin. The result could be called "Paula Wolfert's same-day duck confit" because, as she suggested in the book, it's certainly a suitable alternative. Pair with the celery root and apple puree on page 145. As *Food & Wine* noted, "If you're feeling lazy, you can simply serve the duck with the strained pan juices and forgo the stock and olive sauce altogether."

DUCK

2 teaspoons flaky sea salt

1 teaspoon freshly ground black pepper

1 teaspoon herbes de Provence

1 fresh or thawed frozen whole duck (5 to 6 pounds | 2.2 to 2.7 kg), preferably Pekin

2 yellow onions (1 pound | 450 g total), coarsely chopped

1 large celery rib, sliced

8 garlic cloves, halved

2 bay leaves

¼ cup (5 g) coarsely chopped flat-leaf parsley

1 tablespoon fresh thyme leaves

SAUCE

1 yellow onion, sliced

1 tablespoon tomato paste or Tomato Magic (page 309)

½ cup (120 ml) dry white wine

3 cups (720 ml) water

1 cup (240 ml) lightly salted chicken stock

Pinch of sugar (optional)

1½ cups (225 g) green olives, preferably Picholine, pitted and rinsed (see note, page 91)

Flaky sea salt and freshly ground black pepper

¼ teaspoon herbes de Provence

TO FINISH

Flaky sea salt and freshly ground black pepper

Herbes de Provence, for seasoning

2 teaspoons chopped fresh flat-leaf parsley, for garnish

1 teaspoon fresh thyme leaves, for garnish

Serves 4

The duck cooks for 3½ hours. The duck and sauce can be prepared up to 2 days ahead. Broil the duck just before serving.

Preheat the oven to 475°F (245°C).

To prepare the duck, in a small bowl, stir together the salt, pepper, and herbes de Provence. Using sharp kitchen shears, cut the duck in half lengthwise along its breastbone and backbone; cut off and reserve the backbone, neck, and wing tips for the sauce (or have a butcher do this for you).

recipe continues →

In a 9-by-13-inch (23-by-33-cm) enameled cast-iron or other heavy roasting pan or glass baking dish, make a bed of the onions, celery, garlic, bay leaves, parsley, and thyme, mixing the ingredients well. With the tines of a fork, prick the duck skin every ½ inch (1.25 cm). Rub the duck halves all over with the herbes de Provence mixture. Set the duck halves, skin side up, on top of the vegetables.

Roast the duck, uncovered, for 10 minutes. Lower the oven temperature to 275°F (135°C), cover the pan or dish with foil, and continue to cook until the meat is very tender and most of the fat has rendered, about 3 hours. Turn off the oven and let the duck cool in the receding heat of the oven for 30 minutes.

Meanwhile, begin the sauce. In a 12-inch (30-cm) nonstick frying pan, combine the reserved backbone, neck, and wing tips. Cover and cook over medium-low heat, turning the pieces a few times, until browned, about 20 minutes. Add the onion slices, raise the heat to medium, and cook, uncovered, turning the onion slices occasionally, until glazed and nicely browned, about 15 minutes. Pour off the fat from the pan and reserve for another use, such as duck fat croutons (page 135), duck confit, or roast potatoes.

Add the tomato paste to the pan and stir to coat the duck pieces. Cook, uncovered, turning the pieces a few times, until they are lightly charred, about 3 minutes. Add the wine, raise the heat to high, and bring to a boil, scraping up any browned bits from the pan bottom. Add the water, stock, and sugar (if using) and bring to a boil. Lower the heat to medium and simmer until the stock is reduced to 1 cup (240 ml), about 1 hour. Strain the stock through a fine-mesh sieve into a clear glass pitcher or bowl. Skim off the fat from the surface, reserving 1 tablespoon for the sauce and the remainder for another use (as above). Reserve the stock.

When the duck is tender, transfer the halves to a work surface. Using the kitchen shears or a slicing knife, cut each duck half in half; remove any loose bones, pockets of fat, and vegetable remnants. Transfer the duck quarters, skin side up, to a sheet pan. Strain the juices from the roasting pan through a fine-mesh sieve into a saucepan and discard the contents of the sieve. Skim off any fat from the juices and reserve for another use (as above).

Boil the strained juices until reduced to ¼ cup (60 ml). Add the reserved stock and the olives to the saucepan and simmer for 10 minutes. Season the sauce with salt, pepper, and the herbes de Provence. (At this point the duck and sauce can be covered and refrigerated separately for up to 2 days. Let the duck return to room temperature before proceeding.)

Position an oven rack about 10 inches (25 cm) from the heating element and preheat the broiler. Brush the duck skin with the reserved 1 tablespoon fat and season with more salt, pepper, and herbes de Provence. Broil until the duck is hot and the skin is blistering and crisp, 3 to 5 minutes.

Spoon the sauce onto a warmed platter and set the duck on top. Garnish with the parsley and thyme and serve.

NOTE Be sure your oven is calibrated. If the duck is cooked at a higher temperature it will overcook.

Leblebi

With its customizable components, including runny eggs, briny olives, salty capers, and optional hot sauce, this rich and warming Tunisian street-food soup is a bit like ramen, but instead of noodles it's ladled over chickpeas and bread cubes. As Paula wrote in *The Slow Mediterranean Kitchen*, "In my opinion, the prize for most colorful, balanced, freshest, most delicious, and most exciting of all Mediterranean street foods goes to Tunisian *leblebi.* . . . The dish is usually served as a breakfast and is almost always cooked by men for men. I eat it whenever I go to Tunisia, enjoying the atmosphere of male camaraderie, the delicious flavor, the reasonable price, and its aroma so early in the morning." You can enjoy leblebi any time of the day.

---

1 rounded cup (225 g) dried chickpeas, picked over, soaked overnight in water to cover, drained, and rinsed

2 cups (480 ml) best-quality veal, beef, chicken, or vegetable stock

1 pound (450 g) veal, beef, or lamb bones (optional)

4 garlic cloves, halved

3 tablespoons (45 ml) extra-virgin olive oil, plus more for frying and drizzling

Flaky sea salt and freshly ground black pepper

4 to 8 very fresh medium or large eggs, at room temperature

Four 1-inch-thick (2.5-cm) slices country-style bread, preferably staled overnight

2 to 3 tablespoons hrous (page 312), harissa or other favorite hot sauce (optional)

Ground toasted cumin, for seasoning

24 black olives, preferably kalamata, pitted and rinsed (see note, page 91)

1 heaping tablespoon capers, drained and rinsed

1 red bell pepper, roasted, peeled, and seeded, cut into thin strips or diced

4 to 8 lemon wedges

Serves 4 as a main dish, 8 as a light meal

The chickpeas and broth can be made up to 3 days in advance. Stale the bread overnight and coddle the eggs just before serving.

Preheat the oven to 225°F (110°C). In a deep, heavy pot, combine the chickpeas, stock, bones (if using), garlic, olive oil, pinch of salt, and enough water to cover by 1 inch (2.5 cm); you'll need about 2 cups (480 ml). Bring to a boil over high heat, skimming off any scum that rises to the surface. Remove from the heat, cover, transfer to the oven, and cook until the chickpeas are very tender, about 3 hours.

Remove the chickpeas from the oven. Remove and discard the bones (if used) and garlic. Skim off the fat from the surface. Taste the liquid and adjust the seasoning with salt if needed. Keep the chickpeas in the cooking liquid and reheat to a simmer on the stove top just before serving. (The recipe can be prepared up to this

recipe continues →

point up to 3 days in advance. Let cool, cover, and refrigerate, then return to a simmer on the stove top before proceeding.)

To coddle the eggs, bring a saucepan three-fourths full of water to a simmer over medium heat. While the water is heating, fill a good-size bowl with ice water. Gently lower the eggs in their shells into the simmering water, then remove the pan from the heat. Cover the pan and let stand undisturbed for 6 minutes. Using a slotted spoon, transfer the eggs to the ice water, let stand until cool, and drain. One at a time, gently roll the eggs on a hard surface to crackle the shells all over, then carefully peel the eggs; or partially remove the shell, then use a spoon to gently scoop out the eggs.

To prepare the bread, in a large frying pan, warm ¼ inch (6 mm) of olive oil over medium-high heat. Working with 1 to 2 slices at a time, fry the bread, turning once, until golden brown, adding more oil as needed between slices. Transfer to a work surface and let cool. Tear into 1-inch (2.5-cm) chunks.

To serve, divide the bread evenly among four to eight deep soup bowls. Top with a ladleful of chickpeas and some of the broth. Set an egg on the chickpeas in each bowl. Using kitchen shears, cut each egg so the yolk runs. If using the hrous, thin it with water or olive oil (or a mixture) to a pourable consistency, then drizzle some on each bowl; other hot sauces may not require thinning. Sprinkle with a good pinch each of cumin, salt, and pepper. Scatter on the olives, capers, and roasted pepper. Ladle in more broth if needed. Drizzle each serving with olive oil and then squeeze a wedge of lemon over the top. Serve at once, passing any remaining hrous at the table.

NOTES In her original recipe, Paula called for staled bread cubes, which are more authentic. But frying the bread in oil gives the soup an even richer, more memorable flavor.

Peeling coddled eggs is not easy. If you do not feel up for the challenge, feel free to poach or fry the eggs instead; after transferring them to the soup, cut them in half to let the yolks run.

Omit the bread or replace it with pan-fried or grilled polenta cakes (see note, page 237) for a gluten-free rendition.

For tips on roasting and prepping the bell pepper, see the Ajvar recipe on page 20. A jarred bell pepper also works.

Every Pot
Tells a Story

SONOMA ✤ 2003 to 2011

> "I believe something I was told by my grandmother. . . .
> She insisted that the best daubes were cooked in her
> oldest casseroles, because . . . only a clay pot can keep
> the memory of the love the cook put into it when pre-
> paring the dish."
>
> —Potter Philippe Beltrando in
> *Mediterranean Clay Pot Cooking*

IN LATE 2003, Paula took what would turn out to be one of her last trips to Turkey. She was to spend time with a remarkable Turkish chef named Musa Dagdeviren, who was dedicated to preserving and elevating regional Turkish dishes. She had met him through Ayfer Ünsal at a conference in California; after that meeting, Paula returned to Istanbul where she and Ünsal cowrote a profile about Dagdeviren for *Food & Wine*. Paula and Dagdeviren had much in common: "He is part chef, part culinary anthropologist," the women noted. "And his genius is knowing when to leave these recipes intact and when to add a twist of his own." Dagdeviren shared Paula's love of clay pots and gave her an enormous *çömlek*, a Turkish clay casserole, which she kept safe in her lap during her fifteen-hour flight home to San Francisco.

When she got off the plane, she started to feel so ill that she promptly went to the hospital. Doctors discovered that she had deep vein thrombosis, a blood clot in her leg that could have traveled at any moment to her heart and killed her. Paula immediately began taking a blood thinner, which eventually dissolved the clot.

OPPOSITE:
Paula's first clay
pot, a *triperie*
she purchased in
1958 as a student
of Dione Lucas

But a worse fear had come true. The incident reminded Paula of the Balkan fortune-teller from the 1960s who had warned her not to cross the Atlantic more than twenty-four times. Even though Paula had exceeded that count at least fivefold, crossing the ocean roughly five times a year for twenty-five years, the blood clot spooked her. Never mind that the gypsy had predicted a plane crash, not a blood clot; in 2003 she swore never to fly again—at least not without a business-class ticket to give her room to stretch her legs *and* to store her pots. That decision all but ended her travel.

From 2003 to 2011, she published three more books that demanded little travel: an update of *The Cooking of South-West France*, then *Mediterranean Clay Pot Cooking*, and finally, in a particularly nice symmetry, *The Food of Morocco*, an expanded version of her first book, *Couscous*. The trio lack some of the rawness and vigor of her earlier volumes, but in an example of her career's kismet, they let her complete a kind of circle, to conclude her working life by sharing her last new culinary discoveries on topics and territories she had pursued from her first years as a cookbook writer.

The reissued *Southwest France* (the hyphen in Southwest was dropped for the second edition) celebrated all the wonderful ingredients of the region finally available in the United States, such as Moulard ducks (meatier, fattier, and more flavorful than American Pekin ducks) and domestic foie gras. In another of the many wonderful coincidences of Paula's life, it turned out that one of the country's leading foie gras producers operated right in her town of Sonoma. The owners, Guillermo and Junny Gonzalez, had traveled from their home in El Salvador to Southwest France at the same time Paula had, in the early 1980s, to learn to raise geese for foie gras. In Sonoma, they also operated a small foie gras–centric restaurant, where Paula became a regular.

These developments gave Paula opportunities to deepen and broaden her original book. In the revision, Paula expanded the definition of Southwest to include recipes from the more south-central area where Michel Bras, whom she met after the book came out, is based. She also stretched to the north, to include recipes from Charente, in Cognac country, including *éclade de moules*, a dish in which mussels are cooked under flaming pine needles, preferably in a forest clearing (she had described it briefly in the first edition but had not yet obtained a recipe).

She found some of the most exciting new chefs of Southwest France right in San Francisco, such as Gascon-born Laurent Manrique at Campton Place and Biarritz native Gerald Hirigoyen at his Basque restaurant Piperade, both of whom gave her new recipes.

Lastly, she got help from cooks she met on the food discussion site eGullet.com.

Paula had embraced the Internet with her usual gusto from its earliest days, e-mailing long missives instead of faxing them, tracking down new online food retailers to supplement her mail-order habit, even researching obscure clay pots. Already by the mid-1990s, she had built a reputation as a Web maven. She had poked around a few of the first Internet food groups, but none approached the seriousness of eGullet. Founded in 2001 in New York, the site encouraged home cooks and professional chefs to share know-how on everything from DIY charcuterie to Indian spice blends. Moderators policed discussion threads to keep everyone on topic. Although its popularity peaked in 2005, eGullet helped bring food online, showing bloggers and publications they could have an informed cyber audience. According to eGullet's founders, Paula, whom they named to their board of directors, played a key role in that success.

"Paula was one of our first celebrity contributors," said cofounder Jason Perlow. "She was always our best advocate at various conferences and food-writer gatherings, raising awareness of our existence. She gave us a good idea of who was using the site and what they liked about it. I think the fact [that] she got involved is the reason we got other food stars like Mario Batali involved."

Before Paula arrived, the site already boasted Anthony Bourdain and Eric Ripert as regulars. However, few established cookbook authors had yet gone online in 2003, when Paula typed her first eGullet post, sharing André Guillot's presalting tip in a thread on steak—a tip she had picked up in France in the 1980s. The next few years, through eGullet she created a cyber incarnation of her life as a culinary teacher. She piped up in hundreds of threads, about everything from clay pots to the history of chefs' hats. She found posting reengaged her. "eGullet brought back so many memories for me," she said happily.

Her presence lured other serious cooks to the site and won her some important new fans. For its part, eGullet promoted her books and hosted her in lively Q&A sessions, and Paula became close with many of the site's most active users. It buoyed her to see home cooks tackle complex recipes with gusto, not least her own. At sixty-six, she built a robust community of online fans, long before most authors realized they needed a virtual platform to sell books.

When she got laid up with her blood clot, she asked eGulleteers for help testing her recipes for the new edition of *Southwest France*, offering each of them a signed copy and his or her name in the acknowledgments in exchange. She signed up twenty-six testers around the world. One eGullet participant who went by "nathanm" helped her decipher how to cook duck confit *sous vide*. Another, after testing a fruit terrine, told her it was terrific but a lot of work. She loved their honesty. "There were no ass-kissers," she said. She pulled the terrine from the second edition.

For the acknowledgments, she learned "nathanm" was Nathan Myhrvold, former chief technology officer of Microsoft. In 2011, Myhrvold published his own culinary masterwork, *Modernist Cuisine*, which was inspired by an eGullet thread about *sous vide* cooking. It includes an adapted version of his and Paula's recipe for duck confit *sous vide*.

In food circles, the release of *Southwest France* provoked as much or more excitement than *Slow Kitchen*. "The November reissue of Wolfert's classic created no small buzz," wrote Amy Scattergood in a review of the book in the *Los Angeles Times*. "A lot has happened since 1983. Truffles from Oregon! Confit at your local Whole Foods! Foie gras FedEx'd from D'Artagnan!" Underlining the new adventurous spirit of cooking in America, Scattergood even tackled *éclade de moules* using pine needles from her Christmas tree.

❖

Spurred by the strong sales of *Slow Kitchen* and the second edition of *Southwest France*, in 2005 Paula decided to write a memoir. She had had the title for years: *Confessions of a Clay Pot Junkie*. (For her first e-mail address in the 1990s, she chose claypotjunkie@aol.com.)

The way the rest of us might buy postcards as souvenirs of our travels, Paula had purchased clay pots. She bought her first, a brown potbellied *triperie* (photo, page 262), in 1958, when she was just nineteen and working for Dione Lucas. "I didn't even know what tripe was, but I loved the feel of the earthenware in my hands," she told food writer David Leite in 2003. By 2005, her collection had ballooned to a few hundred. It's possible her grandmother had cooked in clay, she said.

"Ceramic cooking pots speak to me of soothing and nurturing grandmother-style dishes," she wrote.

She sold the memoir to the publisher John Wiley & Sons. But she soon found that writing about herself "felt too me, me, me." The backward reflection clashed with her innate forward momentum. She redirected her focus on to clay pots and all of the unexplored things they could do.

Like foie gras and extended time in the kitchen, clay pots were a niche asset when Paula started her career. In the 1970s, Paula had been forced to omit use of clay vessels from her Moroccan cookbooks, instead adapting her tagines for American casseroles. But by 2005, if not commonplace, clay pots were at least somewhat available. She liked to cite her few online sources as evidence of a coming major trend. "Just wait!" she'd exclaim when we chatted. "Clay pots are going to be huge!"

After fifty years sampling dishes made in clay, she had also become convinced that earthenware made foods taste better. Mediterranean cooks she'd met swore to it. When she conducted side-by-side taste tests in her cooking classes, as she wrote in the book's introduction, clay always won. That added flavor she described as "earthy." It became her ultimate compliment—for a person as well as a dish.

She found this earthiness was strongest in older pots. Unlike metal, for better or for worse, clay retains the flavors of foods cooked in it. "A clay pot remembers its previous tenant," as Paula put it. Moroccans sometimes joked to her that when they cooked tagines in their oldest pots, they didn't need to add any spices, because the seasoned clay provided plenty of flavor. Clay pots also concentrate flavors by evaporation through their porous sides.

She knew she would have to address their shortcomings, especially their fragility: clay pots break if exposed to temperature extremes, such as moving them from a hot oven to a cold countertop without setting them on a room-temperature cloth. They also require a diffuser to shield them from the direct heat of a stovetop burner. She was thrilled to find sturdier cooking vessels made of a type of ceramic called flameware, capable of withstanding sudden temperature swings and direct heat. She also fell in love with durable black clay pots from Colombia (strengthened by the mica in the clay) and with tough, wire-reinforced Chinese sand pots. She figured out a way to cook whole white button mushrooms in a sand pot so slowly that they tasted almost like porcini (recipe, page 276).

Enchanted by the alchemy from all this long, slow cooking in clay, Paula felt surprisingly forlorn about the concurrent explosion of interest in locavore produce. As she was working on the book, in 2005, the year blogger Jessica Prentice coined the word *locavore*, Paula feared the emphasis on fresh and local overemphasized fresh. She wished people would be a little bit more willing to cook, if only to preserve all the bounty. She told *Edible San Francisco* magazine, "When I lived in Morocco, all summer long people were making food for the winter. That's something that we don't even think about anymore—making jarred food. We just don't have an appreciation of that type of cooking with this movement of farmers markets; it's all got to be fresh, fresh, fresh."

More by coincidence than intent, she anticipated a post-2008 trend in artisanal preserved foods, positioning the book as a counterweight to all that freshness. In the back of the book, as she did in many of her books, she included larder recipes for her favorite preserved foods, some of them made in clay, such as *smen*, the Moroccan aged butter (recipe, page 310), preserved lemons (recipe, page 306), duck confit (recipe, page 143), and red wine vinegar. Thinking the book would be her last, she slipped in sentimental favorites adapted for clay, such as a Sicilian eggplant dish (*caponatina*; recipe, page 283) first published in *World of Food*.

Then, shortly before *Clay Pot* went to press, her longtime friend Daniel Halpern, who helmed the publishing imprint Ecco, pitched her about reissuing *Couscous* as a lavish coffee table book. Perhaps surprisingly, Paula waffled.

Halpern had been introduced to Paula by Paul Bowles in 1971, when he moved from Tangier to New York to run their new literary magazine, *Antaeus*, which later spun off a book publishing division then called The Ecco Press. In 1995, Ecco published Paula's updated *Mediterranean Cooking*. For thirty-five years, Halpern, a fellow Morocco-phile, had wanted to publish a more lavish, more richly photographed edition of *Couscous*, to give Moroccan cooking the full-color treatment it deserved. Paula had resisted for many reasons, not least her constant drive to seek out new territory rather than to revisit old.

But by the late 2000s, updating the book made a lot of sense. She could rewrite all her tagine recipes using actual clay pots. She had acquired dozens more Moroccan recipes since *Couscous*, some published in *World of Food*, others in *Grains and Greens*. The United States also finally had access to quality Moroccan ingredients like Moroccan cumin and preserved lemons, thanks to Mustapha's Mediterranean, a new Seattle-based importing company founded by Mustapha Haddouch, a family friend of Paula's and her children's from Tangier. And in another typical Paula coincidence, around the same time Halpern pitched his idea, Oldways called to offer her a free plane trip to Morocco to colead a trip with Ana Sortun. Oldways even agreed to fly her business class, her new requirement since the blood clot.

Yet she hesitated. She feared something was wrong with her mind.

I was one of the people she called. I told her not to worry. Today she likes to tell me I talked her into doing the book. Whatever it was that convinced her, she also agreed to go to Morocco with Oldways. Soon after, my bosses at *Food & Wine* assigned me to travel with her to Marrakech with Quentin Bacon, the book's photographer, to write a story about her time there.

Before we left for Morocco, I visited Paula in Sonoma. Bill took me aside to warn me that her lifelong hypochondria had lately worsened. He coached me in calming her down if she panicked. Sure enough, the reason that she missed our first day there was because of an illness scare: while in Fez with Oldways, right before she was due to meet me in Marrakech, she had become convinced she was having a heart attack and spent the day in the hospital.

The rest of our trip went well. But at home, she had terrible difficulty organizing her thoughts. She roped in close friends to help her test the recipes, including her daughter, Leila, who was still living in the Hudson Valley in New York.

When Halpern asked her to return to Morocco with the photographer for the book's final pictures just eighteen months after our trip, she apologized profusely but explained to him that she could not handle any more extended travel (her friend Haddouch took the photographer around the country instead). Paula felt strangely disoriented even in her beloved kitchen. In 2011, promoting the book on radio programs or at panels, she found she could not follow complex interview queries. Like a skilled politician, she redirected. "That's a great question!" she'd say. "Since we don't have much time, I really want to talk about the magic of the tagine."

She saw several doctors who told her she was fine. In a classic example of the misinformation around dementia (at even the highest levels of medical care), one primary care doctor told her that her symptoms couldn't be related to dementia because she had just written a book. She started to fear public appearances. She grew depressed. She wondered if she had chronic fatigue syndrome, as there were days she lacked the energy to get out of bed.

"It's not me to be lazy, but I'm lazy now," she told me. "I'm scared." Once again I tried to reassure her, suggesting that maybe her disorientation was just an unfortunate part of reaching her seventies. Never did I think she might have dementia. It would have seemed insulting.

Finally, in late 2012, she and Bill were at home together, and he suggested they have omelets for lunch, a dish Paula had mastered under Dione Lucas in 1957.

As Paula recalled, she said to Bill, "Wait a minute, how do you make an omelet?"

Five Masterful
Vegetable Side Dishes,
with or without
a Clay Pot

❖ ❀ ❖

Traveling throughout the Mediterranean, particularly the East and Turkey, Paula acquired a remarkable gift for slow-cooking vegetables, an ability to bring out deep, almost meat-like flavor from even such humble ones as potatoes and white button mushrooms. In her 2008 book *Mediterranean Clay Pot Cooking*, her mastery is on full display. Here are five of the finest vegetable side dishes from the book. Conveniently, of these recipes, only the Sand Pot Mushrooms truly requires a clay pot.

Potato Gratin Dauphinois

Sand Pot Mushrooms

Armenian Cauliflower with Raisins and Pine Nuts

Tuscan White Beans with Sage and Garlic

Caponatina

Potato Gratin Dauphinois

Paula published many enticing scalloped potatoes recipes but this may be the finest expression of the dish ever created. *Gratin dauphinois* is a French classic that originated in the southeastern region of Dauphine. Like cassoulet in the Southwest, there are many iterations, all claiming to be the best. In the early 2000s, Paula researched this one through an official online portal sponsored by the region, gratindauphinois.com, which archives over two hundred officially sanctioned versions.

In her take on the dish, Paula finesses every last step: To give the dish added heft, she pats the potato slices dry but does not rinse them, to preserve their starch. For an extra-velvety sauce, she tempers an egg with the hot milk and cream. At the very end, to let the flavors meld and build, she uses time itself as a seasoning: After baking, she lets the gratin rest, then brushes it with a little more cream for a superior crust, before reheating it and letting it finish baking in the receding heat of the oven.

---

1 garlic clove, halved

2 tablespoons unsalted butter

1½ cups (360 ml) whole milk or half-and-half

1½ cups (360 ml) heavy cream

1 large egg

1 cup (about 105 g) grated Emmentaler, Gruyère, or Comté cheese

1½ teaspoons flaky sea salt

½ teaspoon freshly ground black pepper

¼ teaspoon freshly grated nutmeg

2½ pounds (1.1 kg) Yukon Gold potatoes

Serves 6 to 8

Preheat the oven to 350°F (180°C). Rub the cut sides of the garlic clove all over the inside of an earthenware or glass gratin dish, roughly of 3-quart (3-l) capacity and measuring about 9-by-12 inches (23-by-30 cm). Grease the dish with 1 tablespoon of the butter.

In a large saucepan, combine the milk and 1¼ cups (300 ml) of the cream. Heat over medium-high heat just until small bubbles appear along the sides of the pan. Remove from the heat. While the milk mixture heats, in a bowl, lightly beat the egg until blended. While whisking constantly, pour the hot milk mixture in a slow, steady stream into the egg to temper it.

Pour the egg-milk mixture back into the saucepan and sprinkle in three-fourths of the cheese. Place over medium heat and cook,

recipe continues →

OPPOSITE:
A few of
Paula's favorite
clay pots.

whisking constantly, until the cheese is melted and the mixture is smooth, about 3 minutes. Add the salt, pepper, and nutmeg and stir well. Remove from the heat and cover to keep warm.

Peel the potatoes but do not rinse them. Using a sharp knife, mandoline, or the slicing blade of a food processor, slice the potatoes about ⅛ inch (3 mm) thick. Pat the potato slices dry with paper towels, then add them to the cream sauce and stir to coat evenly.

Scrape the potatoes and sauce into the prepared gratin dish and spread in an even layer. Sprinkle the surface evenly with the remaining cheese. Cut the remaining butter into bits and dot them over the surface of the gratin.

Place the gratin in the oven, raise the temperature to 400°F (200°C), and bake for 1 hour. The potatoes should be golden and tender when pierced with a knife. Remove from the oven. If using an earthenware gratin dish, to prevent cracking, place it on a wooden surface or on a folded kitchen towel. Let cool for 15 minutes. Run a paring knife along the inside edge of the gratin dish to loosen the potatoes. Brush the top of the gratin with the remaining ¼ cup (60 ml) cream.

Return the gratin to the oven and bake for 15 minutes longer. The potatoes should be a rich golden brown. Turn off the heat and let the gratin finish browning in the receding heat of the oven for 30 minutes longer. Serve hot.

NOTE The gratin can be baked in what Paula calls a "clay environment," between two pizza stones or oven-safe quarry tiles set on the upper and lower oven racks. This can result in more even baking and will help to draw moisture out of the gratin, to ensure a richer crust and even more intense flavor.

Sand Pot Mushrooms

In *Clay Pot*, Paula wrote, "When you slow-cook cultivated white mushrooms in a closed clay pot, such as a Chinese sand pot, an extraordinary alchemy takes place. These ordinary mushrooms, which normally taste quite bland, acquire an earthy flavor, almost as deep as that of wild ones. I never cease to be amazed at the transformation, which I attribute to the clay vessel."

After Paula convinced me to spend the fifteen dollars on my own sand pot, I have never bothered to prepare this recipe in anything else, so I do not know if it works in metal. I do know a sand pot is worth the small investment.

---

1 pound (450 g) white mushrooms, caps wiped clean and stem ends trimmed

4 large or 6 medium garlic cloves, very thinly sliced

1½ tablespoons extra-virgin olive oil

2 or 3 fresh thyme sprigs (optional)

Flaky sea salt and freshly ground black pepper

Serves 4

Place the mushrooms in a large bowl. Add the garlic, olive oil, and the thyme sprigs, if using. Season lightly with salt and pepper. Stir to coat. Transfer the mushrooms to a 1- to 2-quart (1- to 2-l) sand pot. Place a piece of crumpled parchment on top of the mushrooms, then cover with the lid.

Cook the mushrooms over low heat, shaking the pot from time to time to stir them, until they are tender when pierced with a sharp knife, about 45 minutes. Taste and adjust the seasoning with salt and pepper if needed. Serve hot or warm.

Armenian Cauliflower with Raisins and Pine Nuts

After seeing Armenia from the Georgian border in 1989, Paula wanted to travel to the country, but conflicts in the region prevented her. Instead, she collected Armenian cookbooks, especially community cookbooks from Armenian churches around the United States. This hearty vegetarian dish is Paula's take on a recipe by Armenian cookbook author Arto Der Haroutunian. It can be made in any ovenproof frying pan, though, Paula prefers a black clay La Chamba roasting pan from Colombia. As she told me for a 2009 *Food & Wine* story, "It imparts sweetness to the dish."

2 tablespoons raisins (not golden ones)

¼ cup (60 ml) extra-virgin olive oil

1 head cauliflower, cut into florets

1 teaspoon sugar (optional)

2 cups (350 g) peeled, seeded, and diced tomatoes (fresh or drained canned)

Pinch of mild red pepper flakes, preferably Marash

Flaky sea salt and freshly ground black pepper

¼ cup (60 ml) hot water

2 tablespoons pine nuts

1 garlic clove, finely chopped

2 tablespoons chopped fresh flat-leaf parsley

1½ tablespoons fresh lemon juice

Serves 4

Preheat the oven to 350°F (180°C). In a small bowl, combine the raisins with warm water to cover and let stand until plump, about 10 minutes. Drain and reserve.

Meanwhile, in a 10- to 12-inch (25- to 30-cm) cazuela, roasting pan, or ovenproof frying pan, heat the olive oil over medium-low heat, using a heat diffuser if using a cazuela. Add the cauliflower and sugar (if using) and cook, stirring, until the cauliflower starts to soften, about 10 minutes. Raise the heat to medium and cook until the cauliflower is lightly browned, about 5 minutes longer. Stir in the tomatoes and red pepper flakes, season with salt and black pepper, and cook until the tomatoes have begun to soften, about 5 minutes.

Add the raisins, hot water, pine nuts, and garlic to the cauliflower and stir well. Transfer to the oven and bake the cauliflower until very tender when pierced with a knife, about 30 minutes.

Remove from the oven, stir in the parsley and lemon juice, and let stand at room temperature for 30 minutes. Serve warm.

Tuscan White Beans with Sage and Garlic

Some of Paula's claims about the flavor-enhancing powers of clay pots seem a little far-fetched. Does a black clay pot from Colombia really make the roasted cauliflower on page 279 taste sweeter? Not all of us have a palate as sensitive as Paula's and can detect the flavors she can. But I have to agree with her that dried beans taste noticeably better slowly cooked in clay. For whatever reason, clay pots give beans a softer, more tender texture. Clay also seems to act like salt, intensifying the flavor both of the bean and the cooking liquor. (Paula also enriches these beans with actual salt, first soaking them in lightly salted water, then cooking them in their soaking water with aromatics and a bit more salt.) These beans can be cooked in any vessel, including a sand pot, but a clay bean pot is worth the splurge.

Seek out heirloom white beans as conventional cannellini fall apart too easily. Italian butter beans are delicious, as are Caballero and Marcella beans from Rancho Gordo New World Specialty Food. The beans taste downright luscious on their own. For a light main course, serve them with a simple tomato sauce, sardines, and fried sage leaves (see the recipe note for details).

---

6 cups (1.5 l) water

Flaky sea salt and freshly ground black pepper

1¼ cups (250 g) dried white beans, preferably an heirloom variety such as butter, Caballero, or Marcella beans

4 garlic cloves, peeled

3 large fresh sage leaves

2 bay leaves

4 tablespoons (60 ml) extra-virgin olive oil

Makes about 3 cups (545 g); serves 4

The beans are soaked overnight before cooking.

In a large bowl, combine the water with ½ teaspoon salt and stir to dissolve. Pick over the beans, then rinse and add them to the salted water. If needed, add more water to cover them by 2 inches (5 cm). Cover and refrigerate overnight.

The next day, drain the beans, reserving the soaking water. In a deep saucepan, preferably earthenware, combine the beans, 1½ teaspoons salt, and enough of the soaking liquid to cover by 1 inch (2.5 cm). Place over medium heat (on a heat diffuser if using an earthenware pot) and bring slowly to a simmer. Add the garlic, sage, bay leaves, and 2 tablespoons of the olive oil. Cover and turn down the heat to low. Cook as slowly as possible until the beans

recipe continues →

still hold their shape but squash easily when pressed between two fingers, about 3 hours.

Drain the beans then discard the garlic and the sage and bay leaves. Season the beans with salt and pepper, drizzle with the remaining 2 tablespoons olive oil, and serve.

NOTE You can turn these Tuscan beans into a simple supper main dish for 2. In a large frying pan, heat 2 tablespoons olive oil over medium heat. Add 1 teaspoon chopped garlic and sauté until fragrant, about 3 minutes. Add 4 large fresh sage leaves, slivered, and 2 tomatoes, peeled, seeded, and diced, and cook, stirring occasionally, until thickened. Add the 1½ cups (275 g) drained cooked beans and cook, stirring occasionally, for 5 minutes longer. Season with salt and pepper and transfer to individual plates.

If desired, drain 2 (4½-ounce | 135-g) cans whole sardines packed in olive oil, preferably Moroccan, then divide the sardines among the plates, arranging them on top of the beans. Drizzle with more olive oil, if you wish. For a lovely add-on, top with some fresh sage leaves fried until crisp in a few tablespoons olive oil. Serve hot or warm with country-style bread.

Caponatina

This meaty Sicilian antipasto, known as caponata or *caponatina* in Palerman, consists of cooked eggplant in a jam-like mixture of onions, celery, and tomato, made tangy yet sweet with the *agrodolce* (sweet-and-sour) combination of red wine vinegar reduced with a little sugar. As one of Paula's all-time favorite eggplant dishes, it is a fitting and poignant final recipe for this book.

She learned this recipe in the 1980s from Maria Sindoni, a Sicilian restaurateur in New York, and published it in *World of Food*. For her later book, *Clay Pot Cooking*, she finessed it, using an earthenware *cazuela* and adding a few more condiments. Soaking the eggplant in salt water draws out bitterness and gives the eggplant a light, pillowy texture. Serve it on its own, on toasted bread, or alongside grilled fish or tofu. It also doubles easily.

---

5 cups (1.25 l) plus ¼ cup (60 ml) water

Flaky sea salt

2 (12-ounce | 350-g) eggplants, peeled and cut into 1-inch (2.5-cm) cubes

1½ tablespoons dried currants or golden raisins

4 tablespoons (60 ml) extra-virgin olive oil, plus more as needed

½ cup (75 g) chopped yellow onion

1½ cups (150 g) diced celery hearts, with some leaves

⅓ cup (90 g) best-quality tomato sauce, canned diced tomatoes, or tomato puree

1½ teaspoons finely chopped sun-dried tomatoes (optional)

3 tablespoons (45 ml) red wine vinegar

1½ teaspoons sugar, or more to taste

Pinch of mild red pepper flakes, preferably Aleppo or Marash, or hot red pepper flakes

6 green olives, preferably Sicilian or Greek, pitted, rinsed (see note, page 91), and coarsely chopped

6 capers, rinsed and drained

2 tablespoons pine nuts, lightly toasted, for garnish

12 large fresh basil leaves, torn, for garnish

Sliced country-style or gluten-free bread, for serving (optional)

Serve 4 as a first course or side dish

🕑 This matures beautifully. Make it up to 4 days ahead. Serve at room temperature.

In a large bowl, combine the 5 cups (1.25 l) water and 1 tablespoon salt and stir to dissolve the salt. Add the eggplant cubes and top with a plate to keep them submerged. Let soak for 45 minutes. Drain and squeeze dry with kitchen towels.

Meanwhile, in a small bowl, combine the currants with enough warm water to cover. Let stand until plump, about 10 minutes. Drain and reserve.

recipe continues →

In a 10- or 12-inch (25- or 30-cm) frying pan (preferably nonstick) or earthenware cazuela, combine 1 tablespoon of the olive oil, the onion, the remaining ¼ cup (60 ml) water, and ½ teaspoon salt. If using a frying pan, place over medium-high heat. If using a cazuela, use a heat diffuser and warm the pan slowly, gradually raising the heat to medium-high. Cook, stirring occasionally, until the water evaporates and the onion is soft and golden, about 20 minutes.

Meanwhile, bring a medium saucepan filled with salted water to a boil over high heat. Add the celery and cook until tender, about 10 minutes. Drain.

When the onion is ready, add the celery, tomato sauce, and, if using, the sun-dried tomatoes, and cook, stirring often, until the mixture sizzles and thickens to a jam-like consistency, 5 to 10 minutes, depending on the consistency of the sauce. Scrape into a wide bowl and let cool.

Without rinsing the pan, add the vinegar and sugar and cook over medium-high heat, stirring, until the sugar dissolves and the syrup has reduced slightly, about 2 minutes. Add the currants, red pepper flakes, olives, and capers, and cook, stirring, for about 2 minutes. Scrape the contents of the pan into the bowl with the onion and celery and let cool.

Rinse out the pan, return the heat to medium-high (raise the heat gradually if using a cazuela), and add the remaining 3 tablespoons (45 ml) oil. When the oil is hot, working in batches, fry the eggplant, turning the pieces occasionally, until golden brown on all sides, about 10 minutes. As each batch is ready, using a slotted spoon, transfer it to paper towels to drain. Repeat with the remaining eggplant, adding more oil to the pan as needed.

Add the eggplant to the onion-celery mixture and stir gently to combine. Let cool to room temperature. Cover and refrigerate for up to 4 days (and return to room temperature before serving) or serve right away, garnished with a shower of the pine nuts and basil leaves. Offer with bread at the table, if desired.

NOTE See page 23 for Paula's tips for selecting eggplants.

Living for
the Now

SONOMA ❖ 2011 to
the Present

DEMENTIA IS IMPOSSIBLE TO DIAGNOSE CONCLUSIVELY without a post-mortem autopsy. But with brain scans and questionnaires, doctors can now get within 90 percent probability of an accurate diagnosis. In early 2013, Bill took Paula to see two of the best neurologists in San Francisco. Paula ultimately obtained three probable diagnoses from three doctors: one for mild cognitive impairment, or MCI; one for early stage Alzheimer's; and one for a variant of Alzheimer's called posterior cortical atrophy, or PCA. Her diagnosis was partly complicated by her vision problems, both her amblyopia and the damage to her visual cortex caused by the brain surgery in the 1960s. Words, she said, had started "floating from the page," but doctors could not say with certainty whether that was due to dementia or brain damage. Nowadays, Paula describes what she has as "mixed dementia." Her primary neurologist says she has Alzheimer's.

Alzheimer's is typically characterized as a disease of forgetting. It's more a dismantling. As we age, our brains naturally develop tangles of tau proteins and clusters of beta-amyloid protein plaques. However, those afflicted with Alzheimer's tend to have them at a higher rate; the tangles and plaques all but attack the brain. The damage happens in the reverse order in which the brain develops, starting with short-term memory and spatial awareness and working backward to basic functions like swallowing.

Paula has probable Alzheimer's, stage four (moderate cognitive decline) with noticeable gaps in memory and requires help with certain efforts—in some ways, like a mature adolescent. Stage six,

OPPOSITE:
In Sonoma in
October 2013,
ten months
after receiving
her dementia
diagnosis, and
overhauling her
diet and daily
routines

severe cognitive decline, is a kind of toddler existence, at which point she will need assistance with daily activities such as getting dressed. Stage seven, very severe, is a brutal kind of infancy.

Paula is determined to stay at stage four for as long as she can. "Today, I live for the now," she often says.

In a strange way, Alzheimer's has soothed her lifelong anxieties like nothing else could. Since 2013, I've never seen her so levelheaded. "I've got a real fear now," she said. "I used to be a hypochondriac, but with Alzheimer's, instead of being afraid of it, I'm *dealing* with it."

She has turned to food as medicine, and it has reinvigorated her. True to form, she has taken her diet to extremes, and it's not for everyone. What's worth emulating is her defiant, take-charge attitude, the same scrappiness and self-reliance she showed as a single mom in New York in the 1970s. Paula is firmly committed to taking care of herself, to experimenting, and to keeping an open mind. I am convinced this flexibility helps her immeasurably. She says she feels better than she has in years. And I see it—she's leaner and lighter, quicker on her feet and to laugh—and, perhaps most noticeably, to forgive mistakes in the kitchen.

In an echo of her cookbooks, her regimen blends the ancient and the cutting edge. She now treats her body like a recipe, to be tested and retested using ever-better ingredients. After a few years of experiments, she has settled on some key approaches (see Paula's Tips for Dementia Worriers and Warriors, page 297). She swears by the medieval practice of fasting—she doesn't eat after seven o'clock in the evening—to spark autophagy, a self-cleaning of her neurons, and to make her cells more resilient by stressing them. For breakfast, she has her version of a trendy concoction called Bulletproof Coffee, for which she mixes coffee, pastured butter, and coconut oil extract. The original was invented by Dave Asprey, a Silicon Valley persona whom Paula follows on Facebook. She insists it keeps her alert well into the afternoon. She has converted her friend and editor Fran McCullough to the drink and continues to try to convert me.

Her other most experimental project is her afternoon smoothie, which she calls her "gritty" because it contains so many nuts, seeds, and vitamin pills. Along with avocado, spices straight out of *Couscous*, and blended greens (à la *Grains and Greens*), it contains a pharmacy's worth of supplements that cost her about two hundred dollars a month, none of which she is confident is helpful. At least she is trying everything she can. Poignantly, the gritty even includes her ultimate memory food, eggplant, in powder form, as part of a superfood-powered supplement called PurpleLogic.

Lunch is Paula's main meal of the day. She avoids gluten, dairy, and sugar, partly on the advice of neurologist David Perlmutter's book *Grain Brain*, which asserts that Alzheimer's is an inflammatory response in part to gluten and casein proteins in wheat and milk, hastened by sugars. He has his skeptics, but everyone supports Paula's diet. She looks for meat and seafood rich in omega-3 fatty acids to nourish her heart and brain, like wild-caught salmon, sardines, and grass-fed beef and chicken liver. Plus loads of vegetables, which she likes to steam-sauté in her favorite dishwasher-safe flameware tagine then assemble with other fresh vegetables to create her "rainbow salad." For probiotics and gut health, she tries to have pickles at every meal, whether kimchi or sauerkraut. As a treat, she has a second cup of coffee after lunch, with a small square of Valrhona dark chocolate. She avoids alcohol.

Cooking is complicated for her. "There's more to life than a good meal," she said at one of our photo shoots. "I didn't used to think that, but now I know." A hallmark of many kinds of dementia, her senses of smell and taste are diminished, not just of food but of smoke. That makes cooking alone prohibitively dangerous, so she only cooks in the company of others. But in other ways, her diminished palate is merely exceptional instead of incomprehensibly good. (And some days it comes back in its full glory. When we made cassoulet together, at the very end she told me to add a little salt. "There's a little bit of emptiness there," she remarked.) At first, she tried cooking a different recipe from her books once a day, "like practicing an instrument," she said. The experience was initially a revelation, as her kitchen skills had also been reduced to mere mortal level. "I can't believe how hard some of my recipes are," she admitted. But it began to depress her; re-creating old recipes also reminded her of what she's lost. Now she cooks other people's recipes she finds online—another first.

Paula works closely with her neurologist to make sure she tries nothing too risky, and she has found one whom she adores, Catherine Madison, who runs the Ray Dolby Brain Health Center in San Francisco (and whose husband supplies beef to some of Paula's favorite chefs). Dr. Madison believes in letting her patients do whatever helps, nothing that harms. She has also connected Paula to a nutritionist who reviews her regimen annually through blood tests and other lab work to assess and adjust Paula's approach.

To my great amazement, Dr. Madison has persuaded Paula to embrace both meditation and exercise, two practices Paula long resisted. Most of her life, whenever she got the urge to exercise, she loved to repeat the old adage, "I just lie down until the feeling passes."

Now, every morning she jogs a twenty-minute mile on the treadmill and meditates for fifteen minutes using an app called Headspace and podcasts by the Buddhist meditation teacher and psychologist Tara Brach. Through a local senior center (which has a network of volunteers to drive seniors like Paula around town), she takes twice-weekly classes in yoga and qigong, to stay active and to help with her balance, which has worsened with her illness. Like t'ai chi, qigong is an ancient Chinese form of exercise that relaxes as it energizes; the version of qigong Paula practices she prefers to t'ai chi because it involves fewer steps. "Qigong is so much better than t'ai chi," she says, only partly joking, "because I don't have to remember any of the moves!"

Clearly, she hasn't lost her sense of humor. "They say that's one thing that never goes," she says, palpably relieved.

A social routine also keeps her engaged. Her calendar is packed: Tuesdays are busiest, always blocked out for a weekly meet up with her Lunch Bunch, as she calls them, a half dozen Sonoma women friends with whom she's kept the standing date since 2002. On Tuesday afternoons in the summer, and Friday mornings year-round, Paula visits all her friends at Sonoma's two main farmers' markets. On Thursdays she checks in via video chat with an international group of fellow dementia advocates she met through the Alzheimer's Association. Facebook has also reunited her with pals around the globe, including former students from her cooking classes.

Politics has also become a later-life passion. She has always been a proud leftist, but she never worked on a presidential campaign before volunteering for Obama at the Sonoma Farmers' Market in 2008 and 2012. In 2016, she's been Feeling the Bern. She and Bill also stream several television shows, such as *House of Cards*, which occasionally cuts into her sleep. "I was up all night binging on season three," she once told me, excusing herself for sounding a bit muddled in our interviews.

Sleep has become a problem. Alzheimer's can throw off a body's natural circadian rhythms and lead to nighttime restlessness. She falls asleep fine but often awakes at two or three o'clock in the morning and can't settle back down. She has read that for optimal brain health, a person needs seven to nine hours of sleep. To achieve that, she has turned to the one drug she successfully avoided despite a decade living among beatnik writers, marijuana. She has obtained an identification card through California's medical marijuana program and has found limited success with sprays, cookies, and brownies infused with the drug. She purchases them online from companies specializing in marijuana-infused "edibles." It's the only part of her regimen not sanctioned by her neurologist, as the treatments, though legal, are not yet approved by the Food and Drug Administration (FDA).

Her biggest struggle so far is research. In her fight for new information on her illness, she must read and reread articles in a fight to retain them. Heartbreakingly for someone so curious, she has serious trouble processing new information. In the early stages, Alzheimer's attacks the hippocampus, the part of the brain that acts as a kind of file clerk, organizing where new information will go and how to find it so it can be recovered later in the form of memories. In this way, Alzheimer's sufferers don't so much lose their short-term memory as lose the ability to form new memories.

While writing this book, I witnessed this one painful day when I asked her to teach me to roll couscous by hand. The lesson began well: she started with a fine semolina from Kalustyan's that she knew well. Then we switched to another brand, without realizing that the slight change in texture would throw her off completely. She could see her couscous pearls were forming too quickly, but she could not connect the problem to the change in flour. "Something is wrong, but I don't know what it is," she said, her panic rising as the grains grew lumpy beneath her unwilling hands. "I am supposed to be the couscous queen!" It was acutely distressing to witness knowledge she so cherished stripped from her.

From then on I kept things simpler. At our photo shoots, instead of asking her to do any of the cooking, I invited her to taste dishes we had prepared, to see what memories their flavors evoked. I encouraged her to dig her hands into familiar textures, like duck confit and herb jam, without her having to bring about the alchemy herself. And I girded myself for the likely possibility that even these simpler experiences might bring nothing up.

Of course, I fantasized that her foods would unlock a flood of memories, the way Proust recalled his childhood by dipping a madeleine in tea. It comforted me to learn, from a book on the neuroscience of flavor, that recalling taste memories requires hard work even in a healthy mind, as Proust himself acknowledged. So when Paula took a bite of some stuffed mushrooms whose country of origin she'd never written down (recipe, page 162), I considered it a victory when she paused for a moment, and then said, "I think these are Tunisian."

❧

Paula's relationship with food has gotten complicated. Today dementia is her new obsession. At first she wanted to share her finds as widely as possible, just as she had her culinary discoveries back in her prime. She wanted to help "the worried and the warriors," as she put it, those fearing they might get the disease and those fighting it. Dementia sufferers and their intimates often struggle to advocate for the disease, feeling both fear and embarrassment—not to mention the debilitating effects of the illness itself. In 2013 she volunteered with the Northern California branch of the Alzheimer's Association on a series of frank, funny YouTube videos about her condition. The national association also tapped her to join its highly select 2014 Early-Stage Advisor Group. As one of twelve patient advisors, she participated in a series of national events, including the annual trip to Washington, DC, where she helped lobby Congress.

Paula was particularly moved in 2014 when some of her favorite chefs, whose work she has most influenced, cooked for separate Alzheimer's fund-raisers in her name in Los Angeles, Oakland, and Phoenix. Among the celebrated participants were Nancy Silverton and Evan Kleiman in Los Angeles, and Mourad Lahlou, Daniel Patterson, and David Kinch, who collaborated on a lavish fund-raising dinner hosted by Russell Moore at his restaurant Camino in Oakland. Paula traveled to each of the dinners.

But travel is now too hard, so she shares her finds on Facebook and Twitter—and keeps the circle local. Once a month she hosts a Memory Cafe at her nearby senior center, where she hopes others will feel safe to come forward. Anyone with memory concerns can share strategies about dementia.

Since the diagnosis, Paula has witnessed the harm that denial can cause. Friends now regularly confess their memory concerns, and when it sounds serious, she urges them to consult with a good neurologist, if only to rule out a tumor or celiac disease, which can cause memory lapses in certain sufferers. In less urgent cases, she recommends an online test for early dementia designed by Ohio State University (see the SAGE test, page 297).

Researching this book, I also witnessed the denial dementia inspires when old friends of hers, during my interviews, would ask me how she was doing but wouldn't call her themselves. Granted, there are good reasons to put off calling her—once you get her on the phone, it's hard to get off—but it was heartbreaking to detect the discomfort and helplessness in their voices.

I understand. Talking to her can break my heart. We often conducted interviews over video—me at my desk in Berkeley, Paula on her iPad in Sonoma. She liked to curl up with her iPad in bed, so it often felt like we were having a sleepover in the middle of the day. It was strange to feel nostalgic for those calls, even as they were taking place, knowing that the time was closing in on us when we could no longer have them. Looking over past transcripts, too, it pained me to see how her vocabulary has diminished along with her memories. For the first time in our decadelong friendship, I'd e-mail her a query in the middle of the night, and she wouldn't write back, forgetting I had written. Paula always e-mails back.

"I have no interest in feeling sorry for myself," she has told me many, many times.

Instead, she pushes on. Just yesterday, she sent me a request to join her network on LinkedIn. She keeps learning.

I am afraid that she may live long enough to reach the last stages of this vicious disease. If that happens, I hope I can find some way to bring her fresh material, to let her know that she is still loved and learning. That is what has fueled her entire life—even the last time she was bedridden, as a child, when she came down with scarlet fever and had to keep to her bed for three months, her entire family quarantined.

"I just fell into my own world," she said, surprisingly happy at the memory. "My mother took care of me and was probably very annoyed that we were living in a quarantine, since nobody could visit us. But my father spent a lot of time teaching me things and telling me stories.

"In a funny way," she continued, her mind making its usual leaps, "that's what I do for a living. The thing that interests me most in my work is what I put in my notebooks—what people tell me: the names of things, how they use them. I'm especially interested in *how* people show me things, because they're showing me a part of *them*."

She sighed, and laughed. "I wish I could make it more intellectual for you, but it's not. It's very earthy."

⊙ ✤ ⊙

Appendix

Seven Keys to Retrieving Food Memories

Connecting through food with someone suffering from dementia has its challenges as well as rewards. Here are seven tips based on what I learned while cooking with Paula for this book.

1. Be open to small successes and potential failure. You're embarking on an experiment, and some experiments don't work. The experience may be frustrating, disappointing, demoralizing—or richly stimulating. No matter what happens, you'll share a meal. You get an A for effort.

2. Although this may seem self-evident, if you want to cook a dish together to see what memories the food might evoke, select a recipe that has meaning, such as specialty of the person or a family heirloom. If there isn't a specific recorded recipe and you're hoping to retrieve a recipe from the person's memory, look over several published equivalents. If it's a dish with a foreign name, look for dishes from other countries that might be similar. Even if they do not share the same name, they may help shed more light.

3. Cooking and eating aren't the only ways a dish can evoke memories. Before shopping or cooking, sit down together in person or over the phone to read through the written recipe—both the ingredients and the instructions. Do any of the words bring up memories? This is an ideal time to ask general questions about the dish, as well, such as what did the person like about it, how did he or she first discover it, or does he or she recall making any ingredient substitutions.

OPPOSITE:
In 2015, two years after her diagnosis and going strong

4. Shopping for ingredients can also spark recollections, even if you're using FaceTime for part of your trip to the store. Using a video conference on one grocery trip, I was able to show Paula that my Berkeley grocery store carried long, curled, pale green *feggous* (Armenian cucumbers), which brought back some of her memories about shopping in the markets of Tangier.

5. When prepping and cooking, I found it almost more helpful to watch what Paula did than listen to what she said. Her hands sometimes knew what to do when her mind did not. Are there tricks that are used in how to peel garlic, flip polenta cakes, or stir batter? Paula would often reveal techniques while insisting she couldn't remember a thing about a dish.

6. As the dish nears completion, ask the person to help guide you as you assess its doneness. For example, if it's roast chicken, has the skin achieved the right color? If it's cooked vegetables, are they the right texture? Sometimes Paula would despair, "I have no idea. I can't remember." But other times the questions restored her confidence, reminding her of her deep cooking expertise—and taught me new ways to judge a dish.

7. When the dish is ready, if it's possible (especially if your cook is as opinionated as Paula), take the first bite to form your own opinion and give yourself an idea of what to ask. Then let your cook take one bite (not several) to focus on the flavor. With Paula, that first bite was often the most revealing. If no recollections come up, feign indifference to help lower the stakes, then encourage another bite or two. If still nothing comes up, sit down and enjoy the meal and talk about something else he or she enjoys, rather than food memories.

Paula's Tips for Dementia Worriers and Warriors

Dementia is a personal disease; everyone has his or her own version. It's important for those afflicted to find a good neurologist who can tailor a program with realistic goals. What follows are strategies that have worked for Paula, which she practices under close supervision of her neurologist, Dr. Catherine Madison.

SAGE test

Although there is no cure, dementia sufferers can gain both physically and emotionally from early intervention. But it can be challenging to find the right doctor. Paula recommends this simple online test to concerned friends. SAGE is an acronym for Self-Administered Gerocognitive Exam, a four-part test designed by Ohio State University that takes about fifteen minutes to complete. The results must be scored by a doctor. It does not replace a diagnosis, but it does offer an informal way to gauge whether deeper attention is needed. Search online for "SAGE test" to learn more.

Diet

Many studies have shown that the Mediterranean diet is good for the mind as well as the heart, for those with and without dementia. A 2015 study in *Alzheimer's & Dementia: The Journal of the Alzheimer's Association* showed that even modest steps toward a whole-foods regimen, such as eating one serving of seafood a week, two servings of berries a week, or two vegetable servings a day, significantly lowered the risk of developing Alzheimer's. At the time of this writing, Paula's diet includes:

- 1 serving (about 1 cup | 145 g) berries every day
- At least 1 serving (about 1 cup | 30 to 65 g) cooked or raw dark green leafy vegetables every day
- 1 handful of walnuts and 1 spoonful each of chia, sunflower, and hemp seeds daily
- 1 avocado almost every day
- 5 to 6 ounces (150 to 180 g) wild-caught salmon or canned sardines two times a week
- 5 to 6 ounces (150 to 180 g) grass-fed beef or pastured poultry two or three times a week

Paula's diet does *not* include simple carbohydrates or sugars. A Harvard study published in the August 2013 *New England Journal of Medicine* showed that even incremental increases in blood sugar levels are linked with an increased risk of dementia. Paula has taken this to an extreme, eliminating virtually all sugars and carbohydrates, what is known as a ketogenic diet. She believes this choice has made her more alert throughout the day. Her neurologist only advises she cut out added sugars.

Exercise

Paula studiously avoided exercise all her life. But many studies show that physically active people are less likely to experience cognitive decline and that exercise may reverse decline in certain cognitive processes. Every morning (after months of building up to this level), Paula proudly jogs a twenty-minute mile on a treadmill. She does qigong four times a week and gentle yoga three times a week. She tends not to walk out of doors because of dementia-related balance issues. But exercise has widened her social circle and has improved her health and self-image and her ability to roll with the punches.

Meditation

A small but exciting Harvard study published in the January 2011 issue of *Psychiatry Research: Neuroimaging* showed that people who meditated about thirty minutes a day for eight weeks experienced slight growth in their hippocampus, the brain's 'file center,' which organizes new information. Paula meditates fifteen to thirty minutes a day, sometimes twice a day, using guided meditations from online sources such as Tara Brach. She has found it improves her mood and emotional equilibrium. She loves to chant the oms.

Intermittent fasting

On the theory that fasting promotes autophagy, or the self-cleaning of her cells, and slows the growth of tau and beta-amyloid proteins in her brain, Paula eats only between the hours of about noon and seven o'clock in the evening and fasts the remaining seventeen hours. Although the practice of fasting is thousands of years old, there is no clinical evidence to support the theory that it impacts brain functioning. Her neurologist does not encourage the practice but sees no harm.

Dietary supplements

Paula works closely with a nutritionist recommended by her neurologist to devise a daily regimen of over thirty supplements, from anti-inflammatory spices like cinnamon, ginger, and turmeric to probiotics, enzymes, and short-chain fatty acids, which she blends in her afternoon smoothie. Although all of them have been cleared by her neurologist, many are inspired by her embrace of functional medicine, an alternative approach to disease prevention created by nutritionist Jeffrey Bland.

Prescription drugs

Paula also embraces traditional Western medicine and takes two medications approved for Alzheimer's that may provide modest benefits in behavior and cognition: donepezil and memantine.

Social activity

Studies have established that socially and mentally active and engaged seniors have better cognitive function and a lower incidence of dementia. Paula has always enjoyed the company of others; because familiar routines are now easier for her to manage than spontaneous gatherings, she picks a few days every week to meet with friends: Tuesdays are her standing date with the Lunch Bunch, a group of local women friends close to her age. On Thursdays she videoconferences with other Alzheimer's activists around the globe. Once a month she volunteers at her local senior center to lead a Memory Cafe, a gathering for the worried and the warriors to learn about dementia.

Openness and activism

Dementia has a punishing stigma attached to it that understandably inspires many sufferers to hide their condition. In certain states such as California, a person with dementia can lose his or her driver's license because doctors are required by law to report the diagnosis to the motor vehicles department. Paula never learned to drive and had already retired when she received her diagnosis, so she did not have to worry about losing her car or a job. She is exceptionally public about her illness and draws tremendous strength from the support of friends, colleagues, and fans.

Online resources

It empowers and engages Paula to keep abreast of the latest developments on dementia and cognitive functioning online. Here are seven of the sites she visits regularly.

alz.org (and alzheimersblog.org)

Paula has found resources for her illness through both the national and the Northern California branches of the Alzheimer's Association, the leading nonprofit advocacy group.

alzforum.org

The news site publishes and archives the latest scientific papers on the disease.

ConsumerLab.com

This private company evaluates nutritional supplements for efficacy and safety. It is not associated with the FDA, but because the FDA does not test nutritional supplements, it's the most reliable source Paula has found outside of her own nutritionist.

Facebook

Paula has discovered a surprising number of resources by simply searching for posts containing the words *Alzheimer's* and *dementia*.

bulletproofexec.com

Aimed at Silicon Valley software engineers and anyone else interested in "the Bulletproof® state of high performance," entrepreneur Dave Asprey's website and Facebook page keep Paula up on the latest in peak cognitive functioning through food.

fourhourworkweek.com

For creative approaches to productivity and mental alertness, Paula follows the blog and podcasts of entrepreneur Timothy Ferriss. Through his interviews she discovered Tara Brach, her meditation guide.

tarabrach.com

Paula has tried many guided meditations and has found this teacher who marries Western psychology with Buddhist practices, among the best.

Additional Resources

- The Mayo Clinic (mayoclinic.org)
- The National Institute on Aging (nia.nih.gov/alzheimers)
- The Ray Dolby Brain Health Center (cpmc.org/advanced /neurosciences/brainhealth)

Three Facts about the Science of Flavor and Memory

Throughout her long career, Paula intuited a few of the ways that our brains perceive flavors, pathways that scientists are only starting to uncover thanks to advances in brain-imaging technologies.

1. **FLAVOR IS MORE THAN JUST TASTE.** Eating is often overlooked as a simple act. But Paula knew instinctively that our relationship to food is incredibly complex, drawing not just on our senses but also on our emotions and intellect. She knew that the best food is about love and learning as much as taste. She articulated this in her 1988 book *Paula Wolfert's World of Food* (see page 159) when she described what she called the Big Taste. She wrote, "While I enjoy eating simple grilled foods, what interests me when I *cook* are dishes with a taste that is fully dimensional . . . that appeals to all the senses." She continued, "I have always loved dishes about which a story can be told. . . . When I come to understand the whys and wherefores behind a dish, I feel a friendship, a kinship with the people who cook it. It is this same kind of friendly bridge I hope to create with my readers."

   Starting in the 1980s, with the discovery of retronasal smell by psychologist Paul Rozin, scientists began to understand the mechanisms behind our perception of flavor. It turns out that our mouths tell us the least about the foods we eat. Our taste buds can detect only the five basic tastes (sweet, salty, bitter, sour, and umami). They send that information to our brain stems to establish only whether a food will kill us or keep us alive. Flavor, on the other hand, is created by the most sophisticated parts of our brain. Flavor starts with the aromatic gases we release by chewing. We don't detect these aromas by smelling them like a rose; rather, they flit up from the back of our mouth to a pair of nasal passages called posterior nares. Wine professionals slurp to aerate their posterior nares. Unlike tastes, these retronasal aromas are processed by the most sophisticated parts of the brain, including the limbic system—the parts that make us human, that form our emotions, subconscious, and memories.

   The next time you take a bite, open your mouth for a moment as you chew. You may be astounded at how that simple action amplifies flavor. Paula often talks with her mouth full, aerating her palate instinctively. It may appear awkward, but there's a certain science behind it.

2. **FLAVOR IS A FACE.** Paula is known for her rigor, for refusing to streamline even the most complex recipes for American home cooks. Thanks to the wonderful book *Neurogastronomy* by Yale neurobiologist Gordon M. Shepherd, I now think she is so protective of her recipes not for the sake of sheer stubbornness (though she's plenty headstrong) but because she relates to them like people. She not only bonds with her recipes, but changing them feels to her as inconceivable as removing an eyebrow from a friend's face.

Shepherd hypothesizes that flavor is so complex that the brain perceives it like it does a human face, forming an irregular but instantly recognizable "flavor image," which incorporates emotions and memory associations as well as sensory data. Just as with human faces, we can recognize a flavor instantly, though we often have difficulty describing it. Paula's ability to articulate flavors comes from long practice and a gifted palate. Her ability to describe them so clearly also deepens her close relationship with them.

3. **IN THE BEST DISHES, TWO PLUS TWO EQUALS MORE THAN FOUR.** Recalling her grandmother's Balkan eggplant spread *ajvar*, Paula told me, "I think I liked it because two plus two equaled so much more than four." Scientists have names for this phenomenon: intramodal enhancement and crossmodal enhancement. When we experience two tastes together, such as sweet and sour (think roasted red bell peppers plus lemon juice), they amplify or "intramodally enhance" each other. In other words, our brains detect more of each taste together than it would if we ate either one alone. Similarly, a taste can be "crossmodally enhanced" by a complementary aroma or texture (think velvety eggplant spiced with aromatic smoked paprika). But these intra- and crossmodal enhancements only work when the contrasts are congruent, that is, they make sense together, whether culturally or intuitively.

Paula craved congruent traditional foods all her life. A key magic of her recipes is that they are loaded with congruent intra- and crossmodal enhancements much more than most recipes. As she wrote in *World of Food*, "When I ask myself why I am so fond of these recipes, it's because they employ ingredients that have traditionally complemented one another and that, when combined, create a flavor different and more pleasing than when served on their own."

Six Lessons from Cooking
Paula Wolfert's Recipes

1. **KEEP CALM AND FOLLOW THE RECIPE.** Despite my two decades in food, I can be a terrible recipe follower. In my impatience, I often miss key instructions because I am reading a recipe too fast or looking for shortcuts. Paula's recipes taught me to slow down. She doesn't always explain the whys, assuming a high level of knowledge on the part of her readers. But to every step there is a reason. If a recipe calls for a thin pan, look for a *thin* pan.

2. **SUBTLE TOUCHES CAN HAVE A BIG IMPACT.** I didn't always think of cooking as hunting for hidden treasures before I discovered Paula's cookbooks. But tucked into many of her recipes are numerous small steps that lead to big flavor. Tossing freshly minced garlic with the lettuce in a salad instead of stirring it into the vinaigrette imparts a milder garlic taste to the dish. Grated onions taste sweeter and softer than chopped or pureed. Eggplants taste lighter and sweeter if salted before cooking, and are downright pillowy if they're soaked in salted water. She doesn't always point them out, but the small techniques are a pleasure to discover.

3. **TIME IS A FLAVORING.** We all know how stews and soups often taste better a day or two after cooking. But Paula's books have taught me many more ways to improve a dish with time. A steak tastes richer if it is lightly salted a day or two before cooking. Chopped greens taste more intense and take on a velvety texture if they're lightly salted, massaged, and then left to drain for an hour or so before sautéing. Roasted vegetables take on sweetness and mellowness if left in the oven's receding heat for a half hour, rather than serving them sizzling hot.

4. **THE TAGINE IS TRULY MAGICAL.** When Paula and I met, she was writing her clay pot book and raved constantly about cooking in earthenware, particularly "the magic of the tagine." A tagine is an investment, but it is worth it. It is the ultimate fix-it-and-forget-it, steam-injected, flavor-intensifying slow cooker. Preheat it for about 15 minutes on a heat diffuser over medium-low heat. Add any roasting-quality vegetable (such as cauliflower or broccoli florets, thick slices of squash or red onion, whole small or quartered large Yukon Gold potatoes, chunks of carrots, wedges of fennel or cabbage), a good glug of olive oil, generous pinches of

salt and pepper (plus Aleppo or Marash red pepper flakes), and some favorite fresh herbs and/or lemon zest. Stir to coat, cover, and let the vegetables cook in the oil and their own juices, turning them occasionally, for 30 minutes to 1 hour. When the vegetables are just tender, turn off the heat and let them continue to cook in the receding heat of the clay. They will emerge intensely flavored, beautifully browned, and surprisingly moist.

5. **GREENS ARE MADE FOR BLENDING.** Thanks to *Mediterranean Grains and Greens*, I cook greens in blends more often than I cook them singly, combining chard with kale, or spinach with arugula (or all four together)—and I cook them for longer than I once did. I've come to realize slow-cooked greens taste meatier than greens that are quickly sautéed. One blend is so good that my husband calls it Magic Greens: In a large, deep pot with a tight-fitting lid, I sauté a thinly sliced onion and/or leek in olive oil and butter over medium heat until soft and sweet, about 15 minutes. Then I add stemmed, chopped greens in order of leaf thickness, seasoning them and cooking them, covered, about 5 minutes after each addition. Collards are first, then kale, next comes chard, and then finally spinach and sometimes a few fistfuls of chopped parsley. I cook the whole mixture, stirring it occasionally, until it has broken down and is dense and richly flavored, about 30 minutes, and then I let it stand for about 15 minutes before serving.

6. **THE BEST HOST IS A RELAXED HOST.** In the past, especially before I cooked my way through *The Slow Mediterranean Kitchen*, whenever I would have friends over for a meal, I tended to serve dishes cooked *à la minute*, like grilled meats or soufflés. Too often this left my guests standing around awkwardly while I cooked (and stressed). I mistakenly had the idea that serving a dish prepared the previous day would feel like putting leftovers on the table. Now I know that make-ahead dishes can be among the most elegant, the most fun to cook, and the most delicious.

An Unforgettable Larder

Today it's a restaurant trope for chefs to boast about their house-made spice blends and preserves. But Paula was way ahead on the idea of building a from-scratch pantry of fantastic flavors. These larder favorites will keep for months and will add nuance and wonder to many dishes, not just the ones in this book.

Preserved Lemons

Paula introduced Americans to Moroccan preserved lemons with her first book, *Couscous*, in 1973. They became one of her signatures, appearing in the pantry sections of several later books. The optional spice mixture comes from the coastal town of Safi. With or without spices, use the lemons in her Moroccan recipes, in cocktails, in cheese sandwiches, and even on pizza.

---

9 or 10 lemons, preferably organic

About ⅓ cup (60 g) kosher salt (see notes)

OPTIONAL SPICE MIXTURE

1 (3-inch | 7.5-cm) cinnamon stick

3 cloves

5 or 6 coriander seeds

3 or 4 black peppercorns

1 bay leaf

Makes 5 lemons

⏱ The lemons must sit for 30 days before using; they will keep for up to 1 year.

Scrub 5 of the lemons well, then soften them by rolling them back and forth on a firm work surface. Quarter each softened lemon from the blossom end to within ¼ inch (6 mm) of the stem end. Spread the salt in a wide, shallow bowl. Sprinkle 1 to 2 teaspoons of the salt on the exposed flesh of the lemons, then reshape the fruits. Halve and squeeze the remaining 4 or 5 lemons to total ½ cup (120 ml) juice. If using the spice mixture, have all the ingredients ready in a small bowl.

Place 1 tablespoon of the salt at the bottom of a large widemouthed glass jar with a tight-fitting lid. Pack the 5 prepared lemons into the jar, adding more salt and the spice mixture, if using, between the lemons. Firmly push down on the lemons so they release their juices. (A cocktail muddler is an ideal tool for this.) Top with the ½ cup (120 ml) fresh lemon juice. The lemons should be completely submerged, with about ½-inch (1.25-cm) headspace between the liquid and the inside of the lid. Add more lemon juice if needed to cover. Screw on the lid.

Let the lemons ripen in a warm place for 30 days, turning the jar upside down every few days to distribute the salt and juice. If necessary, add more lemon juice to keep the lemons covered. Transfer to the refrigerator.

To use the lemons, remove them from their brine as needed, using a wooden spoon or tongs to extract them. Rinse them under running cool water to remove the excess salt. Usually only the rind

recipe continues →

is used, though Paula sometimes also uses the pulp. Cut as directed in individual recipes.

NOTES For the kosher salt, look for a brand with no additives, such as Diamond Crystal.

As Paula wrote in *Couscous*, "Sometimes you will see a sort of lacy, white substance clinging to preserved lemons in their jar; it is perfectly harmless, but should be rinsed off for aesthetic reasons just before the lemons are used."

Saffron Water

Saffron water isn't just an economical way to stretch one of the most expensive spices in the world. Paula was taught that the best saffron "only comes alive when hydrated first." If a recipe calls for saffron water, she will often soak all of the dried spices in the saffron water before adding them to the dish. Saffron and tomatoes have a wonderful affinity, which makes saffron water a terrific addition to tomato-based pasta sauces. It is also good in shellfish stocks, meat loaf, or even a favorite barbecue sauce.

½ teaspoon saffron threads   1 cup (240 ml) warm water

Makes 1 cup (240 ml)

The saffron water can be refrigerated for up to 1 week or frozen for up to 3 months.

Set a small frying pan over low heat until warm but not hot. Rub the saffron threads between your fingers, crumbling them into the warm pan. Toast the saffron over low heat, crushing the threads into filaments with the back of a wooden spoon, until just brittle, about 1 to 2 minutes.

Pour the water into the pan, remove from the heat, and let stand for 5 minutes. The saffron water can be used at once. To store, transfer to a tightly capped jar and refrigerate, or put 2 tablespoons into each section of an ice-cube tray and freeze.

Tomato Magic

Paula invented this vastly superior alternative to canned tomato paste while testing her final book, *The Food of Morocco*.

1 (28-ounce | 800-g) can whole tomatoes, preferably organic and fire-roasted

1 (6- to 8-ounce | 180- to 225-g) jar sun-dried tomatoes packed in olive oil

2 tablespoons water

½ teaspoon flaky sea salt

Extra-virgin olive oil, for topping

In a food processor or blender, combine the tomatoes with their juice, the sun-dried tomatoes with their oil, the water, and the salt and puree until smooth.

Scrape the puree into a wide, heavy stainless-steel or enameled cast-iron saucepan about 8 to 10 inches (20 to 25 cm) wide. Set the saucepan over medium-low heat and cook, stirring often, until the mixture has reduced to a thick jam, about 30 minutes.

Remove from the heat and let cool. The paste can be used at once. To store, transfer it to a jar with a tight-fitting lid, top with a ¼-inch (6-mm) layer of olive oil, cover, and refrigerate; or shape the paste into 1- or 2-tablespoon balls, arrange on a sheet pan, freeze for 10 to 15 minutes, and then transfer the balls to a resealable freezer bag and return to the freezer.

Makes about 1½ cups (395 g)

The paste can be refrigerated for up to 1 month or frozen for up to 3 months.

Smen

Aged clarified butter, or *smen*, is a "quintessentially Moroccan ingredient," Paula wrote in *The Food of Morocco*. It lends dishes a subtle meatiness, a little like miso. This is Paula's recipe for the ultimate traditional version: first you culture cream to make butter, then you clarify the butter, and finally you strain and age it. To rid the butter of all milk solids, which can cause it to go rancid, the clarified butter is is carefully strained through cheesecloth before aging. For a faster version, purchase some clarified butter, transfer it to a clean crock with a lid, cover it, and let it age in a cool, dark cupboard.

---

3 cups (720 ml) heavy cream, preferably organic

2 tablespoons whole-milk plain yogurt (goat's, sheep's or cow's milk)

¾ cup (180 ml) water, chilled with a few ice cubes

2 teaspoons flaky sea salt

Makes about ½ cup (110 g)

🕐 The cream and yogurt are cultured overnight before churning; the butter ages for 2 to 3 days before clarifying. The smen will keep in the refrigerator or in a cool cupboard for up to 4 years.

In a bowl, whisk together the cream and yogurt. Cover with a kitchen towel and let stand overnight at room temperature to culture.

The next day, pour the cultured cream into a food processor and process until the butter solids start to form a ball and throw off the buttermilk, 15 to 25 seconds. Pulse a few more times to help throw off additional liquid.

Set a fine-mesh sieve over a bowl. Pour the buttermilk through the sieve, leaving the butter behind in the bowl of the processor. Reserve the buttermilk for another use, such as for serving with Tunisian couscous (page 231). Return any butter solids from the sieve to the food processor.

To rinse the butter, drizzle about 3 tablespoons (45 ml) of the ice water over the butter and pulse two or three times. Pour off and discard the liquid. Repeat two more times, using about 3 tablespoons (45 ml) ice water each time. The water should run nearly clear. If it doesn't, repeat one more time.

Line a work surface with a kitchen towel. Transfer the butter to the towel and knead the butter with your hands to remove any excess moisture. Transfer the butter to a sheet of parchment paper, sprinkle on the salt, and continue to knead until the salt is evenly incorporated.

Line a large platter or sheet pan with a fresh kitchen towel. Divide the butter into 6 equal pieces. Press each portion into a round ¼ inch (6 mm) thick. Arrange the butter rounds side by side on the towel-lined platter. Cover the rounds with another fresh kitchen towel and let ripen in a cool, dark place for 2 to 3 days.

To clarify the butter, set the rounds in a small, heavy saucepan over very low heat. Allow the butter to melt slowly, without stirring and without browning. Skim off any foam as it bubbles to the surface. When the butter is golden and clear, remove it from the heat and let stand until cool.

Dampen two layers of cheesecloth or one layer of muslin and drape them over a fine-mesh sieve set over a bowl. Carefully ladle the butter through the lined sieve, leaving behind any white sediment at the bottom of the pan. Line the sieve with a fresh double layer of dampened cheesecloth or muslin, place over a clean bowl, and strain the butter a second time (the *smen* must be absolutely clear).

Pour the clarified butter into a clean glass jar or earthenware vessel with a tight-fitting lid, cover, and store in a cool, dark place at room temperature for 1 month before opening. Store in a cool cupboard or the refrigerator after opening. Over time the butter will take on an increasingly grainy texture and meaty flavor.

NOTE If any dark spots appear while the butter ages, the butter has spoiled and must be discarded.

Hrous

If you like hot sauces, especially *harissa*, the Tunisian hot pepper paste, be forewarned: make this sauce once and you may never want anything else. A close cousin of *harissa*, *hrous* has more complexity from its wider blend of seasonings and its unusual base of onions lightly fermented in ground turmeric. Paula liked it so much, she published several versions. This one comes from her updated edition of *Mediterranean Cooking.*

"In a typical southern Tunisian home," she wrote, every June, "the cook will slice about seventy pounds of fresh onions, toss them with salt and turmeric, . . . and leave them for three months." In the fall, once the chiles have ripened and dried, the cook finishes the sauce. Here, Paula ferments the onion for just a few days (the longer it ferments, the more complex the final flavors). The fermenting onion gives off a pungent aroma, but it disappears once the onion is blended with the spices. Dried rosebuds are optional but worth seeking out for their faint sweetness and aroma.

---

1 cup (4 ounces | 115 g) thinly sliced yellow or Vidalia onion

¼ teaspoon ground turmeric

2 tablespoons flaky sea salt

7 dried New Mexico chiles

1 ancho chile

½ teaspoon ground coriander or tabil (see note, page 232)

½ teaspoon ground caraway

½ teaspoon freshly ground black pepper

Generous pinch of ground cinnamon

Generous pinch of food-grade ground dried rosebuds (optional)

3 tablespoons (45 ml) extra-virgin olive oil, plus more for topping if storing

Makes ½ cup (130 g)

🍯 The hrous mellows wonderfully over time; it can be refrigerated for up to 1 year.

In a wide, shallow bowl, combine the onion, turmeric, and salt and mix well. Cover loosely with a paper towel or cheesecloth and let stand at room temperature until soft and very wet, 1 to 3 days.

Working in batches, wrap the onion in cheesecloth, muslin, or a kitchen towel and squeeze tightly until very dry. As each batch is finished, transfer it to the bowl of a food processor. Let the onion sit while you prepare the chiles.

Stem and seed all the chiles and break them up into pieces. Place a small, dry frying pan over low heat, add the chile pieces, and toast them, turning them a few times, just until they are fragrant, about 2 minutes. Immediately remove from the heat to avoid burning and transfer to a plate to cool. Working in batches if needed, transfer to a spice grinder or mini food processor and grind to a powder.

Transfer the ground chiles to the food processor with the onion. Add the coriander, caraway, black pepper, cinnamon, rosebuds (if using), and olive oil and process until smooth.

The sauce can be used at once. To store, pack into a small jar with a tight-fitting lid, top with a ¼-inch (6-mm) layer of olive oil, cover, and refrigerate.

NOTE In Tunisia, this sauce is traditionally made with North African Nabeul chiles. Paula found that a mix of New Mexico and ancho chiles produces the closest approximation.

Svaneti Salt

Savory and faintly sweet with notes of rye bread and garlic, this unusual seasoned salt lends sophistication and mystery to just about anything from roast potatoes or braised brisket to megadarra (page 235) or stuffed eggplant (page 206). Paula learned how to make it in the mountainous Svaneti region of Georgia, where salt is traditionally stretched with spices because it is so valuable. "In fact, in olden times a quart measure of salt was worth an entire cow," she wrote.

---

3 tablespoons flaky sea salt

2 teaspoons ground caraway

1½ teaspoons crushed garlic

1½ teaspoons ground coriander

½ teaspoon freshly ground black pepper

½ teaspoon ground fenugreek

Pinch of cayenne pepper

In a jar with a tight-fitting lid, combine all the ingredients, cover, and shake vigorously until thoroughly mixed and any clumps have broken up. Use at once, or cover and refrigerate.

Makes about ¼ cup (45 g)

🕐 The salt can be refrigerated for up to 1 month.

Pomegranate Concentrate

Paula helped popularize the tangy-sweet Middle Eastern condiments, pomegranate molasses and pomegranate concentrate, when she began reporting on the foods of the region in the late 1980s. Traditionally, pomegranate molasses is made from fresh pomegranate juice cooked down to a syrup with lemon juice and sugar; concentrate is simply reduced fresh pomegranate juice. They are interchangeable in most recipes, Paula says; now that she's on a low-sugar diet, she prefers the concentrate. She typically uses jarred concentrate at home, but she published a recipe for the molasses in *Eastern Mediterranean*, and this one for concentrate in a 1989 story about meze for *Food & Wine*.

---

4 large pomegranates (roughly 15 ounces | 400 g each), or 1½ cups (360 ml) bottled pomegranate juice

Makes about ¼ cup (60 ml)

The concentrate keeps for several weeks in the refrigerator.

If using whole pomegranates, cut each pomegranate into segments. Working over a large bowl in the sink, separate the seeds from the pith. Being careful to leave behind any traces of bitter pith, transfer the seeds in batches to cheesecloth or a kitchen towel and squeeze, working over a clean bowl, to extract the juice. Repeat with the remaining seeds. The juice should measure 1½ cups (360 ml).

In a small stainless-steel saucepan, bring the pomegranate juice to a boil over medium-high heat. Turn down the heat to medium-low and simmer, gently swirling the pan occasionally to prevent scorching, until reduced to ¼ cup (60 ml), about 40 minutes. Alternatively, pour the juice into a 2-cup (480-ml) glass measuring pitcher and microwave on high for 3 to 5 minutes at a time, watching carefully to ensure the concentrate does not boil over, until reduced to ¼ cup (60 ml), about 20 minutes total depending on the power of your microwave.

Pour the concentrate into a small glass jar and let cool, uncovered, to room temperature (it will take on a jelly-like consistency). Use at once, or cap tightly and store in the refrigerator.

Turkish Yogurt Sauce

Among Paula's favorite souvenirs from her many trips to Turkey were its exquisite yogurt sauces. This versatile example, which she published as "Yogurt-Garlic Sauce" in *Eastern Mediterranean*, can be drizzled on grilled vegetables, grain dishes such as Megadarra (page 235), or grilled meats such as Ćevapčići (page 24). Use full-fat yogurt for best flavor and texture. The mint and red pepper flakes are optional but strongly recommended.

---

1 quart (900 g) plain regular yogurt, or 2 cups (450 g) plain Greek yogurt

3 garlic cloves, peeled

Flaky sea salt and freshly ground black pepper

Up to ½ cup (120 ml) water

Pinch of sugar (optional)

Up to 2 teaspoons fresh lemon juice (optional)

Pinch of mild red pepper flakes, preferably Aleppo or Marash (optional)

1 tablespoon crumbled dried mint leaves, pressed through a fine-mesh sieve (optional)

2 tablespoons olive oil, for garnish

Fresh mint leaves, for garnish (optional)

Line a sieve with cheesecloth or muslin and set it over a bowl. Spoon the yogurt into the sieve and let drain at room temperature until it has the texture of very thick sour cream. If using regular yogurt, let drain until 2 cups (450 g) remain. If using Greek yogurt, the total amount with reduce only slightly—not more than a few tablespoons. The regular yogurt will need to drain for 1 to 2 hours and the Greek yogurt for 10 to 20 minutes.

Meanwhile, crush the garlic with ¼ teaspoon salt to form a paste; use a mortar and pestle, the back of a heavy knife and a cutting board, or a mini food processor.

Transfer the yogurt to a shallow bowl. Whisk in the water, a couple of tablespoons at a time, until the mixture is creamy and smooth. Whisk in the garlic paste, ¼ teaspoon at a time, until the desired garlicky taste is achieved. If the sauce tastes acrid, whisk in the sugar. Let the mixture mellow at room temperature for 1 hour.

Add the lemon juice to taste and the red pepper flakes to sharpen the flavor, if desired. Season with salt and black pepper. Whisk in the dried mint, if using. Cover and refrigerate until well chilled, at least 20 minutes or up to overnight.

Just before serving, decorate the yogurt with swirls of olive oil and with the fresh mint, if using.

Makes about 2 cups (480 ml)

The sauce mellows at room temperature for 1 hour and is then refrigerated for at least 20 minutes or up to overnight before serving.

Selected Bibliography

Articles

Claiborne, Craig. "News of Food: Cape Cod Restaurants; French Dishes Offered at Chillingsworth, an East Brewster Inn." *New York Times* 11 August 1959.

Cole, Bruce. "A Conversation with Paula Wolfert Includes Coffee and Canelés." *Edible San Francisco* Fall 2005.

Fletcher, Janet. "The Culinary Sleuth." *San Francisco Chronicle* 1 March 1995; "Display's the Thing." *Metropolitan Home* May/June 2000.

Jenkins, Nancy. "Master Cooks Take to the Road." *New York Times* 10 October 1984.

Knickerbocker, Peggy. "Paula Wolfert's Pursuit of Flavor." *Food & Wine* November 1995.

Kummer, Corby. "What Cooking Classes Teach." *The Atlantic* June 1985.

Lemann, Nicholas. "The Diva: Paula Wolfert is very high maintenance, but she's worth it." *Slate* 18 August 1998.

Julian, Sheryl. "Mistress of the Mediterranean." *Boston Globe* 16 September 1998.

Leite, David. "La Bouche Speaks: An Interview with Paula Wolfert." *Leite's Culinaria* 22 November 2003.

Nathan, Joan. "Private Lessons: The Kitchen's Got Class." *Washington Post* 21 October 1979.

O'Neill, Molly. "Fresh Pepper." *New York Times Magazine* 26 June 1994.

Robertson, Nan. "Students of Mrs. Lucas Have a Choice of 123 Recipes to Attempt." *New York Times* 25 October 1958.

Parsons, Russ. "Easy polenta that doesn't skimp on flavor." *Los Angeles Times* 18 February 2010.

Sidhom, S.A. "Couscous and Other Good Food from Morocco." *Minnesota Daily* 26 November 1973.

Scattergood, Amy. "Extreme Wolfert? Mais Oui!" *Los Angeles Times* 25 January 2006.

Steingarten, Jeffrey. "Out of North Africa." *Vogue* March 1994.

Books

Barr, Luke. *Provence 1970: M.F.K. Fisher, Julia Child, James Beard, and the Reinvention of American Taste*. New York: Clarkson Potter, 2013.

Belasco, Warren. *Appetite for Change: How the Counterculture Took on the Food Industry*. Ithaca and London: Cornell University Press, 1989 and 2007.

Blanch, Leslie. *The Wilder Shores of Love*. New York: Simon & Schuster, 1952 and 1982.

Clark, Robert. *The Solace of Food: A Life of James Beard*. South Royalton, VT: Steerforth Press, 1993.

Dillon, Millicent. *A Little Original Sin: The Life and Works of Jane Bowles*. New York: Holt, Rinehart, and Winston, 1981.

Driasma, Douwe. *The Nostalgia Factory*. Translated by Liz Waters. New Haven and London: Yale University Press, 2013.

Edwards, Brian T. *Morocco Bound: Disorienting America's Maghreb, from Casablanca to the Orient Express*. Durham, NC: Duke University Press, 2005.

Ephron, Nora. "The Food Establishment: Life in the Land of the Rising Soufflé (or Is It the Meringue?)" *New York*, September 1968, anthologized in *Wallflower at the Orgy*. New York: Bantam Reprint Edition, 2011.

Goldstein, Joyce. *Inside the California Food Revolution*. Berkeley: University of California Press, 2013.

Jones, Evan. *Epicurean Delight: The Life and Times of James Beard*. New York: Simon & Schuster, 1990.

Hess, John L. and Karen. *The Taste of America*. New York: Penguin Books, 1972.

Kamp, David. *The United States of Arugula: How We Became a Gourmet Nation*. New York: Clarkson Potter, 2006.

Kuh, Patric. *The Last Days of Haute Cuisine*. New York: Viking, 2001; *Finding the Flavors We Lost*. New York: Ecco, 2016.

Lang, George. *Nobody Knows the Truffles I've Seen*. Lincoln, NE: Authors Choice Press, 2005.

McNamee, Thomas. *Alice Waters and Chez Panisse*. New York: Penguin Press, 2007; *The Man Who Changed the Way We Eat: Craig Claiborne and the American Food Renaissance*. New York: Free Press, 2012.

Rubin, David C. *Memory in Oral Traditions: The Cognitive Psychology of Epic, Ballads, and Counting-out Rhymes*. New York: Oxford University Press, 1995.

Shepherd, Gordon M. *Neurogastronomy: How the Brain Creates Flavor and Why It Matters*. New York: Columbia University Press, 2012.

Shenk, David. *The Forgetting: Alzheimer's: Portrait of an Epidemic*. New York: Doubleday, 2001.

Van Aken, Norman. *No Experience Necessary*. Lanham, MD: Taylor Trade Publishing, 2014.

Villas, James. *Between Bites: Memoirs of a Hungry Hedonist*. New York: John Wiley & Sons, 2002.

Acknowledgments

FIRST, TO PAULA, for your bravery, trust, humor, leisurely Sonoma lunches, clay pots, hundreds of e-mails, fifty interviews over five years, seven decades of backup materials, and so much more. Writing your life story was an adventure of a lifetime.

Second, to Team Unforgettable: Eric, who encouraged us all to be bold with this project, starting with the suggestion that we Kickstart it ourselves, then saw Paula's food like no one else; Andrea, our majordomo, keen editor, and gifted teacher, for giving us a master class in writing cookbooks; and Toni, for transforming it all into this breathtaking book. You all inspired me more than I dreamed possible. Without you, nothing.

To everyone else who so generously helped make this book a reality (in chronological order):

To Susan McCreight Lindeborg, my beloved chef who first showed me Paula's cookbooks on the line at the Morrison-Clark Inn; to all my mentors and friends at *Food & Wine*, especially Dana Cowin, Tina Ujlaki, and Pamela Kaufman, for assigning me to be Paula's editor, sending me to Marrakech with her, and encouraging this endeavor in manifold ways; Joe Yonan and Bonnie Benwick, for assigning Eric and me to break the news of Paula's dementia in the *Washington Post*, which led to this book; Melanie Jackson, for encouraging me to think big; Barbara Haber and Paula Hamilton, for a crucial push; Patricia Cogley, Kristen Donnelly, Lori Galvin, Scott Hocker, Steven Kotok, Joyce Lee, Molly Stevens, Nicholas Wolfert, and Leila Wolfert, for supporting the idea early and often.

To Nick Fauchald, Anna Watson Carl, Holly Muñoz, and Maris Kreizman, for shining a light on the mysteries of Kickstarter; Pete Lee, for our unforgettable video; to everyone who helped spread word of the campaign, especially Yotam Ottolenghi, Michael Pollan, Alice Waters, Dorie Greenspan, Ruth Reichl, Michael Ruhlman, Evan Kleiman, Marcia Gagliardi, and Kim Severson, as well as many others;

to the San Francisco chapter of Les Dames d'Escoffier, for their clarion call; Kathy Strahs, for her sound ideas; and the good people at BackerKit.

To all who spoke or e-mailed with me about their adventures with Paula: Stewart Aledort, Ann Amernick, Colman Andrews, Sara Baer-Sinnott, Ariane Batterberry, Michel Bras, Jerilyn Brusseau, Donna Coughlin, André Daguin, Ariane Daguin, Greg Drescher, Loretta Foye, Susan Friedland, Gael Greene, Montse Guillén, Dan Halpern, Abderrazak Haouari, Filiz Hösükoğlu, Janet Jaidi, Nancy Harmon Jenkins, Thomas Keller, Diana Kennedy, Peggy Knickerbocker, Aglaia Kremezi, Mourad Lahlou, Julia Logue-Riordan, Judy Lundblad, Catherine Madison, Tony May, Fran McCullough, Joan Nathan, Daniel Patterson, Jacques Pépin, Jason Perlow, Anne Otterson, Russ Parsons, Ruth Reichl, Charles Sahadi, Christine Sahadi, David Scantland, Ted Siegel, Arthur Schwartz, Gordon M. Shepherd, Michael Solomonov, Ana Sortun, Carolyn Tillie, Ayfer Ünsal, James Villas, Alice Waters, Ari Weinzweig, and Ann Willan.

To Nancy Lang, for shining her light; Nathalie Christian, for her awe-inspiring hard work and perceptiveness at the stove; Karen Shinto, for couscous; Alma Espinola, for more than there is room to list here; Connor Bruce, photographer's assistant extraordinaire.

To all who advised on crafting the book, especially Aaron Wehner, as well as Francis Lam, Whitney Peeling, Celia Sack, Heidi Swanson, and Jenny Wapner; Katherine Sharpe, for helping me find the outline; Cary Groner, for his illuminating edit; Sharon Silva, for her enlightening copyedit; Suzanne Fass for brilliant proofing and indexing; Chris Hemesath, Michelle Duggan, and the team at Weldon Owen for its invaluable help printing it; Olga Katsnelson and crew at Postcard Communications for so generously promoting it; Kate Leahy for thorough proofreading and inspiration; and Jan Newberry and the team at Sun Basket for their support in the final stages.

To Kari Stuart and Anna Stein at ICM for their exceptional vision and determination; and to Karen Murgolo, Andy Dodds, and everyone at Grand Central Life & Style for continuing the journey with us, to bring the book into the wider world in such glorious fashion.

To Bill Bayer, for his fact finding, photographs, unsparing critiques, and faith.

To my parents, Hannah Jopling and Bob Kaiser; my in-laws, Carole and Jay Thelin; my sister Charlotte, brother-in-law Nick, nephew Linus, and all my extended Kaiser and Thelin relations for cheering me on.

Last, to Josh and Avidel, who make it all possible. I love you.

❧

To the luminaries who generously donated dinners and other delights to our Kickstarter campaign:

Jeff Bareilles	David Kinch	Steve Sando
Mario Batali	Eric Korsh	Ana Sortun
April Bloomfield	Mourad Lahlou	Craig Stoll
Rebecca Boice	Nathan Myhrvold	James Syhabout
Kyle Connaughton	Daniel Patterson	Pim Techamuanvivit
Thomas Keller	Gilbert Pilgram	Ten Speed Press

To the exceptional Kickstarter backers who pledged $250 or more, to help make our campaign such a blazing success:

Elizabeth Andoh	Joe Hargrave	Charles Phan
Robert Arndt	Jonathan Marshall Harris	Jacquey and Alain Piallat
Marlene and Ralph Bennett	Alexandra Holbrook	Kelly and Tamara Puleio-Costa
Sue Conley	Filiz Ç. Hösükoğlu	Gil Rafael
Dana Cowin	Laura Fisher Kaiser and Michael Kaiser	Bryan M. Read
Andrew Dornenburg	Tamara Kaiser	Julee Rosso
Nancy Errebo	Dorothy Kalins	Tracey Ryder and Carole Topalian
Joyce Goldstein	Rebecca Katz	Amaryll Schwertner
Susan Tefs Goodwin, along with Diana & Eric Burns	Steven Kotok	Peggy Smith
Warner and Iris de Gooijer	M	Vicki Snyder
Gael Greene	Hilary Markow	Martin Terry Stein
Barbara Haber	Chef Amos Miller	Zanne Early Stewart
Larry Halff and Randy Windham	Barbara Passino and John Kuhlmann	Patricia Storace
Lara Hamilton	Paula Perlis and Sarah Perlis Riley	Margot Walk
		Nach Waxman

Deepest gratitude to Alicia Walter, Michael Stern, Cynthia Walk, and Charlie Wolfinger.

⊙ ❖ ⊙

The Complete Works
of Paula Wolfert

Couscous and Other Good Food from Morocco, 1973

Mediterranean Cooking, 1st ed., 1977; 2nd ed., 1994

The Cooking of Southwest France, 1st ed., 1983; 2nd ed., 2005

Paula Wolfert's World of Food, 1988

The Cooking of the Eastern Mediterranean, 1994

Mediterranean Grains and Greens, 1998

The Slow Mediterranean Kitchen, 2003

Mediterranean Clay Pot Cooking, 2009

The Food of Morocco, 2011

Subject Index

Page numbers in *italics* refer to photographs

Hirigoyen, Gerald
  (Piperade), 264
Hirsheimer, Christopher,
  246
Hösükoğlu, Filiz,
  189–90, 227
hrous, 214, 227, 258

I, J
Indonesian food, 24, 59,
  65–67, 68, 71, 72, 75
Jaffrey, Madhur, 3, 119
Jaidi, Abdeslam, 68, 78, 83
Jaidi, Janet, 78
Jaidi, Mme. Khadija, 68, *76*,
  79–81, 117, 159, 190,
  217, 243
Julian, Sheryl, 215

K
Kadir, Omar, 82
Kafka, Barbara, 118, 119
Kalins, Dorothy, 220
Kalustyan's, 219
Keller, Thomas, 3–4, 181
Kennedy, Diana, 3, 12, 13,
  68, 69, 83, 127
Kerouac, Jack, 29, 35, 40
Kinch, David, 292
Kleiman, Evan, 292
Knickerbocker, Peggy, 14,
  215, 216
Kremezi, Aglaia, *178*,
  186–88, 189, 193,
  217–18, 245
Kummer, Corby, 117–18

L
Lahlou, Mourad, 77–78,
  181, 292
Lambraki, Mirsini, 218
Lang, George, 115–16,
  119, 243
Le Plaisir, 119, 120, 121,
  125, 131
Leite, David, 266
Lejanou, Pierrette, 124, 136
Lemann, Nicholas, 221

Lenôtre, Gaston, 116,
  120–21, 123–24
Lucas, Dione, 32–34, 35,
  36, 39, 42, 51, 52, 54,
  56, 60, 64, 81, 263,
  266, 269
Lundblad, Judy, 242
Lundy's restaurant, 14,
  19, 27

M
Mack, Patricia, 241
Madison, Dr. Catherine,
  289, 297
Manrique, Laurent
  (Campton Place),
  246, 264
Marrakech, Morocco, 1, 2,
  13, 49, 50, 52, 78, 84,
  110, 128, 220
Mastering the Art of French
  Cooking, 3, 55
May, Tony, 68–69
McCullough, Fran, 69,
  84–85, 87, 125, 130,
  154, 216, 224, 288
*Mediterranean Clay Pot
  Cooking* (2009),
  27, 40, 263, 264,
  266–67, 268, 271,
  276, 283, 303
Mediterranean Cooking,
  1e (1977), 12, 87, 119,
  156, 180
Mediterranean Cooking,
  2e (1994), 87, 203,
  268, 312
*Mediterranean Grains and
  Greens* (1998), 6, 49,
  90, 193, 213, 214,
  221, 268, 288, 304
megadarra, 313, 315
Mendel, Janet, 40, 219
Miller, Mark, 157
Minnesota Daily, 85
Mrabet, Mohammed, 85
muhammara, 3
Myhrvold, Nathan, 266

N
Natsvlishvili, Tsino, 183
New York, 60, 64, 85, 115,
  118, 119
New York Times, 32, 33, 36,
  65, 85, 87, 131, 159,
  179, 242
no-stir polenta, 219,
  230, 260
nouvelle cuisine, 115, 121,
  146, 157

O
Oldways Preservation &
  Exchange Trust,
  191–92, 217, 220,
  268–69
O'Neill, Molly, 179, 193
onion-parsley salad, 209
Orlovsky, Peter, 29, 51
Otterson, Anne, 116, 117,
  120, 128
Ottolenghi, Yotam, 4, 181
oven-steamed salmon,
  153, 202

P
Palladin, Jean-Louis, *122*,
  123, 124, 127, 128,
  146, 158
Patterson, Daniel, 153,
  213, 292
*Paula Wolfert's World of
  Food* (1988), 6, 94,
  131, 153–56, 159, 162,
  172, 181, 186, 253,
  268, 283, 301, 302
Peck, Paula, 34
Pépin, Jacques, 116–17, 119
peppers (Aleppo, Marash,
  Urfa), 3, 4, 179,
  180, 185, 190, 192,
  242, 304
Perlmutter, David, 289
pomegranate concentrate,
  196, 202, 209
pomegranate molasses, 3,
  179, 196, 242, 314
pork chops with cornichon
  butter, 158

Recipe Index

About the Author

EMILY KAISER THELIN is a writer, editor, and former restaurant cook. A two-time finalist for James Beard awards, and a former editor at *Food & Wine*, her work has also appeared in *Oprah*, *Dwell*, the *New York Times*, *Wall Street Journal*, and the *Washington Post*. For five years during and after college Emily worked as a professional chef: as a prep cook in London, a private chef in France, and a line cook in Washington, DC. She currently works for the meal kit delivery service, Sun Basket, and lives in Berkeley with her husband and daughter.